VYGOTSKY AND MARX

Toward a Marxist Psychology

*Edited by Carl Ratner and
Daniele Nunes Henrique Silva*

Routledge
Taylor & Francis Group

LONDON AND NEW YORK

First published 2017
by Routledge
2 Park Square, Milton Park, Abingdon, Oxon OX14 4RN

and by Routledge
711 Third Avenue, New York, NY 10017

Routledge is an imprint of the Taylor & Francis Group, an informa business

British Library Cataloguing in Publication Data
A catalogue record for this book is available from the British Library

Library of Congress Cataloging in Publication Data
A catalog record for this book has been requested

ISBN: 978-1-138-24480-1 (hbk)
ISBN: 978-1-138-24481-8 (pbk)
ISBN: 978-1-315-27663-2 (ebk)

Typeset in Bembo
by Saxon Graphics Ltd, Derby

In loving appreciation of my parents' inspiration to follow the ideas of Karl Marx

Carl Ratner

To Professors Angel Pino, Maria Cecilia Rafael de Góes and Ana Luiza Smolka for inspiring my Marxist and Vygotskyan commitment

Daniele Nunes Henrique Silva

"Marxist psychology" … [is] the only genuine psychology as a science. A psychology other than this cannot exist. And the other way around: everything that was and is genuinely scientific belongs to Marxist psychology. This concept is broader than the concept of [scientific] school or even current. It coincides with the concept scientific per se, no matter where and by whom it may have been developed.

(Vygotsky, *Crisis*)

CONTENTS

CONTRIBUTORS

Andy Blunden – Independent Researcher, Australia

Peter Feigenbaum – Professor of Education and Director of Institutional Research, Fordham University, New York, USA

James P. Lantolf – Professor of Linguistics, Center for Language Acquisition, The Pennsylvania State University, USA

Ilana Lemos de Paiva – Professor of Psychology, Federal University of Rio Grande do Norte, Brazil

Lavínia Lopes Salomão Magiolino – Professor of Education, State University of Campinas, Brazil

Kátia Maheirie – Professor of Psychology, Federal University of Santa Catarina, Brazil

Lígia Márcia Martins – Professor of Educational Psychology at the Universidade Estadual Paulista, São Paulo, Brazil.

Eduardo Moura da Costa – State University of Maringá, Brazil

Carl Ratner – Director of the Institute for Cultural Research and Education, USA

Daniele Nunes Henrique Silva – Professor of Psychology, University of Brasilia, Brazil

Silvana Calvo Tuleski – Professor of Psychology, State University of Maringá, Brazil

Andréa Vieira Zanella – Professor of Psychology, Federal University of Santa Catarina, Brazil

INTRODUCTION

Recovering and advancing Vygotsky's Marxist psychology

Carl Ratner and Daniele Nunes Henrique Silva

The ultimate objective of this book is to stimulate and guide the cultivation of a Marxist psychology – that is, a psychological discipline based upon Marx's social philosophy and politics. A Marxist psychology is a necessary element of both Marxist scientific social theory and revolutionary politics. Scientifically, Marxist psychology is also crucial for contributing to social analysis and social transformation to a fulfilling, just, democratic, cooperative society. Marx's intellectual pursuits were always driven by this kind of revolutionary political improvement in society. Thus, a work on Marxist psychology represents both a scientific act and a political act for human improvement.

Lev Vygotsky (1896–1934) was the most important pioneer of Marxist psychology. This is why we endeavor to explore his distinctive contribution to this field. Vygotsky explicitly said that developing Marxist psychology was his goal and, indeed, should be the goal of all scientific psychologists. We make the development of Marxist psychology by Vygotsky the central theme of this book. The book is not concerned with Vygotsky the person, Vygotsky the intellectual scholar (see Yasnitzky and van der Veer, 2016, for these kinds of insights), or even Vygotsky the psychologist with his contributions to many psychological topics. We are concerned with Vygotsky the Marxist psychologist. We are concerned with ways that Vygotsky fits within Marxist psychology and how he utilized Marxist concepts to understand and advance psychology. We are also concerned with ways that he did not accomplish these goals and how his Marxist psychology needs to be deepened.

We argue that Vygotsky's Marxism is Janus-faced: it faces outward to enrich Marxist psychology and it also faces inward to enrich Vygotsky's psychological ideas. His Marxism is neither a diversion from nor a reduction of his broad, varied intellectual interests. It informs them, as he said himself. Conversely, Vygotsky's fertile mind extended Marxism to psychological and cultural issues that had hitherto been beyond the ken of Marxism. This book seeks to inspire a full analysis of these issues.

This book's strong position of Vygotsky's Marxism

There are different estimations of Vygotsky's Marxism. We take a "strong view"; that is, Marx's influence on Vygotsky was strong. Others take a weaker view. For example, some comments in *The Cambridge Handbook of Cultural-Historical Psychology* deny Vygotsky's Marxism:

> Although as did all the citizens of USSR, Vygotsky had to obey the totalitarian government, his relations with Marxism were only polite: he liked Karl Marx as well as his friend, the great poet, Heinrich Heine, for their ironic judgments of the bourgeois society, but his quotations from the other official texts were made mostly for tactical reasons.
>
> *(Yasnitsky et al., 2014, p. 505)*

This serious charge is proclaimed in a single sentence with no documentation or argumentation.[1]

Our book does not survey all views on this question. Instead, we focus on articulating and advancing the strong position. Our reason is that although a strong view is warranted, it has never been rigorously explained or verified with evidence.

In the strong view, Marx was a central influence on Vygotsky, though that is not to say he was the only influence. It is well known that Vygotsky followed Spinoza's philosophy in certain ways. In focusing on Vygotsky's Marxism – in his scientific work as well as in his political sympathies – we believe that Marxism *informed* Vygotsky's diverse interests in other philosophers and social scientists. We believe that Vygotsky was attracted to elements of their works that are compatible with Marxism and which enabled him to advance Marxism. For example, some scholars, such as Hardt and Negri (2000) and Sawaia (2009), argue that some Marxian ideas were prefigured by Spinoza.

Vygotsky was the most important pioneer of Marxist psychology because he used the essence of Marxism to explore the intricacies of psychology as a distinctive order of reality. He informed psychology with Marxism without reducing psychology to Marxist politics or economics (which were Marx's main concerns). He extended Marxism to psychology in new, creative ways. He thus used psychology to enrich Marxism and he used Marxism to enrich psychology.

He gave full play to the issues of cognition, emotion, imagination, perception, memory, concept formation, developmental psychology, experience, subjectivity, personality, educational psychology, and the relation between biology and psychology. He developed theories of their internal operations, and he developed methodologies for researching them. Vygotsky immersed himself in the discipline of psychology. He drew upon and critiqued numerous psychological theories and methodologies. He identified and solved contradictions and conundrums within these. He explained the details of psychological phenomena in new ways. He worked within the discipline as a Marxist. He did not stand outside psychology and pontificate Marxist terms that would override actual psychological processes. He made Marxism consistent with psychology. This made Marxism vibrant in new ways (psychological), and it made psychology vibrant in new ways (Marxist).

These contributions of Vygotsky are explored in the current book.

Our approach to demonstrating the strong view of Vygotsky's Marxism is to identify Marxist concepts in Vygotsky's work. Our chapters examine specific Marxist constructs in diverse topics researched by Vygotsky. We believe this is a reliable and valid way of estimating the depth of Marxism in his work.

We believe this is a more reliable and vivid way of examining Vygotsky's Marxism than discussing general historical intellectual contexts surrounding his life. We cannot deduce the influence of a social environment on one individual's activity; we must apprehend this environment *in* individual activity to see its resulting effects. We concentrate on Marxism within Vygotsky's work rather than Marxism in Vygotsky's society.

Vygotsky did not simply refer to Marxist concepts in a general way as useful ideas for understanding psychology and culture. He utilized them as foundational ideas for his general sociocultural theory and his empirical research. This is true in his first writings and lectures: "I want to learn from Marx's whole method how to build a science, how to approach the investigation of the mind. ... We do not need fortuitous utterances, but a method: not dialectical materialism, but historical materialism" (Vygotsky, 1997a, p. 331). In *The Psychology of Art*, Vygotsky (1925/1971) explains, "I propose to remain content with the methodological and theoretical laws of the psychological examination of art, along with every other attempt, pointing out the essential importance of finding a place within the Marxist doctrine of art."

In his private notebooks, far from the eyes of any officials, Vygotsky professes his passion for the Russian Revolution: "The Revolution is our supreme cause ... I speak on behalf of the Revolution" (van der Veer and Zavershneva, 2011, p. 466).

The Marxist thrust to Vygotsky's cultural psychology has been detected by several of his followers.

Luria writes, "Vygotsky set a great example of how to master the historical method; he showed us how to apply Marx and Lenin's methodology to concrete studies in one of the most formidable fields of knowledge [psychology]" (cited in Levitin, 1982, p. 173). He also describes Vygotsky as the "leading Marxist theoretician among us" (Luria, 1979, Chapter 3). He says that

My entire generation was infused with the energy of revolutionary change—the liberating energy people feel when they are part of a society that is able to make tremendous progress in a very short time. ... The limits of our restricted, private world were broken down by the Revolution, and new vistas opened before us. We were swept up in a great historical movement. Our private interests were consumed by the wider social goals of a new, collective society.

This atmosphere immediately following the Revolution provided the energy for many ambitious ventures. An entire society was liberated to turn its creative powers to constructing a new kind of life for everyone.

(Ibid., Chapter 1)

Marxist philosophy, one of the world's more complex systems of thought, was assimilated slowly by Soviet scholars, myself included. Properly speaking, I never really mastered Marxism to the degree I would have liked. I still consider this to have been a major shortcoming in my education.

(Ibid., Chapter 2)

Van der Veer and Valsiner note that "Vygotsky sincerely believed in the utopian ideas of the communist world-view, he was actively involved in the organizations linked with the Communist Party, and he attempted to incorporate the communist world-view in his research" (1991, p. 374). Indeed, Vygotsky was a representative of the Bolshevik government in Gomel from 1919 to 1923.

Cole affirms Vygotsky's Marxist point of view: "Vygotsky began with *Das Kapital*. When Engels' *Dialectics of Nature* appeared in 1925, Vygotsky immediately incorporated it into his thinking" (cited in Levitin, 1982, p. 54).

Gielen and Jeshmaridian write:

Vygotsky considered himself first and foremost as a Marxist thinker who wished to contribute in theory and praxis to the construction of the newly evolving socialist society. He never doubted his commitment to Marxism and to the new society, and when toward the end of his brief life he was confronted with the threat of "excommunication" he grew despondent and disintegrated psychologically and physically.

(1999, p. 276)

Unable to understand why this should be so, Vygotsky nevertheless realized that he was now considered to be outside Marxism. In this context, Bluma Zeigarnik, Vygotsky's assistant in a psychiatric clinic, remembers how Vygotsky ran to and fro in the clinic, saying, "I do not want to live any more, they do not want to consider me a Marxist." For the sensitive and highly social Vygotsky, Communism provided a philosophy of life that provided hope and meaning to his suffering. When he realized that he had been placed outside this home, his hopes dwindled, the meaning of his existence evaporated, and he had to face death alone.

(Ibid., p. 284)

Intellectual breaches in the field of Vygotskyian Marxism

Despite plentiful evidence of Vygotsky's strong use of Marxism, from Vygotsky's own statements and those of several Vygotskyian scholars, this issue has received little attention from most of Vygotsky's followers. In order to correct this problem (which is the *raison d'être* and objective of our book), we must understand it. The remainder of this Introduction documents the problem with examples. We document ways that many Vygotskyians have failed to address, understand, utilize, and advance Marxian concepts in their treatment of Vygotsky's work.

Neglecting Vygotsky's Marxism

Most treatments of Vygotsky's cultural psychology, or cultural-historical psychology, ignore his Marxism. *The Cambridge Handbook of Cultural-Historical Psychology* (Yasnitsky *et al.*, 2014) is devoted to contemporary Vygotskyian scholarship. Marx, Engels, and Marxism are cited 17 times in the index of this 533-page tome. With the exception of Grigorenko's one-page discussion of this issue, the citations are limited to mentioning Marx's or Engels' name, one of their books, or one of their sentences, or to citation of Marx by other Soviet figures such as Eisenstein, or to just a one-sentence comment on Vygotsky's Marxism. They do not discuss or describe Vygotsky's Marxism.

Gielen and Jeshmaridian (1999, pp. 275–276) describe the breadth of this kind of neglect:

> Our emphasis on Vygotsky's Marxist identity derives in part from the observation that this central aspect of his identity has frequently been neglected by his American followers. When beginning in the 1960s, American psychologists began to rediscover Vygotsky they often shoved aside the Marxist basis of his theorizing. We may note, for instance, that when his important work *Thought and Language* … was first translated into English it was shorn of its Marxist references. Perhaps this is not too surprising in a country that had just gone through the rabidly anti-Communist McCarthy era. Other Vygotskyites in the West have considered his Marxist ideas to be of limited intellectual value when compared to the richness of his psychological legacy. Today, many of the more pragmatically oriented American psychologists treat Vygotsky's work as a kind of psychological gold mine that exists to be plundered for nuggets of insight and wisdom and hints for new research. In contrast, they tend to pay insufficient attention to the question how and for what purpose this gold mine came into being in the first place.
>
> An example may suffice. Recently, many American psychologists have appropriated Vygotsky's concept of a Zone of Proximal Development, together with his idea that learning leads development. They use this concept to explain how under the guidance of adults children learn to accomplish actions that they later accomplish independently. … For the Marxist educator Vygotsky—but not for modern American psychologists—the idea of a Zone of Proximal Development contained political implications. … The idea could be used to lend support to the proclaimed goal of Soviet education: to

create the new Soviet Man, the kind of being that would be needed in the Soviet society of the future.[2]

Packer (2008, pp. 8–9) similarly states:

> When Vygotsky's texts were first translated into English, some psychologists in the United States noted that his work had strong connections to Marx's analysis of capitalism, but since then these connections have often gone unnoticed and "many interpretations of Vygotsky have not attempted to position him within a Marxist framework" (Robbins, 1999, p. vi). Translations of Vygotsky's work have often omitted references to Marx and Engels, or treated these as "a forced concession to official ideology" (Yaroshevsky, 1989, p. 20). Consequently ...
>
>> the political context of his work is virtually ignored by modern scholars concerned to recover it. Vygotsky is portrayed not so much as a Marxist theorist who negotiated a tense political environment and whose work was a victim of Stalin's purges, but as a thinker whose genius "transcend[s] historical, social and cultural barriers" (Bakhurst, 2005, p. 178).
>
> [...] Important and early exceptions to this tendency to ignore or downplay Vygotsky's debt to Marx include Toulmin (1978) who, in the *New York Review of Books* article in which he famously dubbed Vygotsky "the Mozart of psychology," wrote that "the general frame provided by 'historical-materialist' philosophy gave him the basis he needed for developing an integrated account of the relations between developmental psychology and clinical neurology, cultural anthropology and the psychology of art." A second exception was the introduction to *Mind in Society* by Cole and Scribner (1978), who wrote that the Marxist theoretical framework was a "valuable scientific resource" for Vygotsky, that he used "the methods and principles of dialectical materialism" and intended "to create one's own *Capital*." More recently, Cole *et al.* (2006) proposed that "Vygotsky, Luria, and Leontiev undertook the wholesale reformulation of psychology along Marxist lines ... (p. 244).

Inadequate treatments of Vygotsky's Marxism

A few treatments of Vygotsky's cultural psychology mention his sympathy with Marxism. However, they do not provide any detailed, thorough discussion of it. This would require that they explain in detail the meaning of specific, distinctive Marxist concepts; for example, how did Marx conceptualize dialectics, dialectical materialism, alienation, money, historical materialism, private property, wage labor, capitalism, socialism? These Marxist concepts would then need to be identified in Vygotsky's work as he explicitly named them and also as he implicitly used them without naming them.

Pursuing Vygotsky's Marxism would also include identifying topics where Vygotsky failed to utilize Marxist concepts even though he could have done so in ways that would have enriched his explanation. In addition, creative uses of Marxism would be proposed for topics that Vygotsky did not discuss so as to extend his Marxist cultural psychology to those subjects. Sexuality is one example.

Pursuit of Vygotsky's Marxism would also require developing a Marxian social theory or theory about the nature of culture. Vygotsky drew upon historical materialism as his guiding social theory. This social theory is necessary to establish a Marxist foundation to cultural psychology.

Vygotsky (1998, p. 43) adopts historical materialism in his developmental psychology:

> the basic change in the environment consists of the fact that it expands to participation in societal production. On this basis, in the content of thinking, societal ideology is represented most of all as connected with one position or another in societal production. The history of the school-age child and the youth is the history of very intensive development and formulation of class psychology and ideology. … Usually, reference is made to the instinct of imitation as the basic mechanism for the origin and formulation of the content of thinking in the adolescent. However, reference to the instinct of imitation undoubtedly obscures understanding the formation of class psychology in the child.

Only a few of Vygotsky's followers, such as Veresov (2005), Newton Duarte (2000), and Angel Pino (2000) among others, have pursued these avenues. Most followers treat Vygotsky's use of Marxist concepts superficially, incompletely, and incorrectly (Tuleski, 2015, Chapter 1). They generally reduce Marxist concepts to simple, abstract notions that are deprived of Marxist content and refilled with non-Marxist content. This has adverse scientific and political affects. We identify problems in the way Vygotsky's followers have treated both his Marxism and Marxism more generally. Our intention is constructive – to overcome the problems and to indicate a more adequate direction for developing Marxist psychology. Vygotsky engages in this kind of critique of Marxist psychologists in his work "The historical meaning of the crisis in psychology." Here, he complains: "many 'Marxists' are not able to indicate the difference between theirs and an idealistic theory of psychological knowledge, because it [the difference] does not exist. […] We claim that the viewpoint of our 'Marxists' is *Machism in psychology*" (Vygotsky, 1997a, pp. 323–324). Vygotsky is so critical of his colleagues' Marxism that he dismisses it through his use of the grammatical form "Marxist." He regards the situation as so grave that the entire science of psychology must be reorganized:

> Following Spinoza, we have compared our science to a mortally ill patient who looks for an unreliable medicine. Now we see that it is only the surgeon's knife which can save the situation. A bloody operation is immanent.

Many textbooks we will have to rend in twain, many phrases will lose their head or legs, other theories will be slit in the belly.

(Ibid., p. 324)

We provide a similar treatment to some of the existing presentations of Vygotsky's Marxism and Marxist psychology below.

1) Elena Grigorenko

Elena Grigorenko (2014), a Russian Vygotskyian psychologist, acknowledges that Vygotsky was a disciple of Marx; yet she construes Vygotsky's Marxism as consisting of "transformative collaborative practices." One example of this in her work is: "development, learning, and teaching, together and separately, are contributors and outcomes of collaborative transformative practices" (ibid., p. 205). Another Marxist notion is that "culture is not a collection of ancient artefacts, but a globally uninterrupted continuous stream of transformed and transforming practices that penetrate human history" (ibid.). Another frequently mentioned Marxist concept is Vygotsky's conception of psychology as a tool that mediates our interactions with nature.

These are only superficially Marxist concepts. They do not refer to concrete social systems, structures, collectives, institutions, artefacts, collaboration, or politics. They do not refer to concrete capitalism – e.g., neoliberalism – or to transformative politics and collaboration oriented toward socialism. Nor do they concretize globally continuous institutional practices in neoliberal capitalism promulgated by The World Bank, The World Trade Organization, or global trade agreements such as NAFTA (none of which are mentioned in the *Cambridge Handbook*'s index).

Reducing Marxism to general, abstract concepts such as collaboration and transformation leaves it ill-defined and blurs its most important ideas. Collaborative, transformative practices in education can include anything, even agreeing to eliminate all homework and reading assignments. It can include the exclusion of evolution from the school curriculum.

Abstract collaboration and transformation, in some nondescript form, are not specific to Marxism and add no specific Marxist character to culture or psychology.

2) Seth Chaiklin

Chaiklin's (2012) discussion of Vygotsky and Marx describes some common concepts they utilized. He usefully tells us that "Marx understands freedom in a historical way: freedom is a consequence of the conditions of human life, and the development of human capabilities in relation to those conditions" (ibid., p. 35). However, Chaiklin does not explore what conditions are concretely. He does not mention that freedom for Marx exists in a socialist political economy that requires the eradication of private property, class structure, capital, money, commodity production, and wage labor.

Chaiklin lists some ideas about the dialectical tradition and historical understanding shared by Hegel, Marx, and Vygotsky, including being "committed to a scientific approach," needing to "pay attention to the whole," needing "to understand the interactions that form objects," using "a historical approach," being "oriented toward the concept of freedom and full human development," and recognizing that "persons transform their conditions" (ibid., pp. 30–32).

It is unclear what these abstractions mean. Transforming conditions can range from polluting the oceans to a social revolution. Leaving this nebulous prevents it from enriching cultural-historical activity theory. It leaves us without direction about what to research. It grants anyone license to include any trivial or destructive transformation within the rubric of cultural-historical activity theory.

Likewise, which "interactions" must we study in the formation of social systems and psychological phenomena? Are these interpersonal interactions or geopolitical interactions?

What aspects of "history" should we focus on? Whose history is it? Is it official history or "people's history"? Is it the history that claims the US frees people from autocracy, or is it the history of the American Empire that oppresses people?

What is "the whole" when we study society or psychology? Is it a unified, homogenous whole, or is it riddled with contradictions? Are some elements of the whole more dominant, or are they all equal? Is the whole a sequence of elements or a gestalt?

Marx and Vygotsky provide concrete answers to these questions, but this is overlooked by Chaiklin as he remains at the level of general abstractions.

Marx uses abstractions cautiously as general frameworks to be filled in with concrete features. He discusses the nature of "the social whole," for example, in concrete terms: "the whole internal structure of the nation itself depends on the stage of development reached by its production" (in Marx and Engels, 1932/1968, p. 11).

> Neither legal relations nor political forms could be comprehended whether by themselves or on the basis of a so-called general development of the human mind, but on the contrary they originate in the material conditions of life, the totality of which Hegel, following the example of English and French thinkers of the eighteenth century, embraces within the term "civil society"; that the anatomy of this civil society, however, has to be sought in political economy.
>
> *(Marx, 1859/1999, Preface)*

Chaiklin omits the political-economic core of the social whole that determines its essential character and comprises the determination of psychology and all social activity.

Marx similarly concretizes history:

> This conception of history depends on our ability to expound the real process of production, starting out from the material production of life itself, and to

comprehend the form of intercourse connected with this and created by this *mode of production as the basis of all history.*

> *(In Marx and Engels, 1932/1968, p. 28, emphasis added)*

He says that "The *history of industry and the established objective existence of industry* are the open book of man's essential powers, the perceptibly existing human psychology" (in Marx and Engels, 1975, p. 302, emphasis added). This concreteness is overlooked by Chaiklin.

Vygotsky emphasizes this specificity in his psychological work. He reiterates Marx's words in articulating "the whole": "each person is to some degree a measure of the society, or rather class, to which he belongs, for the whole totality of social relationships is reflected in him" (1997a, p. 317).

Vygotsky also adopts Marx's historical materialism in articulating history. He grounds the development of concepts in specific social conditions and corresponding social consciousness: the "thinking of the adolescent is not an instinctive peculiarity of the adolescent, but is the inevitable result of the formation of concepts within the sphere of a specific societal ideology" (1998, p. 44). Societal ideology, like social whole, is a concrete, political construct.

Dialectics also has concrete dimensions at the hands of Marx and Vygotsky. Max Horkheimer (1993, p. 116) explains it thusly:

> Marx and Engels took up the dialectic in a materialist sense. They remained faithful to Hegel's belief in the existence of supraindividual dynamic structures and tendencies in historical development but rejected the belief in an independent spiritual power operating in history.

Marx describes a *necessary dialectic* that *has to* utilize the socialized infrastructure of capitalism as the basis for a viable, comprehensive alternative to capitalism. All of this has a bearing on psychological change. Vygotsky agrees with this in his essay entitled "The socialist alteration of man" (1994b).

Marx's dialectics is based upon Hegel's conception of objective, necessary, dialectical possibilities and movement: "what is really possible can no longer be otherwise; under the particular conditions and circumstances something else cannot follow. Real possibility and necessity are therefore only *seemingly* different"; the identity of possibility and necessity "is already *presupposed* and lies at their base" (Hegel, 1969, p. 549). "Real possibility does ... become necessity" (ibid., p. 550). Chaiklin and other cultural-historical activity theorists do not appreciate this sense of determinate, necessary history and dialectics that Marx and Vygotsky use.

This is both a scientific breach and a political breach for it eradicates the practical, political, revolutionary thrust of Marxism that negates capitalism with concrete socialist social relations. General abstractions lead to treating war, peace, poverty, crime, etc. as purged of concrete content and history. They lead to bemoaning "the complexity and tragedy of war" instead of concrete political-economic interests (e.g., imperialism, religious conquests such as the Crusades) that drive it and that must be concretely negated.

3) Fred Newman and Lois Holzman

Newman and Holzman (2014) consider Vygotsky to be a Marxist, yet they construe this in humanistic, interpersonal terms devoid of concrete historical, political dimensions. They say, "We wanted to show a Vygotsky closely aligned methodologically with the historical-materialist Marx" (ibid., pp. ix–x). To truly show this, they would have to identify Marx's historical materialism and then explain how its specific points appear in Vygotsky's works. Some of those points include Marx's grounding of society and consciousness in the means and relations of production: "Consciousness must be explained from the contradictions of material life, from the conflict existing between the social forces of production and the relations of production" (Marx, 1859/1999, Preface).

Newman and Holzman eschew this kind of formulation; they replace it with a populist, indefinite notion of people working together interpersonally to remake their social activities. There is no historical context or historical outcome to this process. For us, there is nothing political about it; there is nothing systemic about it.

They fall back on Vygotsky's notion of zone of proximal development, which emphasizes how interpersonal interaction helps individuals develop their competencies. Newman and Holzman seem to confine their discussion of Vygotsky's Marxism to this notion of individuals developing themselves through social interaction. This is a micro-level abstraction that they interpret as being (current) develops into becoming (future).

> Another area of psychology in which Vygotsky is beginning to make his mark is the study of the lives of young people and of outside of school interventions designed to promote youth development. As a field of inquiry and practice … youth development engages young people in productive and constructive activities through programs and organizations that provide opportunities for creativity and leadership. … Vygotsky's major contribution to this field is his understanding of the socialness of learning-and-development, and the critical importance of relationships with caring adults and with peers in effective programming. For some youth development practitioners, the Vygotsky of [*Lev Vygotsky: Revolutionary Scientist*] has led them to see and further organize their work so as to support young people to perform ahead of themselves, as who they are and other than who they are simultaneously.
>
> *(Newman and Holzman, 2014, p. xiii)*

This statement is all about self-development, becoming, caring, and engaging young people in productive and constructive activities that promote leadership and creativity. These are all empty abstractions. No cultural-historical social system is mentioned, no problems or contradictions with the social system are mentioned, no politics or power are mentioned, and no concrete negations of the current social system into a new mode of production are mentioned. Leadership, creativity, and development are all left indefinite or defined in instrumental ways as organizational psychology. This makes them acceptable to existing social relations.

Newman and Holzman appear to forget Vygotsky's principle tenet, which Luria articulates as follows:

> Vygotsky made it his life's task to bring home to every scientist that the history of these higher psychological functions is the prime subject of psychology. He claimed that genuine scientific analysis of the human mind always involved not the reduction of the human psyche to abstract elements in which the specific traits of the psyche are lost, but analysis in terms of actual units that preserve in the simplest form all the richness and peculiarities of the whole.
>
> *(Cited in Levitin, 1982, p. 171)*

By "whole," Vygotsky means the full historical content of psychological elements that are grounded in material conditions, civil society, and the mode of production. Newman and Holzman discard all of Luria's cautions as they emphasize abstractions devoid of concrete culture and history, much less power and politics.

The authors distort Marx and Vygotsky in places. They say, "Marx must be *postmodernized* if he is to be understood in postmodern times" (Newman and Holzman, 2014, p. xv). This says that Marx must be made congruent with capitalism in order to be understood in capitalist society. It is as absurd as saying that Marxist dialectics must be converted into formal logic in order to be understood by (and made relevant to) Anglo-American students. Or that art should be reduced to advertising to be understood in, and relevant to, consumerist society. This destroys the entire radical, critical essence of Marxism. Marxism developed a counter-capitalist philosophy and political economy in order to understand capitalism more deeply than its own spokespeople and in order to criticize it and transform it. Following Newman and Holzman leads to destroying all of this oppositional essence and adapting Marxism to capitalism. We can never critique and transform capitalism if we are thinking within its terms. This is the one-dimensional thinking that Marcuse exposed and criticized so well. How bizarre that self-proclaimed Marxist Vygotskyians promote capitalist, one-dimensional thinking.

Newman and Holzman misinterpret Marxism by advancing the slogan of "All Power to the Developing" (ibid., p. xvi) in place of Marx's slogan of all power to the proletariat. This makes social change a matter of promoting "development" – indefinite, contentless, formless, abstract development. All historical, political content of such development has been eschewed. This wipes socialism off the historical agenda.

The authors exemplify their distorted Marxism and Vygotskyianism in their practice of social therapy: "Social therapists work with the capacity that groups of people have to transform how they feel and relate to themselves and others, an

application of the Vygotskyian 'principle' that 'You can't develop on your own.'"
Their therapy groups consist of diverse genders, ages, ethnicities, sexual orientations,
and class backgrounds "in order to challenge people's notion of a fixed identity.
Additionally, the varieties of diversity among … members give the [groups] rich
material to create emotional growth" (ibid., p. xvi).

Again we see indefinite, abstract notions devoid of historical or political content.
Marxism, and cultural-historical psychology, are postmodernized into simplistic
notions of transforming how we feel and relate to ourselves and to others,
challenging fixed identities, and creating emotional growth. All without any
political or economic change in the social structure or the psyche. Presumably, the
social structure will be unerringly improved by creative, emotive, flexible, self-
reflexive, developing (becoming), caring individuals without direction from
nonindividual factors.

4) Michael Cole and Yrjö Engeström

While acknowledging Vygotsky's Marxism, Cole and Engeström state that "the
analysis of human psychological functions must be situated in historically
accumulated forms of human activity" (2007, p. 486). This is the same kind of
abstraction that Chaiklin proffers about history. It is abstract because it does not
indicate the nature of historical forms of psychological functions. This leaves them
up to the discretion and opinion and "sense" of the researcher. There is no
guideline about whether the researcher should focus on intergenerational personal
narratives within a single family – for example, about "why we have always gone
horseback riding on Sunday mornings" – or whether to pay attention to official
historical narratives that are mass-distributed in the form of textbooks, which
reflect political-economic interests of educational, political, and business leaders.
Anything qualifies as the historical form of psychological processes. This enables
cultural psychologists to exclude official, objectified, politicized, mass, historical
activities from their research if they so desire.

Additionally, it is not clear how accumulated historical forms actually relate to
psychology. Are they a "setting" or do they specifically form and direct psychology?
Luria says that historical culture forms perceptual codes that structure our perceptions.
Lukács (1924/1970) gives a similar example of historical shaping of psychology:

> the Social Democrats' [pragmatic, revisionist] attitude to the war was not the
> result of a momentary-aberration or of cowardice, but was a necessary
> consequence of their immediate past … *to be understood within the context of the*
> *history of the labour movement.*

Thus, the Social Democrats' revisionist participation in the history of the labor
movement conditioned their consciousness to adopt a revisionist attitude toward
the war. Abstract concepts of history do not include this kind of historical-
materialist, formative analysis.

But Vygotsky did. He says, "Once we acknowledge the historical character of verbal thought, we must consider it subject to all the premises of historical materialism, which are valid for any historical phenomenon in human society" (Vygotsky, 1986, pp. 94–95). In this statement, Vygotsky immediately concretizes the general statement "we acknowledge the historical character of verbal thought" by explaining that the historical character of verbal thought consists in its following the premises of Marx's historical materialism. Historical materialism is a specific historical theory and process composed of specific factors; it is not simply accumulations of past experiences.

Cole and Engeström confine attention (both their own and the reader's) to the first part of Vygotsky's statement, which says social stimuli and human behavior are historically codified, and omit the message of the second part – that the historical character is concrete class character. They thereby present an incomplete picture of human activity and of Vygotsky's view of activity.

Vygotsky utilizes historical materialism to specify the nature of historically accumulated experiences, their causes, and their interpretation:

> By ideology we will understand all the social stimuli that have become hardened in the form of legal statutes, moral precepts, artistic tastes, and so on. These standards are permeated through and through with the class structure of society that generated them and serve as the class organization of production. *They are responsible for all of human behavior*, and in this sense we are justified in speaking of man's class behavior.
>
> *(1926/1997b, pp. 211–212, emphasis added)*

Vygotsky mentions the historical codification of social stimuli in particular cultural-historical forms that have a class character which is rooted in the mode of production and class structure. As Luria says, historical social stimuli are responsible for individual behavior; they are not merely means for individuals to utilize as they wish to regulate their own interactions.

The inadequacy of free-floating, unframed, cultural abstractions (such as "historically accumulated forms of human activity"; Cole and Engeström, 2007, p. 486) is that they transcend and disregard concrete cultural facts about real social and psychological life. Abstractions blind us to the fact that in 2015, the wealthiest 62 individuals in the world had more wealth than the poorest 3.5 billion people. These concrete facts are precisely what Marx and Vygotsky sought to highlight in order to bring about social transformation. Social transformation is made at the concrete macro cultural level by negating concrete political-economic social relations that are revealed in concrete facts. This is the *politics of abstraction and concreteness* (Paolucci, 2012).[3]

Marx criticized abstractions that are severed from concrete determinations. He says,

> The population is an abstraction if I leave out, for example, the classes of which it is composed. These classes, in turn, are an empty phrase if I am not

familiar with the elements on which they rest. E.g. wage labour, capital, etc. These latter in turn presuppose exchange, division of labor, prices, etc. For example, capital is nothing without wage labour, without value, money, price, etc.

(Marx, 1939/1973, p. 100)

Similarly, in referring to "the people," Marx follows with: "or to replace this broad and vague expression by a definite one, the proletariat" (in Marx and Engels, 1976, p. 222). Poverty and wealth are similar kinds of abstractions that are devoid of concrete contradiction and lead to no specific solution. In *The Economic and Philosophical Manuscripts*, he says,

> The antithesis between *lack of property* and *property*, so long as it is not comprehended as the antithesis of *labour* and *capital*, remains an indifferent antithesis, not grasped in its *active connection*, in its *internal* relation, not yet grasped as a *contradiction*. ... But labour [concretely conceived] as exclusion of property ... and capital as ... exclusion of labor constitute *private property* as its developed state of contradiction – hence a dynamic relationship driving towards resolution.
>
> *(In Marx and Engels, 1975, pp. 293–294)*

Concrete features generate concrete resolving of their problems.

Marx carefully demonstrated how general historical references need to be filled in with concrete, political-economic content. He says,

> The *forming* of the five senses is a labor of the entire history of the world down to the present. The *sense* caught up in crude practical need has only a *restricted* sense. ... The care-burdened poverty-stricken man has no *sense* for the finest play.
>
> *(Ibid., p. 302)*

Here, Marx makes a general statement about the historical forming of senses and immediately concretizes it in negative terms.

Vygotsky (1989) followed Marx's emphasis in writing about "concrete psychology." His followers rarely take this step toward Marxist psychology.

Marx used abstractions to identify general, ideal, essential aspects of culture and psychology; however, he always filled them out with concrete features. This was important to him on scientific grounds and on political grounds in terms of effecting social improvement.

An example can be found in his discussion of human labor, consciousness, and sociality in his *Manuscripts*. Here, Marx begins with general, abstract statements about human activity vis-à-vis animal activity. He immediately fills out this description with concrete features that are produced by capitalist social relations.

The animal is immediately one with its life activity. It does not distinguish itself from it. It is *its life activity*. Man makes his life activity itself the object of his will and of his consciousness. He has conscious life activity. … [I]t is only because he is a species-being that he is a conscious being, i.e., that his own life is an object for him. Only because of that is his activity free activity.

[…] It is just in his work upon the objective world, therefore, that man really proves himself to be a *species-being*. This production is his active species-life. Through this production, nature appears as *his* work and his reality. … Estranged labor reverses this relationship. … In tearing away from man the object of his production, estranged labor tears from him his *species-life*, his real objectivity as a member of the species and transforms his advantage over animals into the disadvantage that his inorganic body, nature, is taken from him.

Similarly, in degrading spontaneous, free activity to a means, estranged labor makes man's species-life a means to his physical existence.

[…] Estranged labor turns … *Man's species-being* into a being *alien* to him, into a *means* to his *individual existence*. It estranges from man his own body, as well as external nature and his spiritual aspect, his *human* aspect. … An immediate consequence of the fact that man is estranged from the product of his labor, from his life activity, from his species-being, is the *estrangement of man* from *man*.

(In Marx and Engels, 1975, pp. 276–277)

Marx envisions the ideal state of human activity, which is to produce itself consciously as an object of its will. This conscious, willful production is *free activity* that unites the individual with his species. It is *active species life*. However, this ideal abstraction is contradicted by real, estranged, concrete labor of capitalist society. Concrete, estranged labor is not freely produced by the laborer; it does not unite him with his species; it does not express or fulfill him; it is not *his* work but is, rather, controlled and imposed by his boss. Because species-being and life activity do not exist in their ideal, true, fulfilling form, they must be made so. And this cannot be accomplished abstractly through exhortations to "feel connected," "get involved," or "own your behavior." It can only be accomplished through changing material conditions; for example, macro cultural factors such as the political economy, artifacts (forces of production), and concepts (collective representations). Marx and Engels (1932/1968, p. 68) say,

proletarians of the present day, who are completely shut off from all self-activity, are in a position to achieve a complete and no longer restricted self-activity, which consists in the appropriation of a totality of productive forces and in the thus postulated development of a totality of capacities.

Working people must develop their self-activity in a political-economic revolution in which they appropriate the broad organization of the productive forces in vast social international networks.

Marx's abstractions are ideals that negate and improve on concrete, momentary reality (see Ilyenkov, 1960/1982). Abstractions such as labor and production are curtailed and falsified by concrete reality. Abstractions must be realized in the future through eliminating estranged labor and replacing it with democratic, collective labor. When Marx says, "all forms of state have democracy *for* their truth, and they are therefore untrue insofar as they are not democracy" (in Marx and Engels, 1975, p. 31), he means that this truth must be developed for their becoming genuine states. Existing states are not yet democratic, genuine states. Democracy is a transcendent, teleological ideal of the true, genuine state. This is the negative dialectics of Hegel and Marx that the Frankfurt School explain.

Vygotsky adopted this Marxian-Hegelian dialectical thinking that genuine, ideal forms of life/behavior must be developed through social transformation. They do not exist in current society. For example, consider creativity and education: "Life becomes creation only when it is finally freed of all the social forms that distort and disfigure it. Questions of education will have been resolved when questions of life will have been solved" (Vygotsky, 1926/1997b, p. 350).

If Marx had not concretized the abstraction labor, it would have implied that community is readily available as any multiple social interaction or that labor *now* is free, willful, conscious, fulfilling, and socially unifying. The present incomplete, untrue reality would have been misrepresented as ideal, fulfilling, and free. This legitimation of the present would have obviated the need to humanize labor.[4]

This is what the abstractions of Vygotsky's followers do. Wertsch quotes Marx's discussion of labor as "a process in which man, through his own activity, initiates, regulates and controls the material reactions between himself and nature" (in Levitin, 1982, p. 67). Cole and Engeström (2007, p. 485) similarly say

> The initial premise of the Russian cultural-historical school was that human psychological processes entail a form of behavior in which material objects are modified by human beings as a means of regulating their interactions with the world and each other. ... An application of this was to provide an adult suffering from Parkinsonism with bits of paper, by means of which he was able to walk across a floor.

This implies that labor is already the free expression and realization of the laborer through the utilization of things for his own purpose. Wertsch, Cole, and Engeström omit Marx's crucial qualification that this is an ideal that must be created through social transformation; extant labor is estranged and prevents the worker's control over his own activity.

These scholars therefore omit Marx's crucial call for political transformation in order to realize the ideal state of nature. Their connotation of all labor as self-activity blunts the need for political change, and it accepts the alienated status quo as fulfilling.

Resisting Vygotsky's Marxist psychology

Although Vygotskyian scholars, such as Cole, Wertsch, Valsiner, van der Veer, Bruner, Kozulin, Tulviste, Daniels, and Chaiklin, acknowledge Vygotsky's Marxism and admire his work, claiming to follow and develop it, they fail to follow and develop its Marxism.

They have rarely explained what the Marxist concepts mean, how Vygotsky utilized these concepts, and how these could be advanced. They have not addressed political aspects of human psychology, nor have they addressed political aspects of the discipline of psychology.[5]

These Vygotskyians have never sought to reformulate psychology along Marxist lines as Vygotsky did.

Particularly glaring in the retreat from Marxism is the neglect of politics by Vygotsky's followers. They neglect political aspects of psychological phenomena; they neglect political aspects of the discipline of psychology; and they neglect political aspects of culture. Whereas Marx geared all of his concepts toward reflecting cultural factors, critiquing them, and improving them, Vygotskyians do not focus their theories, methodologies, interventions, or research questions on this political direction. This is evident in their abstract concepts that overlook concrete, political themes. They forgo Marx's revolutionary role for social science, which he states in his closing lines to *The Poverty of Philosophy*: "the last word of social science will always be … combat or death; bloody struggle or extinction" (1847/2008, p. 191). (Bourdieu embraces this in his famous statement that sociology is a combat sport.)

Advancing Vygotsky's Marxist psychology requires confronting the intellectual impediments to it, recovering Vygotsky's ideas about it, and probing the work of Marxists to deepen and extend Marxist psychology beyond Vygotsky's pioneering work. That is the mission of this book.

The science and politics of Marxist psychology

We propose that these issues are not purely intellectual; they are political as well. This is an important element of a Marxist critique of social science and ideology.

We propose that the resistance to, retreat from, and revision of Vygotsky's Marxist psychology is based upon a mistaken politics of freedom (see O'Boyle and McDonough, 2016). This must be reconceptualized before the intellectual issues of Marxist psychology can be appreciated and advanced.

The mistaken politics of freedom that underlie mistaken intellectual issues consist of defining freedom as individual autonomy/agency. This is evidenced in frequent statements about the importance of expressing personal agency and complaints about the cultural structuring of psychology as mechanistic, depersonalizing, and static. Vygotskyian educator Daniels complains that "Durkheim's notion of collective representation allowed for the social interpretation of human cognition, on the other hand it failed to resolve the issue as to how the collective representation is interpreted by the individual" (2012, p. 48). By "individual interpretation," Daniels means idiosyncratic inventions of meanings, as in what it means to you or me as individuals, how we impose our personal stamp on it. He does not mean personal incarnations of social meanings; i.e., which social meanings have been adopted by you or me because of various social pressures. Critics of Bourdieu's social structural organizing of the *habitus* employ the same terminology. A typical complaint is that Bourdieu's strategic model of social action remains too narrow to allow for the possibility of autonomous agency and an emancipatory political praxis. This is what drives the search for, and invention of, individual acts and psychology. Social structure and politics must be rejected as the basis of psychology because they do not afford the political phenomenon of autonomous agency-freedom. Chomsky developed his nativist theory of universal grammar for a similar politics of freedom. He sought to oppose the behavioristic manipulation of behavior by social authority, and a biologically programmed, intra-individual grammar was such an antidote. It functions like universal human rights do to oppose certain oppressive practices.

Revisionist Vygotskyians invert his statement that "The environment is a factor in the realm of personality development, and its role is to act as the source of this development ... not its context" (Vygotsky, 1994a, p. 348).

Revisionists reduce the social environment to a context that is interpreted and utilized and modified by individuals as they assert their individual autonomy. This is achieved by reducing culture to indefinite contexts and interpersonal interactions and dialogues wherein people are of similar status and power and assert their personal agency in mutual negotiation of desires. For example,

> In Engeström's (1996) work within activity theory, which to some considerable extent has a Vygotskyian root, the production of ... discourse is not analyzed in terms of the context of its production that is the rules, community, and division of labor which regulate the activity.
> [...] The application of Vygotsky by many social scientists has been limited to relatively small-scale interactional contexts. ... [T]he focus is on the creation and negotiation of social order by participants.
>
> *(Daniels, 2012, p. 49)*

Cole and Engeström's (2007, p. 488) example of a patient using pieces of paper to orient himself in walking is this level of personal use of social artifacts.[6]

In contrast, Marxist psychology is driven by a politics of concrete, social structural change. This requires identifying the social structural organization and reorganization of behavior. Vygotsky opposes the individualism and subjectivism that his followers laud: "Not in the narrow confines of his own personal life and his own personal affairs will one become a true creator in the future" (Vygotsky, 1926/1997b, p. 350).

Different political philosophies of emancipation are the basis of different psychological approaches.[7]

The book chapters and their authors

The chapters of this book generally focus on the way in which Vygotsky and his colleagues utilized specific Marxist concepts in their psychological work. The focus is on Vygotsky's Marxism. The chapters explain how these Marxist concepts enabled Vygotsky to gain certain insights into psychological issues. They indicate the value of Marxist psychology. A few chapters apply this theme to the authors' own original work within the Vygotskyian tradition. These authors advance Marxist psychology to new realms.

Part I takes a different approach to Vygotsky's Marxism. It articulates a broad architecture of Marxist psychology based on Marx's concepts. It situates Vygotsky within this architecture of Marxism that prefigures Vygotsky and develops beyond him. Vygotsky is not the focus of this chapter as he is in the other chapters.

The chapter explains how cultural psychology (specifically macro cultural psychology) is a powerful discipline, well suited to refining and extending Marxist psychology. Vygotsky's contribution to Marxist psychology is introduced in this discipline.

Part I provides a background for the other chapters, which focus on Vygotsky and do not have the space to address the broad issue of Marxist psychology in general.

Part II discusses the relationship between Marx's epistemological and ontological concepts, and ways they are linked to Vygotsk's ideas. The authors demonstrate how it is impossible to read Vygotsky without knowing Marx. The chapters demonstrate how Marx's category of work is fundamental to understanding Vygotsky's conception of the subject. And how Vygotsky's work on the formation of higher psychological functioning and mediative processes, that are constitutive of the human psyche, reflect and advance Marx's conception of the relation between nature and consciousness.

Part III analyzes applications of Vygotsky's Marxism to specific psychological topics. The questions of imagination, language, bilingualism among others are in the center of the discussions.

This book has been written by an international group of scholars who are uniquely equipped to address the relationship between Vygotsky's cultural-historical psychology and Marxism. Each contributor is an erudite Vygotskyian scholar and also a Marxist scholar. We feel this dual expertise is essential for discussing Vygotsky's Marxism intelligently – and for discussing Marxist psychology intelligently.

We also believe our scholarship more than compensates for our lack of reading Russian works by Vygotsky. Given the wealth of translated material, it is unreasonable to expect that scholarly research on Vygotsky is done only by Russian readers. Russian readers of Vygotsky are not necessarily (or usually) experts in Marxism. Their linguistic fluency does not translate into social theory fluency concerning the embedded meanings of Marxist concepts.

The necessary combination of expertise in Marxism and Vygotsky is strong in Vygotskyian studies in Brazil. This is a legacy of the strong tradition of left-wing, political liberation psychology and liberation theology (Proença, 2016; Tuleski, 2015, 2016). Brazil contains more Marxist Vygotskyians than any other country in the world. Our book is unique in presenting this important Brazilian perspective on Vygotsky to the English-speaking world.

Notes

1   The fact that Stalin's regime required nominal endorsement of Marxism does not mean that all scholars who endorsed Marxism did so for this reason and that nobody really believed in Marxism. An entire generation of social scientists and philosophers and artists genuinely believed in Marxism.

2   Gielen and Jeshmaridian condemn Marxism as misguided and stultifying, and they castigate Vygotsky for naively embracing it.

They fall into the common mistake of equating Stalinism and Marxism. This leads them to condemn the latter in the same terms as the former. Vygotsky and Luria grasped the gross corruption of Marxism that Stalinism effected, and they correctly continued to accept Marxism.

3   Bilingualism follows the same pattern. It is construed as broadening perceptual and cognitive competencies. In fact, perceptual and cognitive effects depend entirely on the social status of the two languages learned. The abstraction "bilingualism" has no particular effects. High-status languages (e.g., in India, English and Hindi) have positive psychological effects; however, low-status languages (e.g., Kui and Oriya) have negative effects (Ratner, 2012, pp. 228–230).

Gender is similarly an empty psychological abstraction that is only meaningful when concretized with concrete social roles. Valuing gender *per se* tacitly values the concrete social roles which are unstated and are often oppressive and destructive. Valuing women for political office is often touted as a positive act for producing female role models for children. However, this ignores the concrete activities of political office, which are oppressive, exploitive, imperialist, and pro-corporate. Thus, female political leaders such as Margaret Thatcher, Hillary Clinton, and Condi Rice actually model women-as-imperialists, women-as-corporate-apologists, women-as-liars, women-as-oppressors of poor people. This is the full female political role model that these women promote and that children perceive and imitate. Lauding female political leadership as enhancing the image of women smuggles concrete cultural evils of the political role of women into this ideal. These evils are not mentioned; however, they do exist and they inspire girls to applaud or assume the role of imperialist, apologist, oppressor, and liar – which are all disguised by the lauded category "woman leader."

Ignoring (and accepting) concrete facts makes abstract formulations acceptable to the status quo. Imperialism, oppression, hypocrisy, etc. can all be tacitly promoted by promoting "women's leadership," which tacitly contains status quo activities. Promoting women as leaders in this context is thus actually a bad role model because of the invidious concrete behaviors it includes.

Role modeling as political strategy for social mobility and equality is a sham. It is a personalistic strategy that assumes a successful role model will inspire disadvantaged others to become motivated to achieve the same success. This implies that opportunities are waiting to be filled; all that is lacking is motivation to take advantage of them. No structural change or support is necessary. Role modeling is based upon a false, psychologistic theory of behavior; it ignores structural obstacles to success that must be overcome by structural-political transformation.

4 In the same way, the abstraction "culture = civilization" is a future ideal, not concrete, existing reality. A great deal of existing culture de-civilizes people. This is true for slavery, dictatorship, neoliberalism, and others. Culture must be made civilizing through social transformation.

Similarly, the abstraction "schooling = education" is an ideal that must be created through social reorganization. The phrase contradicts and improves on existing schooling that does *not* educate people and cultivate high-level cognitive functions. In 2015, only 4 percent of Detroit public school eighth graders were proficient in math and only 7 percent in reading (Higgins, 2015).

5 One way to extend and advance Vygotsky's concepts would be to enter debates about the causes and treatments of intelligence, identity, emotions, cognitive reasoning, child development, sexuality, or mental illness. Vygotskyians could elaborate on the cultural basis of these competencies and rebut nativist, biological, and personal-subjective causation. Marxist scientists in the 1970s and 1980s, such as Lewontin, Levins, and Gould, wrote powerful Marxist critiques of nativist theory and research (such as sociobiology) concerning intelligence, gender, sexual orientation, and mental illness. For instance, Lewontin, Rose, and Kamin (1984, pp. 152–153) write:

> Lesbians, it was argued, should have higher androgen and/or lower estrogen levels than heterosexuals. Yet no such relationships exist. Nor would we have expected them to: the very assumption implies a reification and biological reductionism which insists that all sexual activities and proclivities can be dichotomized into hetero- or homo-directed, and that showing one or the other proclivity is an all or none state of the individual, rather than a statement about a person in a particular social context at a particular time in his or her history.

Levins and Lewontin (1985) wrote a profound critique of biologism relating it to capitalist social relations, ideology, and the commoditization of science. In this vein, Marxist Vygotskyians should refute postmodernism, liberalism, social constructionism, subjectivism, and neoliberalism in the same principled manner in which earlier Marxists rebutted sociobiology, behaviorism, psychiatry, psychoanalysis, and positivism.

Vygotskyians should additionally advance Vygotsky's concepts by entering the debate over Freudo-Marxism. Vygotsky (1997a, pp. 258–269) wrote a culture-based, Marxist attack on Freudian psychoanalysis. Vygotskyians should expand and refine the cultural-Marxist elements of this critique (see Lichtman, 1982, for example). Chapter 1 of this book advances this critique.

6 Cole and Engeström make this kind of personal, micro-level activity central to developmental theory: "developmental change is promoted by having people with different kinds of knowledge and ability engage jointly in a variety of culturally organized, sanctioned activities" (2007, p. 488). This is an abstract statement: interpersonal interactions among diverse individuals, devoid of any particular content, devoid of any particular direction of change, and divorced from concrete macro cultural factors are construed as useful for development. Of course, this is not true. Useful developmental change depends upon the specific kinds of knowledge and ability that caretakers possess, as well as the concrete school, neighborhood, and occupational conditions that surround and permeate interpersonal relations. Vygotsky explains that "The various internal contradictions which are to be found in different

social systems find their expression both in the type of personality and in the structure of human psychology in that historical period" (1994b, p. 176).

Positive developmental change also depends upon systematically transforming deleterious social conditions. Individuals must be prepared to seek social-political-economic transformation to bring about their psychological development. This is what Freire meant by conscientization. Cole's intervention for psychological enrichment ignores this. It focuses on children playing computer games to stimulate cognitive skills (see Ratner, forthcoming, for additional critique).

7   The politics of Marxist psychology are rather similar in China. Curiously, this socialist country, governed by the Chinese Communist Party (CCP), has *no* Marxist psychology (not even cultural psychology or Vygotsky's psychology) – not in Communist Party Schools, not in Marxist Institutes, not in Marxist university departments or the Chinese Academy of Social Sciences, and not in public health and psychological interventions. Chinese academic psychology is a slavish imitation of American mainstream psychology (which now includes cross-cultural psychology).

This is a telling *political* event. All Western Marxists roundly criticize American social science – especially psychology – for obfuscating cultural features of psychology that need to be elucidated, critiqued, and changed. Marx states in *The Poverty of Philosophy* that "economic categories are only the theoretical expressions, the abstractions, of the social relations of production" (1847/2008, p. 119); "economists are the scientific representatives of the bourgeois class" (ibid., p. 186); clearly, psychologists perform the same function. Foucault extends this critique of the human sciences as forms of knowledge that recapitulate practices of power in government and the management of individuals. Yet socialist China and its ruling CCP avidly follow American psychology without a word of criticism and without searching for a Marxist alternative. China's acceptance of American psychology also contrasts with its suspicion and censoring of Western news, magazines, websites, and entertainment. Why does the Marxist Communist Party afford such a unique, exalted position to an American psychology – especially since it is criticized by Marxists around the world?

The reason is that American psychology is a sociopolitical *gatekeeper* of social knowledge. It removes deep, penetrating, critical research on the social system. The CCP fears this kind of research because it offers an alternative understanding of Chinese society and psychology to the Party line. (For the role that Marxist anthropology plays in challenging official discourse, see Lem and Marcus, 2016). This is the same reason that the CCP prohibits an independent press and why it controls civil society associations.

The CCP uses the *epistemological-political function of American psychology* to block deep, penetrating, critical thinking about society (Yang, 2016). The advantage is that psychology does its job as a scientific discipline. It requires no overt, external, political censoring by the government. It is a *nonpolitical form* of repression that has a *political function*. It is a nonpolitical legitimation of political governmentality. It is thus more effective than overt political legitimation through CCP censorship and ostentatious self-praise.

References

Chaiklin, S. (2012). Dialectics, politics, and contemporary cultural-historical research, exemplified through Marx and Vygotsky. In H. Edwards (Ed.), *Vygotsky and sociology* (pp. 24–44). London: Routledge.

Cole, M., and Engeström, Y. (2007). Cultural-historical approaches to designing for development. In J. Valsiner and A. Rosa (Eds.), *The Cambridge handbook of sociocultural psychology* (pp. 484–507). New York: Cambridge University Press.

Cole, M., Levitin, K., and Luria, A. (2006). *The autobiography of Alexander Luria: A dialogue with The Making of Mind*. Mahwah, NJ: Lawrence Erlbaum Associates.

Daniels, H. (2012). *Vygotsky and sociology*. London: Routledge.

Duarte, Newton (2000). The man anatomy is the key to the monkey anatomy: the dialectics in Vigotski and in Marx and the issue about objective knowledge in school education. *Educ. Soc.* [online], 21 (71), 79-115. Available at: http://dx.doi.org/10.1590/S0101-73302000000200004.

Gielen, G., and Jeshmaridian, S. (1999). Lev S. Vygotsky: The man and the era. *International Journal of Group Tensions*, 28 (3–4), 273–301. Available at: http://lchc.ucsd.edu/mca/Paper/Vytogsky-the_man_and_the_era.pdf (accessed December 1, 2016).

Grigorenko, E. (2014). Tracing the untraceable: The nature-nurture controversy in cultural-historical psychology. In A. Yasnitsky, R. van der Veer, and M. Ferrari (Eds.), *The Cambridge handbook of cultural-historical psychology* (pp. 203–216). New York: Cambridge University Press.

Hardt, M., and Negri, A. (2000). *Empire*. Cambridge, MA: Harvard University Press.

Hegel, G. (1969). *Science of logic*. New York: Humanities Press.

Higgins, L. (2015). Michigan's black students lag behind the nation. *Detroit Free Press*, December 10. Available at: www.freep.com/story/news/local/michigan/2015/12/10/michigans-black-students-academic-performance/77099294/ (accessed November 20, 2016).

Horkheimer, M. (1993). History and psychology. In *Between philosophy and social science: Selected early writings*, trans. M. S. Kramer, G. F. Hunter, and J. Torpey (pp. 111–128). Cambridge, MA: MIT Press.

Ilyenkov, E. (1982). *The dialectics of the abstract and the concrete in Marx's Capital*. Moscow: Progress Publishers. (Original work published 1960).

Lem, W., and Marcus, A. (2016). The Marxist tradition as a dialectical anthropology. *Dialectical Anthropology*, 40 (2), 57–58.

Levins, R., and Lewontin, R. (1985). *The dialectical biologist*. Cambridge, MA: Harvard University Press.

Levitin, K. (1982). *One is not born a personality*. Moscow: Progress Publishers.

Lewontin, R. C., Rose, S., and Kamin, L. (1984). *Not in our genes: Biology, ideology, and human nature*. New York: Pantheon.

Lichtman, R. (1982). *The production of desire: The integration of psychoanalysis into Marxist theory*. New York: Free Press.

Lukács, G. (1970). *Lenin: A study on the unity of his thought*, trans. N. Jacobs. London: New Left Books. (Original work published 1924). Available at: https://www.marxists.org/archive/lukacs/works/1924/lenin/ch04.htm (accessed December 1, 2016).

Luria, A. (1979). *The making of mind: A personal account of Soviet psychology*. Cambridge, MA: Harvard University Press. Available at: https://www.marxists.org/archive/luria/works/1979/mind/ (accessed December 1, 2016).

Marx, K. (1973). *Grundrisse: Foundations of the critique of political economy*, trans. M. Nicolaus. London: Penguin Books. (Original work published 1939).

Marx, K. (1999). *A contribution to the critique of political economy*, trans. S. W. Ryazanskaya. Moscow: Progress Publishers. (Original work published 1859). Available at: https://www.

marxists.org/archive/marx/works/1859/critique-pol-economy/ (accessed December 1, 2016).

Marx, K. (2008). *The poverty of philosophy*, trans. H. Quelch. New York: Cosmio. (Original work published 1847).

Marx, K., and Engels, F. (1968). *The German ideology*. Moscow: Progress Publishers. (Original work published 1932).

Marx, K., and Engels, F. (1975). *Karl Marx Frederick Engels collected works: Volume 3*. New York: International Publishers.

Marx, K., and Engels, F. (1976). *Karl Marx Frederick Engels collected works: Volume 6*. New York: International Publishers.

Newman, F., and Holzman, L. (2014). *Lev Vygotsky: Revolutionary Scientist*. London: Psychology Press.

O'Boyle, B., and McDonough, T. (2016). Critical realism and the Althusserian legacy. *Journal of the Theory of Social Behaviour*, 46 (2), 143–164.

Packer, M. J. (2008). Is Vygotsky relevant? Vygotsky's Marxist psychology. *Mind, Culture, and Activity*, 15 (1), 8–31. DOI: 10.1080/10749030701798607

Paolucci, P. (2012). *Marx and the politics of abstraction*. Chicago: Haymarket Books.

Pino, A. (2000). The social and the cultural in Vygotsky's work. *Educ. Soc.* [online], 21 (71), 45-78. Available at: http://dx.doi.org/10.1590/S0101-73302000000200003.

Proença, M. (2016). School psychology from a critical historical perspective: In search of a theoretical-methodological construction. In M. Proença, R. de Souza, G. Toassa, and K. Bautheney (Eds.), *Psychology, society and education: Critical perspectives in Brazil* (pp. 3–30). New York: Nova Publishers.

Ratner, C. (2012). *Macro cultural psychology: A political philosophy of mind*. New York: Oxford University Press.

Ratner, C. (2015). Classic and revisionist sociocultural theory and their analyses of expressive language: An empirical assessment. *Language and Sociocultural Theory*, 2 (1), 51–83.

Ratner, C. (2016). Culture-centric vs. person-centered cultural psychology and political philosophy. *Language and Sociocultural Theory*, 3 (1), 11–26.

Ratner, C. (forthcoming). Trends in sociocultural theory: The utility of "cultural capital" for sociocultural theory. In J. Lantolf, M. Poehenr, and M. Swain (Eds.), *Routledge handbook of sociocultural theory and second language learning and teaching*.

Sawaia, B. B. (2009). Psychology and social inequality: A reflection on freedom and social transformation. *Psicologia & Sociedade*, 21 (3), 364–372. http://dx.doi.org/10.1590/S0102-71822009000300010

Tuleski, S. (2015). *Vygotsky and Leontiev: The construction of a Marxist psychology*. New York: Nova Publishers.

Tuleski, S. (Ed.) (2016). *Liberation psychology in Brazil*. New York: Nova Publishers.

van der Veer, R., and Valsiner, J. (1991). *Understanding Vygotsky: A quest for synthesis*. New York: Blackwell.

van der Veer, R., and Zavershneva, E. (2011). To Moscow with love: Partial reconstruction of Vygotsky's trip to London. *Integrative Psychological and Behavioral Science*, 45 (4), 458–474. DOI: 10.1007/s12124-011-9173-8. (This article is published with open access at Springerlink.com).

Veresov, N. (2005). Marxist and non-Marxist aspects of the cultural-historical psychology of L. S. Vygotsky. *Outlines: Critical Practice Studies*, 7 (1), 31–50.

Vygotsky, L. S. (1971). *The Psychology of Art*. Cambridge, MA: The MIT Press (Original work published 1925). Available at: https://www.marxists.org/archive/vygotsky/works/1925/preface.htm (accessed December 1, 2016).

Vygotsky, L. S. (1986). *Thought and language*. Cambridge, MA: The MIT Press.

Vygotsky, L. S. (1989). Concrete human psychology. *Soviet Psychology*, 27 (2), 53–77.

Vygotsky, L. S. (1994a). The problem of the environment. In R. van der Veer and J. Valsiner (Eds.), *The Vygotsky reader* (pp. 338–354). Cambridge: Blackwell.

Vygotsky, L. S. (1994b). The socialist alteration of man. In R. van der Veer and J. Valsiner (Eds.), *The Vygotsky reader* (pp. 175–184). Cambridge: Blackwell.

Vygotsky, L. S. (1997a). *The collected works of L. S. Vygotsky. Volume 3: Problems of the theory and history of psychology*, ed. R.W. Rieber and J. Wollock, trans. R. van der Veer. New York: Plenum.

Vygotsky, L. S. (1997b). *Educational psychology*, trans. R. Silverman. Boca Raton, FL: St. Lucie Press. (Original work published 1926).

Vygotsky, L. S. (1998). *The collected works of L. S. Vygotsky. Volume 5: Child psychology*, ed. R.W. Rieber, trans. M. J. Hall. New York: Plenum.

Yang, J. (2016). The politics and regulation of anger in urban China. *Culture, Medicine, Psychiatry*, 40 (1), 100–123. DOI 10.1007/s11013-015-9476-1

Yasnitsky, A., and van der Veer, R. (2016). *Revisionist revolution in Vygotsky studies*. Hove: Routledge.

Yasnitsky, A., van der Veer, R., and Ferrari, M. (2014). *The Cambridge handbook of cultural-historical psychology*. New York: Cambridge University Press.

1

MARXIST PSYCHOLOGY, VYGOTSKY'S CULTURAL PSYCHOLOGY, AND PSYCHOANALYSIS

The double helix of science and politics

Carl Ratner

I. Marx, Marxist psychology, and Vygotsky

Whereas most treatment of Vygotsky's relation to Marxism explores the manner in which he utilized Marx's concepts and methodology, here, I invert this and explore the manner in which Marxist psychology can utilize Vygotsky's concepts and methodology.

This chapter explains how a Marxist psychology can be constructed that draws on Marx's social theory regarding the structure of society, the relation of psychology to social structure, and human nature. Vygotsky is used for his important contribution to fleshing out some of these elements.

Marx and Vygotsky are shown to enrich each other. On the one hand, Vygotsky adds the crucial psychological dimension to Marxism through his brilliant theorizing about the academic discipline of psychology and his empirical research on specific psychological processes. On the other hand, Marxism provides the foundation for Vygotsky's Marxist psychology and indicates how it can be developed beyond what Vygotsky accomplished. Vygotsky was unable to fully apply Marxist political philosophy to all psychological topics, or even to all of the topics that he touched upon. As Luria says: "The system of human psychology on which Vygotsky worked all his life was never completed. He did not leave us a personally completed and rebuilt science" (in Levitin, 1982, p. 173). It is thus necessary for us to thoroughly articulate Marxist political philosophy so that it can deepen Vygotsky's work and be extended to psychological phenomena in general.

For instance, Vygotsky emphasized language as the basis of thought. Marx and Engels cautioned that language is grounded in social life and reflects its features; it is not an independent realm. In *The German Ideology*, they say,

One of the most difficult tasks confronting philosophers is to descend from the world of thought to the actual world. Language is [construed as] the immediate actuality of thought. Just as philosophers have given thought an independent existence, so they were bound to make language into an independent realm. This is the secret of philosophical language, in which thoughts in the form of words have their own content. The problem of descending from the world of thoughts to the actual world is turned into the problem of descending from language to life.

We have shown that thoughts and ideas acquire an independent existence in consequence of the personal circumstances and relations of individuals acquiring independent existence. We have shown that exclusive, systematic occupation with these thoughts on the part of ideologists and philosophers, and hence the systematisation of these thoughts, is a consequence of division of labour, and that, in particular, German philosophy is a consequence of German petty-bourgeois conditions. The philosophers have only to dissolve their language into the ordinary language, from which it is abstracted, in order to recognise it, as the distorted language of the actual world, and to realise that neither thoughts nor language in themselves form a realm of their own, that they are only manifestations of actual life.

(Marx and Engels, 1932/1968, Chapter 3)

Advancing Vygotsky's Marxism must utilize Marx and Engels' criticism of philosophical idealism to develop a historical-materialist conception of language as the basis of psychology.

Marxist psychology is a dialectical integration of two fields: Marxism and psychology. It is faithful to both and corrective of both. Marxist social theory is extended to the distinctive domain of psychology where it initiates fruitful hypotheses, corrects theoretical issues, and identifies methodological errors (with both positivism and postmodernist/individualistic qualitative methodology). Marxist psychology is an internal development of psychology that fills its intellectual voids, corrects its errors, and resolves its contradictions and controversies. Conversely, psychology is extended to Marxism, where it contributes specific theories and research about phenomena such as emotions, memory, learning, socialization, mental illness, and developmental processes. These correct certain Marxist concepts that are psychologically uninformed. Of course, the psychological theories, conclusions, and methodologies are adjusted to Marxist principles and, reciprocally, introduce adjustments to those principles.

Marxist psychology avoids reducing psychological theory and methodology to Marxist economic formulations or political activism. On the contrary, Marxist psychology retains the distinctive contributions of psychology and utilizes these to enrich Marxism. Yaroshevsky put this as follows:

Vygotskiy viewed Marxist psychology not as a school but as the only scientific psychology. … Vygotsky believed that transformation of psychology on the basis of Marxism did not in any way mean abandoning all previous [academic] work. Every effort thought to gain insight into the psyche … would necessarily be incorporated into it [Marxist psychology] in a modified form.

(Cited in Levitin, 1982, p. 53)

This is illustrated in Figure 1.1.

Marxist psychology must be developed by Marxists who are grounded in the discipline of psychology – its theories, methodologies, research findings, and interventions. Marxist psychology cannot be developed on the purely philosophical level of Marxian-Hegelian theory, or Freudian or Lacanian theory, that is ignorant of these psychological details.

Vygotsky saw Marxism as a model whereby a philosophical doctrine is applied to a concrete science. That task could not be tackled by the direct introduction of the universal categories and laws of dialectical materialism into the concrete sciences. Equally fruitless was the approach whereby isolated utterances from Marxist works were thought to provide a ready-made psychology, i.e., a solution to the question of the specifics and laws of the human psyche. To apply Marxism to a particular science, it was necessary to work out a methodology, i.e., a system of concepts which could be applied to that particular science.

(Levitin, 1982, p. 54)

FIGURE 1.1   Marxist psychological science

Vygotsky states this as follows:

> The *direct* application of the theory of *dialectical materialism* to the problems of psychology *is impossible*. ... Like history, sociology is in need of the intermediate *special theory* of historical materialism which explains the *concrete* meaning for the given group of phenomena of the abstract laws of dialectical materialism. In exactly the same way, we are in need of an as yet undeveloped but inevitable theory of psychological materialism as an intermediate science which explains the concrete application of the abstract theses of dialectical materialism to the given field of phenomena.
>
> [...] In order to create such intermediate theories – methodologies, general sciences – we must reveal the *essence* of the given area of phenomena, the laws of their change, their qualitative and quantitative characteristics, their causality; we must create categories and concepts appropriate to it, in short, we must create our *own Das Kapital* – its own concepts of class, basis, value, etc. – in which it might express, describe, and study its object.
>
> *(1997a, p. 330)*

> Dialectical materialism is a most abstract science. The direct application of dialectical materialism to the biological sciences and psychology, as is common nowadays, does not go beyond the formal logical, scholastic, verbal subsumption of particular phenomena, whose internal sense and relation is unknown, under general, abstract, universal categories.
>
> *(Ibid., p. 331)*

Vygotsky is saying that dialectical philosophy cannot suffice as a psychological theory because it is devoid of concrete knowledge of psychological phenomena, just as it is devoid of biological knowledge. Consequently, it is limited to general, abstract dialectical categories. "We do not need fortuitous utterances, but a method; not dialectical materialism, but historical materialism" (ibid., p. 331).

Vygotsky implies that even historical materialism is insufficient for constructing a complete psychological theory because it is ignorant of concrete psychological processes, the essence of the given area of phenomena, the laws of their change, their qualitative and quantitative characteristics, and their causality. Historical materialism does not contain categories and concepts appropriate to psychology. This is why Vygotsky says we must create a specifically *psychological* theory that he calls "psychological materialism." It is based upon dialectical materialism and historical materialism; however, it contributes a specifically psychological dimension to these. This is how Marxist psychology enriches Marxism.

In *The Psychology of Art*, Vygotsky (1925/1971) explains the relationship between art and Marxism:

> I propose to remain content with the methodological and theoretical laws of the psychological examination of art, along with every other attempt,

pointing out the essential importance of finding a place within the Marxist doctrine of art. Here my guideline has been the well-known Marxist position that the sociological view of art does not deny its aesthetic consideration; on the contrary, it opens wide the door to it and presupposes it, in Plekhanov's words, as its complement.

Vygotsky emphasizes the distinctive, "emergent" nature of the esthetic realm and advocates that Marxism make a space for it without reducing it to the political economy.

Vygotsky made important advances in psychology and in Marxism by developing the distinctive features of psychology that force Marxism to expand to incorporate them in its theory. Where Marx and Engels say, "language is practical consciousness," Vygotsky uses language as the basis of thought/cognition. Vygotsky took Marx and Engels' (1932/1968, p. 42) statement that "consciousness takes the place of instinct" in humans, and expanded consciousness as the entire basis of psychology: "Development of thinking has a central, key, decisive significance for all the other [psychological] functions and processes.... All other special functions are intellectualized, reformed, and reconstructed under the influence of these crucial successes that thinking achieves" (Vygotsky, 1998, p. 81). This is a psychological insight made by a psychologist steeped in the field of psychology; it extends Marxism into the full nature of human psychology.

Vygotsky developed psychology along Marxist lines (infused with Marxist thinking) more profoundly and scientifically than anyone ever has. Consequently, while Vygotsky argues that Marxist psychology is the only scientific psychology, we must add that Vygotskyian psychology is the only adequate Marxist psychology. Marxist psychology (i.e., scientific psychology), which certainly incorporates ideas from various scholars, must be based upon Vygotsky's ideas. It is impossible for psychoanalytically oriented psychologists, or critical psychologists, to engage with Marxist psychology while disregarding Vygotsky. It is intellectually irresponsible as well to ignore the best scientific contribution to Marxist psychology.

Marxist psychology uses Marxism and psychology to enrich each other without reducing either to the other. Marxist psychology must research psychological issues that extend Marxism and psychology beyond their traditional domains.

We need:

- a Marxist psychology of emotions
- a Marxist psychology of sexuality/gender
- a Marxist psychology of memory
- a Marxist psychology of intelligence
- a Marxist psychology of perception
- a Marxist psychology of development
- a Marxist psychology of language
- a Marxist psychology of self/personality
- a Marxist psychology of the body

- a Marxist psychology of mental disorders
- a Marxist psychology of psychobiological processes. For example, Marxist psychology needs a psychology of brain localization of psychological phenomena. This is far removed from conventional Marxist topics; however, it enriches Marxism. The question is whether emotions, memory, self-concept, attention, problem-solving, mental illness, and language are localized in prefigured brain centers (modules) with unique neurophysiological properties capable of processing unique psychological features, or whether the cortex is a general, flexible, unspecified processing apparatus in which any psychological function can be processed in any location. This technical matter is relevant to Marxism because it concerns the question of whether psychological functions are preformed modules that are biologically determined through localized, distinctive physiological factors or whether the cortex does not determine psychology's features through the inherent properties of cortical centers but is, rather, a general information processing center of psychological features that are cultural in nature, origin, formation, and function. Evidence is on the side of the latter, which makes brain localization (modularity) an interesting and important support for Marxist psychology. This is an important example of how technical, psychobiological, non-Marxist psychological issues have a strong bearing on Marxist theory and science.
- a Marxist psychology that explains why and how psychological phenomena are formed by cultural factors and processes. This is crucial for extending Marxism to subjectivity and consciousness. It avoids empiricism that simply correlates phenotypical psychological expressions with social events without explaining how or why the correlation exists.

Central to Marxist psychology is the revolutionary politics of Marxism that critiques the existing social system and directs its reorganization toward a more fulfilling one. This must be built into the theory, constructs, methodology, and interventions of psychology; it must permeate, structure, and direct all of these scientific elements. This political dimension makes Marxist scientific psychology unique. It *enhances* scientific psychology; it does not detract from it. This is a point of emphasis in this chapter.

I argue that cultural psychology is the most fruitful psychological approach for linking psychology and Marxism in a Marxist psychology. Cultural psychology is consistent with Marxist psychology, which enables it to utilize Marxist concepts in cultural psychology, and academic psychology, and enables it to introduce psychological theories, methodologies, interventions, and data into Marxism. This, of course, was Vygotsky's goal in developing his cultural-historical psychology.

After explaining this use of cultural psychology for Marxist psychology, I discuss how Marxist psychology must deal with incompatible theories, methodologies, and interventions. These cannot be directly incorporated into Marxist psychology as cultural psychology can. Incompatible approaches to Marxist psychology must be reorganized and reframed in Marxian terms. I illustrate this with Freudian psychoanalysis.

II. Principles of Marx's theory of social consciousness: the double helix of science and revolution

A Marxist psychology must grow out of Marx's ideas about social consciousness and its grounding in a social structure of social conditions for that is as close as Marx came to discussing psychology. After we examine Marx on social consciousness, we will possess a firm understanding of important elements of a Marxist psychology, which we outline with the help of cultural psychology – especially Vygotsky's.

All of Marx's scientific scholarship about social activity and consciousness was rooted in an antipathy toward capitalist exploitation and his desire to overthrow it in favor of a cooperative, democratic, collective social system. His scientific social science is unique and important in integrating science with emancipatory politics. We must understand both elements of this double helix when examining his ideas on social consciousness.[1]

Marx's discussion of psychological issues within social consciousness has advantages and disadvantages for psychologists.

Its *advantages* are the emphasis on the social bases, organization, and function of psychological phenomena. Social consciousness emphasizes social-political aspects of consciousness such as its social oppression and social liberation. Marxism is the deepest and most comprehensive description and explanation of these aspects of consciousness. We present examples momentarily.

The *disadvantages* of treating psychology within social-political consciousness include the fact that it distracts away from important details of psychological phenomena unrelated to their social oppression and emancipation. It does not formulate essential, comprehensive theories of particular psychological phenomena such as emotions, self-concept, cognition, perception, and mental illness. Instead, these are restricted to practical considerations of social oppression and emancipation. This is an important observation of the social constitution of the senses; however, it is not a general theory of senses that psychologists strive to develop – concerning why sense is social, what the social function and requirement of sense is, what makes sense social whereas animal sense is biologically determined, what the human biology of sense is compared with the biology of animal sense, and what the structural relation is between sense, cognition, emotion, and perception.

Specific principles of Marx's theory of consciousness

1) Social consciousness is conditional on and conditioned by social conditions.

Marx's theory of social consciousness is unusual in that it rests consciousness *completely* upon social conditions. Social conditions are the key to all aspects of social consciousness. They are the origin of social consciousness, its *raison d'être*, its necessity, its function, its operating mechanisms, its *telos*, dynamics, formation, organization/structure, its stimulus and support system. Social conditions explain all forms of consciousness. They explain what we perceive and do as well as what we misperceive and misunderstand. Marx and Engels also grant to social conditions the potential of transforming psychology in the future. Thus, the social conditionality and conditioning of consciousness is *a general theory of consciousness that explains diverse features in terms of essential, consistent, parsimonious concepts.* We explain that this is an environmental theory of consciousness that is Darwinian in orientation — though not in its details.

Social conditions — what I call macro cultural factors — are formed by individual humans utilizing their consciousness and subjectivity. However, conditions and macro cultural factors are emergent, holistic phenomena that transcend their individual founders. A university, an army, a hospital, a slum, a church are collective objectifications of individual agencies that entail institutional forms and features, institutional rules and administration, institutional logics (*telos*) and dynamics. These are all integrated gestalts that are more than the sum of their individual participants. Holistic social conditions constitute the scientific aspects of consciousness as well as the politics of consciousness. These emergent social gestalts, or collective objectifications, become the conditions that require and inspire new ideas, practices, and conditions. They also form the environment that selects in favor of viable ideas, practices, and conditions and prevents (weeds out) others from propagating.

Social consciousness is always embedded in social structures, systems, conditions, objectifications, and dynamics, and it embeds them within itself. Consciousness is a function of these conditions, it is selected, required, stimulated, and supported by social conditions, and it is functional for maintaining them. Our mental competencies are required by, selected by, stimulated by, and supported by university admissions departments, university professors, and textbooks, by supervisors at work, by army sergeants, by dating norms, etc. If you adapt your psyche to these conditions, you will succeed and you will reproduce them. If you do not develop socially appropriate competencies, you will be excluded from participating in these institutions and receiving the benefits they bestow. In this "structural-functional" model, failure itself is necessary, encouraged, supported, and functional for exploitive social systems. To fail is to succeed in performing and reproducing the lower-class social role and function. This is necessary for the class system. To challenge failure in the lower class is to challenge the success of the class structure; it represents failure of the system to maintain itself. This is why it is *discouraged* in numerous ways.

Life activity, including consciousness, is so dependent upon conditions that Marx and Engels define communism in these terms: "Communism is the doctrine of the conditions of the emancipation of the proletariat" (1976, p. 341). Communism is not emancipation incarnate. It is the conditions that allow for people to become emancipated as they comprehend and draw upon social conditions propitious for transforming social life.

Marx and Engels' theory of social consciousness incorporates Hegel's dialectical formulation of *non-identity* (Kosok, 1972). According to Hegel, every thing is more than itself; it is not identical with itself but has an otherness contained in itself. "The existent thing has no being of its own, but only in something else; in this other, however, is its self-relation" (Hegel, 1817/1965, p. 245). Culture is this otherness to subjectivity that makes subjectivity what it is. Reciprocally, social conditions need consciousness; they do not exist as mechanical, natural forms devoid of consciousness.

These points are evident in Marx's statements:

> As the conscious representative of this movement [of capital], the possessor of money becomes a capitalist. His person, or rather his pocket, is the point from which the money starts and to which it returns. The expansion of value, which is the objective basis or main-spring of the circulation M–C–M, becomes his subjective aim, and it is only in so far as the appropriation of ever more and more wealth in the abstract becomes the sole motive of his operations, that he functions as a capitalist, that is, as capital personified and endowed with consciousness and a will.
>
> *(Marx, 1867/1961, pp. 108–109)*

> We have seen that *the capitalist process of production is a historically determined form of the social process of production in general.* The latter is as much a production process of material conditions of human life as a process taking place under specific historical and economic production relations, *producing and reproducing these production relations themselves, and thereby also the bearers of this process, their material conditions of existence and their mutual relations, i.e., their particular socio-economic form.* For the aggregate of these relations, in which the agents of this production stand with respect to Nature and to one another, and in which they produce, is precisely society, considered from the standpoint of its economic structure. Like all its predecessors, the capitalist process of production proceeds under *definite material conditions, which are, however, simultaneously the bearers of definite social relations entered into by individuals in the process of reproducing their life.* Those conditions, like these relations, are on the one hand prerequisites, on the other hand results and creations of the capitalist process of production; they are produced and reproduced by it.
>
> *(Marx, 1894/1962, emphasis added)*

> The principal agents of this mode of production itself, the capitalist and the wage-labourer, are as such merely embodiments, personifications of capital and wage-labour; definite social characteristics stamped upon individuals by the process of social production; the products of these definite social production relations.
>
> *(Ibid., Chapter 51)*

> The advance of *capitalist production develops a working class* which by education, tradition and habit looks upon the requirements of that mode of production

as self-evident natural laws. The organization of the capitalist process of production, once it is fully developed, breaks down all resistance.

(Marx, 1867/1977, p. *899, emphasis added*)

These passages express a) how consciousness is conditional and conditioned through social relations and b) how social conditions are themselves conditional on and conditioned by other social and physical conditions. (Momentarily, we see how current conditions generate their own transformation.) It is social conditions all the way down.

A contemporary example of the integration of consciousness with social conditions is a high school student who wants to avail herself of the benefits of an advanced education. She systematically works on herself to gear her cognitive and social skills to conform to Harvard's admission requirements. She becomes Harvard personified, endowed with consciousness and will, such that her operations have no other propelling drive than the progressive appropriation of Harvard competencies. If she stands out because of her absolute thirst for academic enrichment, this is because her soul is "that of Harvard," and "Harvard has but one instinct: the instinct to increase, to create intellectual value." She wants to represent Harvard, which means reproducing its standards in her behavior. This is how she gets to develop herself intellectually, it is how she gets to succeed in society, and it is how Harvard – and society – maintain themselves by having individuals striving to embody their standards.

Following Marx and Engels, we can see how private property *makes* people self-centered; it gives them the social *right* to be so, the social value and justification to be so. Your neighbor can cut down a beautiful tree next to the property line with your house without considering the fact that you love to look at it. She has the legal and ethical right to cut down her tree, and this insulates her from thinking about you; it is not your business. If you become upset about it, it is your problem; you have no *right* to become angry because it is her property and you have nothing to do with it; you should not concern yourself with her business, legally or psychologically. If you express anger at her, you are infringing on her privacy; you will be punished for interfering with her; she will not be punished for interfering with you because she has acted within her private property. She has no obligation to be concerned with you because it is *her property*. Private property forms the contour of our consciousness: anything on our side of the property line is our business, concerns only us, and insulates us from thinking of outsiders. Communal property would form an expansive contour of consciousness that would include all the members who jointly owned the tree and property. The communal social consciousness would prevent us from thinking of it as "my" tree and not considering all the other owners of that tree.

2) Marxist behavioral theory is a form of Darwinian environmentalism.

Marxist theory that consciousness/behavior is conditional on and conditioned by social conditions is a Darwinian revolution in psychology, or a Copernican shift, away from traditional psychology. Darwin says, "as diverging peculiarities are transmitted to the new generations, nature itself does the choosing, and a new generation will arise having changed peculiarities." Here, Darwin uses environmental conditions as the basis for selecting individual features. Individual members do not choose and select their own features. Environmentalism encompasses individual change through changes in the environment and the attributes it selects.

Marx and Engels admired Darwin's theory. Marx sent Darwin a copy of *Capital* as a token of his appreciation. Marx (2010, pp. 246–247) wrote to Lassalle in 1861:

> Darwin's work is most important and suits my purpose in that it provides a basis in natural science for the class struggle in history. One has to put up with the crude English method of development [i.e., struggle for survival], of course. Despite all deficiencies, not only is the death-blow dealt here for the first time to "teleology" in the natural sciences but their rational meaning is empirically explained.

Marx and Engels admire Darwin for explaining change objectively and materially and for disproving metaphysical, spiritual, teleological explanations. These range from god's will to Hegelian spirit to human will.

In *Capital, Volume 1*, Marx explains his regard for Darwin's materialistic explanation of change:

> Darwin has interested us in the history of Nature's Technology, i.e., in the formation of the organs of plants and animals, which organs serve as instruments of production for sustaining life. Does not the history of *the productive organs of man, of organs that are the material basis of all social organization*, deserve equal attention? And would not such a history be easier to compile, since, as Vico says, human history differs from natural history in this, that we have made the former, but not the latter?
>
> *(Marx, 1867/1961, p. 372, fn. 3, emphasis added)*[2]

Marx emphasizes that human behavior is different from physical anatomy and that the processes that generate psychological/behavioral capabilities, support them, and select for them by weeding out misfits are different. Processes that generate the environment also differ. The human environment is constructed by humans in conscious acts. The natural environment of nonhuman organisms is a function of natural forces. However, the dependence of capabilities on a generating, supportive, and selective environment is an overarching principle in both social and natural life. Actually, Marx's environmentalism is more determining of behavior than is Darwin's since Darwinism postulates the mechanisms of behavior to be rooted in the individual's biology – e.g., random genetic changes. The environment selects from among these which ones are to be maintained and proliferated. Marx argues that social processes form the behavioral mechanisms and content that individuals assume; conditions do not simply select from intraindividual mechanisms.

Vygotsky embraces this social extension of Darwinian environmentalism. He writes:

> The point of public education may be defined with scientific exactitude as that of a kind of social selection which education produces from out of the wealth of potentialities within the child.
>
> *(1926/1997b, p. 317)*

> Into that chaotic melange of the newborn infant's uncoordinated and disorganized movements, discipline, meaning, order, and succession are introduced through the methodical educational influence of the environment.
>
> *(Ibid., p. 316)*

> Development is achieved under particular conditions of interaction with the environment, where the ideal and final form of development is already there in the environment and actually exerts a real influence on the primary form, on the first steps of the child's development. *Something which is only supposed to take shape at the very end of development somehow influences the very first steps in this development.*
>
> *(Vygotsky, 1994a, p. 348)*

> If no appropriate ideal form can be found in the environment, and the development of the child, for whatever reasons, has to take place outside those specific conditions, i.e., without any interaction with the final form, then this proper form will fail to develop properly in the child.
>
> *(Ibid., p. 349)*

Marx's environmentalism generates an organic integration of consciousness and social conditions – just as Darwinism generates an organic integration of anatomy, behavior, and environment. Environment forms, requires, supports, and stimulates congruent consciousness, and it weeds out incongruent consciousness. In this sense, Darwinian environmentalism is quintessential cultural psychology and vice versa. Behavior is functional for an environment. Environment sustains consciousness and consciousness sustains the environment by reproducing it.

Marx and Engels use their theory of conditional, conditioned consciousness to explain social illusions such as religion. This is an important advance of Marxist psychology. It explains misperceptions in the same terms as veridical perceptions. This parsimonious explanation of diverse phenomena is a central element of scientific explanation. Marx and Engels explain that misperceptions originate in, and are functional for, normal social conditions. They are not produced by cognitive deficiencies of the individual psyche.

Man is the world of man – state, society. This state and this society produce religion, which is an inverted consciousness of the world, because they are an inverted world. Religion is the general theory of this world, its encyclopaedic compendium, its logic in popular form, its spiritual point d'honneur, its enthusiasm, its moral sanction, its solemn complement, and its universal basis of consolation and justification. It is the fantastic realization of the human essence since the human essence has not acquired any true reality. The struggle against religion is, therefore, indirectly the struggle against that world whose spiritual aroma is religion.

Religious suffering is, at one and the same time, the expression of real suffering and a protest against real suffering. Religion is the sigh of the oppressed creature, the heart of a heartless world, and the soul of soulless conditions. It is the opium of the people.

(Marx, 1843; see also Marx's section on the
fetishism of commodities, 1867/1961, p. 79)

Marx's social theory traces illusion and mystification to the exploitive, unfulfilling, "untrue" (using Hegel's term), "inverted" state and society. These conditions do not afford genuine fulfillment; so people construct an escapist, mystical fulfillment in a domain of spiritual chimeras. Marx does not blame religious devotees for their illusions; rather, he indicts the state and society as alienated, inverted, untrue, and reified.

Marx and Engels explain that conditions are not simple, singular, or transparent. They do not lead to direct reflection of their true exploitive character in consciousness. Conditions determine the extent to which they can readily be apprehended or not. Inverted conditions generate inverted perceptions, or illusions. *Illusions are objective, not subjective. Subjective illusions reflect objective mystifications.*[3] Ending illusions requires changing the conditions that spawn them.

Religion is not a creation by individual citizens utilizing psychic mechanisms. Religion is systematically cultivated by social authorities with the objective of distracting attention away from concrete social issues and transformation. This is a social-political process, not a personal, individual, psychic process. Religion is generally a mechanism of governmentality; it is not originally or essentially a personal quest for meaning.

Marx explains other illusions that are based in the economic form of capitalism, particularly the commodity:

A commodity is a mysterious thing simply because in it the social character of men's labor appears to them as an objective character stamped upon the product of that labor. … A definite social relation between men assumes in their eyes the fantastic form of a relation between things. … This Fetishism is inseparable from the production of commodities.

(Marx, 1867/1961, p. 72)

Marx is saying that producers' social contact, or social relations, with people is always mediated by the exchange of products. Social relations thus appear to be forms, or byproducts, of object-exchange. This reverses the true situation, which has social relations (of private ownership and production) determining the production of objects (commodities). "Value converts every product into a social hieroglyphic" (ibid., p. 74) that obscures its true nature and origin. "Capital becomes a mystic being since all of labor's social productive forces appear to be due to capital rather than labor" (Marx, 1894/1962, p. 806). Marx adds that "estranged, irrational forms of capital – interest, land rent, and wage labor – are forms of illusion in which agents of production [workers] move about" (ibid., p. 810).

Marx argues that treating labor as a commodity is an important source of mystification. Commodities are things that are exchanged for equal value and are paid for according to their value; consequently, the commodity form of labor presumes that the value of labor is equivalent to the wage that is paid for it. However, this conceals the fact that the wage only covers a portion of the worker's labor; an additional portion is not paid for and is surplus value that forms the capitalist's profit. Capitalist profit comes from the free labor of the worker, not his paid labor. Thus, wage labor "actually conceals, instead of disclosing, the social character of individual labor" (Marx, 1867/1961, p. 97).

> We may therefore understand the decisive importance of the transformation of the value and price of labour power into the form of wages, or into the value and price of labour itself. All the notions of justice held by both the worker and capitalist, all the mystifications of the capitalist mode of production, all capitalism's illusions about freedom, all the apologetic tricks of vulgar economics, have as their basis the form of appearance discussed above, which makes the actual relation invisible, and indeed presents to the eye the precise opposite of that relation.
>
> *(Ibid., p. 540)*

Marcuse (1968, pp. 84–85) expands on Marx's objective explanation of illusions as being grounded in social conditions:

> To the consciousness of men dominated by reified social relations, the latter appear in a distorted form which does not correspond to their true content – their origin and their actual function in this process. But they are not by that token in any way "unreal." It is precisely in their distorted form and as motives and "foci" in the calculating consciousness of those groups who control the process of production that they are very real factors. ... Theory, which aims at overcoming this distortion, has the task of moving beyond appearance to essence and explicating its content as it appears to true consciousness.

See Engster (2016) for discussion of the Frankfurt School's critical theory, which conceptualized the inseparability of the economy and subjectivity.

Relating illusions to normal social conditions deepens our understanding of the latter. It reveals that one of their characteristics is to misrepresent themselves and thereby mystify consciousness. This is an important addition to the exploitive character of social conditions.

Comprehending a mode of production and a culture includes comprehending its own myths and obfuscations and illusions and deceptions. We do not assume that culturally formed psychology comprehends the mode of production in which it originates for psychology's cultural origins and characteristics are self-obscuring. The Frankfurt School of critical theory emphasizes this:

> For Critical Theory this capitalist economy – if it produces not only objects but also subjects – must also be in some way decisive for the crisis of this subject. Or rather, the crisis already exists at the beginning – already with this constitutive connection between the economy and subjectivity – because although it might be obvious that the capitalist economy is socially constituted and developed throughout history, this capitalist economy and its categories nevertheless appear as ahistorical and assume an independent second nature. Thus, subjectivity right from the start is problematic when it cannot exactly grasp the social constitution and historical specificity of its own economy – and hence of its own subjectivity. Rather, subjectivity is this misunderstanding; it is this looking at the economy and its own subjectivity as if both were not only separate but naturally given.
>
> This dialectic between normality and crisis in Critical Theory also applies to subjectivity: there is no such thing as a normal, stable and healthy subjectivity for which crisis is an external, individual interruption. Rather, just as in the economy, crisis is a part of reproducing subjectivity and a part of its normality.
>
> (Engster, 2016, p. 78)

This is why an objective, external, critical Marxist psychology is called for. It does not accept culture's self-presentation; it studies the objective workings of culture from an external standpoint. This is what Marx did with regard to capitalism. This opposes "indigenous psychology" that does accept a people's indigenous, culture-bound conception of their psychology and their society. Indigenous psychology fails to recognize indigenous cultural oppression that generates illusions, deceptions, and mystifications of consciousness (see Vygotsky, 1997a, 325–328).

3) Marx's grounding of consciousness in social conditions is a revolutionary social-psychological theory of social and psychological revolution.

The organic integration of consciousness with environment is revolutionary, not static and passive. The reason is that the model requires changing the environment in order to change the consciousness that the environment forms. Behavioral/

psychological change requires a new stimulating, supportive, selective environment that weeds out competing behavior (i.e., existing debilitating behavior). Consciousness cannot be changed on its own because it is social consciousness. Dialectical thinking comprehends that determinism leads to liberation. Radical social change to improve social conditions and consciousness was Marx's driving motivation in his scientific work and his political work.

The inverse dialectic is that the less consciousness (construed as being) is integrated with social conditions and oppression and the more it can survive by transcending and circumventing them rather than transforming them, the less need there is for revolutionary, thorough social transformation. This is the conservative politics of individualistic approaches to psychology that claim individuals are autonomous and create their own social-psychological life-spaces and meanings or which postulate biological determinants of consciousness.

Marx and Engels call for changing the mode of production in order to eradicate mystification, illusion, reification, alienation, and psychological oppression.

> The abolition of religion as the illusory happiness of the people is the demand for their real happiness. To call on them to give up their illusions about their condition is to call on them to give up a condition that requires illusions. The criticism of religion is, therefore, in embryo, the criticism of that vale of tears of which religion is the halo.
>
> Criticism has plucked the imaginary flowers on the chain not in order that man shall continue to bear that chain without fantasy or consolation, but so that he shall throw off the chain and pluck the living flower. The criticism of religion disillusions man, so that he will think, act, and fashion his reality like a man who has discarded his illusions and regained his senses, so that he will move around himself as his own true Sun. Religion is only the illusory Sun which revolves around man as long as he does not revolve around himself.
>
> It is, therefore, the task of history, once the other-world of truth has vanished, to establish the truth of this world. It is the immediate task of philosophy, which is in the service of history, to unmask self-estrangement in its unholy forms once the holy form of human self-estrangement has been unmasked. Thus, the criticism of Heaven turns into the criticism of Earth, the criticism of religion into the criticism of law, and the criticism of theology into the criticism of politics.
>
> *(Marx, 1843; see also Marx, 1867/1961, p. 79)*

While social oppression is tragic, it dialectically calls for comprehending and transforming its conditions to achieve subjective fulfillment/emancipation. Oppression and revolution are dialectical complements; they are not antinomies. In "Contribution to Hegel's philosophy of law," Marx put it this way: "No class in civil society has any need or capacity for general emancipation until it is forced by its *immediate* condition, by *material* necessity, by its *very chains*" (in Marx and

Engels, 1975, p. 186). The depths of social oppression make us realize the necessity for social transformation and the breadth that it must take. The depths of social oppression make us achieve the heights of liberation.

In a subsequent section, we explain how the environmental-structural forming of consciousness a) elucidates the *necessity* for radical societal change in order to enrich consciousness, b) provides propitious conditions that provide the *possibility* for effecting viable societal change, and c) constitutes the *direction* that societal change must pursue in order to humanize society and enrich psychology.

4) Marx's specification of social conditions that organize psychology and underlie change.

Because social conditions stimulate, support, and organize consciousness, as well as calling for, affording, and directing enriched consciousness and cultural factors, it is imperative to comprehend what social conditions are and how they are organized. This provides direction for researching and explaining and predicting the factors that bear on consciousness/psychology. Without this concrete, comprehensive understanding of social conditions, we are incapable of understanding the conditionality and conditioning of consciousness/psychology. We would be left at the level of abstractions such as "historically accumulated customs," and "a concern with the whole." This would eviscerate Marxist psychology of any meaningful, concrete, insightful understanding of cultural psychology.

Marx developed a comprehensive social theory that articulates the structure and dynamics of social conditions. Marx's theory of society is *historical materialism*. This construes society as an organized system of macro cultural factors, with some more central, influential, and powerful than others. The most powerful, fundamental, and central factor is the political economy, or mode of production. "The form of this [social] intercourse [of individuals] … is determined by production" (Marx, 1968, p. 37). Moreover, "the whole internal structure of the nation itself depends on the stage of development reached by its production" (ibid., p. 38). "Capital is the all-dominating economic power of bourgeois society. It must form the starting-point as well as the finishing-point" (Marx, 1939/1973, pp. 106–107). As early as his "Economic and philosophical manuscripts of 1844," Marx had formulated this social theory: "Religion, family, state, law, morality, science, art, etc. are only *particular modes of production, and fall under its general law*" (in Marx and Engels, 1975, p. 297). The productive basis of society constitutes the fundamental materialism of Marx's social theory.

Marx's social system may be diagrammed as a cone with the mode of production at the base and diverse cultural domains radiating out from it up to the mouth of the cone.

These include education, religion, natural science, social science, philosophy, family, government, art, and news. These diverse domains extend the mode of production in distinctive ways. They are internal developments of the mode of production in diverse forms. We may say that the mode of production develops itself in diverse forms such as education, religion, etc. It needs to educate people to form their competencies to participate in the central, basic mode of production. It needs to cultivate a self-concept and entertainment and new outlets that similarly organize the breadth of human activity in accordance with the mode of production. This organization is necessary to solidify the mode of production that provides the means of subsistence and fulfillment for people.

The conical model of society emphasizes diversity and mediation of the mode of production. Mode of production provides a basic, underlying coherence of diverse cultural factors. Diversity exists within unity/coherence, and unity/coherence is diversified in distinctive macro cultural factors. Neither unity nor diversity is absolute. Each is mediated by the other.

The social cone specifies what the "social whole" is. It is the integration of all macro cultural factors within a cone that has a single central basis. Since all elements of this cone are interrelated and interdependent, each one crystallizes the whole (cone) in its own distinctive way. Anthropologist Marcel Mauss calls this kind of social element "a total social phenomenon … at once legal, economic, religious, esthetic, morphological, and so on" (1967, p. 76). Lukács (1924/1970) makes this point: "Marx always pictured capitalist development as a whole. This enabled him to see both its totality in any one of its phenomena, and the dynamic of its structure."

Each element provides insight into the whole through its distinctive position in the whole. For instance, childhood crystallizes and reveals society in the ways that social elements treat, or mediate, childhood. This is a different "take" on society from that provided by a different element such as religion, foreign policy, sexuality, romantic love, privacy, artistic taste.

Marx's conical model of society is confirmed by his opponents – neoliberal businessmen and government officials. Neoliberals have systematically drawn every single cultural domain into the capitalist political economy. Education, health care, prisons, scientific research, news, entertainment, sports, dating, the exploration of outer space, government agencies, politics, and national security are all now thoroughly corporatized and dominated by the capitalist political economy. (Corporate lobbyists are now the main source of information on political issues for American congressional staffers who advise legislators. Lobbyists write laws and also propaganda points for legislators to use in gaining support for corporate-written laws.) Moreover, capitalists and their political representatives have established a wide-ranging institutional structure of think tanks and centers for developing corporate-friendly policies (Mayer, 2016; Brown, 2015).

The corporate control of education is revealed in the fact that billionaire capitalists – Bill Gates, Eli Broad, and the Walton family who own Walmart – have poured billions of dollars into privatizing schools and turning them into neoliberal institutions. They have given several billion dollars to neoliberal, privatizing, educational organizations and politicians. Carrie Walton Penner sits on the board of the foundation connected to the prominent KIPP charter school chain – on which the Walton Family Foundation has lavished many millions in donations – and is also a member of the California Charter Schools Association. Carrie's husband, Greg Penner is one of the directors of the Charter Growth Fund, which a nonprofit venture capital fund that invests in charter schools. US Secretary of Education Arnie Duncan was on the board of the Eli and Edythe Broad Foundation. "The result is that the K-12 policy of these megafoundations is pretty much the K-12 policy of the USA" (Massing, 2015, pp. 66–67; see also Miller, 2016).

The Charles Koch Foundation granted $6.6 million to Florida State University's economics department from 2008 to 2013. The contract stipulated that five faculty would be hired to teach "The value of free enterprise," with oversight by an advisory board chosen by the Kochs. The board not only gave the foundation authority on hiring, but also allowed it to "review the work of the professors to make sure it complied with the objectives and purposes of the foundation." (American Association of University Professors, cited in Bader, 2015). Although many on campus argued that this was a gross infringement of academic freedom, the administration seemingly had no qualms about accepting the donation (Bader, 2015).

Capitalists understand a fundamental feature of social life – that it must be coherent among its elements in order strengthen each of them and the social whole. This would be undermined if diverse elements were unrelated to, or antithetical to, each other. There could be no social order or strength in such a case. A tightly organized society has each part reinforcing others in a common direction and interest. This produces a unified social fabric that emanates from a mode of production. This is why capitalists strengthen the mode of production by ensuring that diverse social elements cohere around it.

Moreover, capitalists recognize that people's psychology must be congruent with the political-economic base in order to maintain it through their individual, personal, private acts. Brown (2015) explains that neoliberalism is far more than economic practices. It is a form of political reason and governing that reaches from the capitalist state to the soul. It casts people as human capital, having to constantly tend to their own present and future value.

Marx's conical social structure, or system, is central to making it scientific. A conical structure is necessary to meet the scientific requirement known as the law of parsimony. This law states that the panoply of diverse elements of any phenomenon must be coherently explained by a few basic, encompassing, explanatory constructs. This avoids fragmentary, accidental elements and relationships.

Parsimony and coherence of a system are not reductionistic because they include diverse extensions of core factors in a rich, dynamic system of cultural and psychological factors. Marx carefully explained how fundamental constructs such as political economy develop themselves into emergent social forms. He opposed reducing diverse forms to a single one.

I. I. Rubin – an economist of Vygotsky's generation, killed by Stalin in the late 1930s – explains Marx's methodology in his article "Abstract labour and value in Marx's system." He cites Marx as saying, "starting from the most abstract concepts, show how these develop to lead us on to more concrete forms, more concrete concepts" (Rubin, 1978). How is it, for example, that general human labor becomes concretized in wage labor? And in our case of the social cone, we would explain how the mode of production becomes concretely variegated in family relations, gender roles, religion, and so on.

Any particular element (macro factor) of the social cone is complex because it consists of:

1. its distinctive quality as art, science, athletics, religion, family;
2. in conjunction with the political economic core that extends throughout social conditions; and
3. features of other factors, or social domains, with which it is interdependent.

5) Psychology and social transformation.

When Marx speaks of social conditions organizing aspects of consciousness, he is referring ultimately to the organization of conditions in a conical pattern that is centralized in the mode of production, or political economy. Aspects of consciousness are complex because they embody the (foregoing) three features of macro cultural factors that organize them.

Marx's conical social system is central to making it transformative and emancipatory as well as scientific. The reason is that the mode of production comprises a basic, central element that can transform the entire system into a fulfilling one. Apprehending and reorganizing the mode of production and the productive forces initiates reorganizing of the factors that depend upon it in the social cone. This makes comprehensive, thorough, deep social change possible. It is the only effective way to produce this kind of radical change.[4]

Marx's scientific-political conception of society as a cone that can be transformed into an emancipatory alternative cone is illustrated in Figure 1.2. The figure schematically depicts the existing social-psychological cone on the left side, a transition to a new social cone, and the depiction of that social-psychological cone on the right side. The figure depicts a Marxist-psychological methodology for identifying macro cultural factors that form psychology and for identifying new cultural factors that will generate a fulfilling, emancipatory consciousness/ psychology. Marxist, historical-materialist methodology reverses the causal historical-materialist chain that produces cultural factors and psychology. All science works from effects back to causes, reversing the causal process in which effects are produced.

Each of the categories of Figure 1.2 includes scientific, cultural, and interventionist elements.

Tracing psychological deficiencies to macro cultural factors that are grounded in a mode of production is a scientific conception of psychology and social organization; it is also a cultural analysis of psychology; and it is a political analysis insofar as psychology and culture are grounded in political economy that imbues them with political features and functions. This analysis has an interventionist objective of improving psychological functioning and culture.

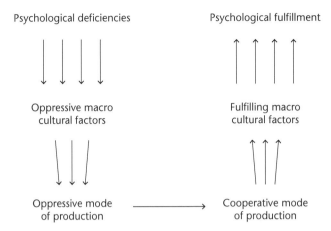

FIGURE 1.2 Marxist-psychological methodology for comprehending and enriching the social organization of consciousness/psychology

The bottom row of Figure 1.2 aims at superseding the given oppressive mode of production with a democratic, cooperative one. This is clearly an interventionist objective. It is also a political act that changes culture and psychology. It is also a scientific analysis concerning what kind of alternative social system can enhance culture and psychology, and it is also a comprehensive, essential, viable negation of the given one.

Moving up from a new cooperative mode of production to enriched psychology is a thoroughgoing intervention. It introduces a new politics into cultural factors and, through them, into psychology. This is all based upon a scientific analysis of the political-economic basis of culture and the cultural basis of psychology.

Figure 1.2 shows that psychological deficiency can only be improved through a social-political "detour" "down" to the mode of production, transitioning to a new mode and social system. (Academic psychologists have dubbed this kind of problem-solving the "Umweg problem.") Psychological deficiency cannot be improved at the psychological level alone; i.e., horizontally. Even oppressive macro cultural factors cannot be corrected on their own level. Correction must be made at deeper levels of the social structure, in the mode of production. Liberation must focus on understanding and developing an objective mode of production that is a complete, concrete negation of capitalism and which can support a new social system that will generate new social consciousness.

Reforming psychology and macro cultural factors without transforming the political economy is the definition of liberal reformism, as opposed to revolutionary transformation. It benefits some people; however, it also leaves them oppressed by the essential elements of the system – social class, commodification, alienation, precariousness, depersonalization. And reform does not benefit the majority of the population. Mid-range reform (in Figure 1.2) is debilitating in the sense that it exaggerates both the importance of mid-range factors in determining social-psychological life and the capacity of reform to improve social-psychological life. It distracts attention from the necessity to transform the political economy to solve basic problems.

Parenting in the US exemplifies this point. Middle-class parents spend billions of dollars on parenting advice and equipment. Outside this interpersonal, familial interaction, US social institutions provide less support to children than those of any other developed country. There is no mandatory paid maternity or paternity leave, no help at home after childbirth, no childcare for working parents. The emphasis on familial parenting distracts from this structural nonsupport (irresponsibility) and allows it to subvert good parenting. The US has the highest rates of infant mortality and child poverty in the developed world (Angell, 2016, p. 8). Good structural support for children would provide for better developmental outcomes than "parenting" alone does, and it would render most of the parenting industry unnecessary.

The emphasis on educational reform exemplifies these points. An entire industry of educational training has developed, focusing on interpersonal relations between teachers and students; i.e., on how knowledge is communicated. A Marxist analysis emphasizes that educational psychology is affected more by the political economy than by classroom interactions. The history of literacy confirms this perspective. According to Cressey, "The social distribution of literacy in preindustrial England was more closely associated with economic activities than with anything else" (cited in Ratner, 2012a, p. 24).

Reading was associated with particular occupations.

> The gentry, professional men, and merchants were virtually all in possession of literacy, and they used reading and writing in all their affairs – to get rich and stay that way, to solidify ideas and gain access to others, and to service and extend their hegemony. ... In the next cluster, at some distance, would be found yeomen and tradesmen, who in turn maintained a solid superiority [in the rate of literacy] over humbler artisans, husbandmen, and laborers.
>
> *(Ibid.)*

For people who had no practical economic need for literacy,

> however persuasive the rhetoric, it foundered on the indifference to literacy of the bulk of the population who saw no practical need for those abilities. Where people needed little literacy to manage their affairs ... it was difficult to persuade them to embrace a skill which was, for all practical purposes superfluous.
>
> *(Ibid.)*

In this economic demographic of literacy, there is no reason to think that pedagogy of literacy played a decisive role. It is not plausible that those who were literate required any particular pedagogy; nor does it seem likely that some special pedagogy could have helped people with no economic incentive or opportunity to learn literacy. Yet this is what the education industry today claims as educators focus on technique/method without considering economic incentives or opportunities. (Of course, certain pedagogical methods may fine-tune learning that is stimulated by broader macro economic factors.)

The true objective of mid-range interventions is to expand capitalism to include some marginalized, disadvantaged individuals; it is not to transform capitalism into an alternative political economy that liberates the populace as a whole.[5]

It is futile to demand "respect," "consideration," "validation," "commiseration," "acceptance of diversity," "inclusiveness," "self-expression," "agency," "voice," "rights," "the end of mass incarceration," "better jobs," "democratic education," etc. within existing social conditions and power relations. This is what *protest* seeks. It appeals to the powers that be to change. The goal should be to devise a new social system (social cone, mode of production) that can generate and sustain these.

Demanding these things *now* distracts from devising the conditions that are necessary to generate them. It assumes that they can be implemented in the status quo, given enough pressure from the people. It also assumes that current forms of these issues are inherently liberating.

Both of these assumptions are erroneous. The truth is that these demands can only be realized through transforming social conditions/mode of production. In addition, new conditions will generate new *forms* of demands, as Figure 1.2 shows. Democracy, respect, justice, better jobs, and even cooperation and community are not abstract universals that can simply be dropped into place in a society. They have cultural-political forms that reflect concrete social conditions. Demands for reform now, within the status quo, insidiously retain current cultural-political forms. For those are all that we know at this point. Current cultural forms actually subvert genuine, fulfilling forms. Emancipatory labor, democracy, and community must be constructed in particular cultural-political forms that will be different from current forms which suit the capitalist mode of production. Engels' work "The principles of communism" describes the process by which social conditions generate social and psychological transformation/emancipation.

> Just as the peasants and manufacturing workers of the last century changed their whole way of life and became quite different people when they were drawn into big industry, in the same way, communal control over production by society as a whole, and the resulting new development, will require an entirely different kind of human material.
>
> People will no longer be, as they are today, subordinated to a single branch of production, bound to it, exploited by it; they will no longer develop one of their faculties at the expense of all others; they will no longer know only one branch, or one branch of a single branch, of production as a whole. Even industry as it is today is finding such people less and less useful.
>
> Industry controlled by society as a whole, and operated according to a plan, presupposes well-rounded human beings, their faculties developed in balanced fashion, able to see the system of production in its entirety.

> *The form of the division of labor which makes one a peasant, another a cobbler, a third a factory worker, a fourth a stock-market operator, has already been undermined by machinery* and will completely disappear. Education will enable young people quickly to familiarize themselves with the whole system of production and to pass from one branch of production to another in response to the needs of society or their own inclinations. It will, therefore, free them from the one-sided character which the present-day division of labor impresses upon every individual. Communist society will, in this way, make it possible for its members to put their comprehensively developed faculties to full use. But, when this happens, classes will necessarily disappear. It follows that society organized on a communist basis is incompatible with the existence of classes on the one hand, and that the very building of such a society provides the means of abolishing class differences on the other.
>
> The general co-operation of all members of society for the purpose of planned exploitation of the forces of production, the expansion of production to the point where it will satisfy the needs of all, the abolition of a situation in which the needs of some are satisfied at the expense of the needs of others, the complete liquidation of classes and their conflicts, the rounded development of the capacities of all members of society through the elimination of the present division of labor, through industrial education, through engaging in varying activities, through the participation by all in the enjoyments produced by all, through the combination of city and country – these are the main consequences of the abolition of private property.
>
> *(In Marx and Engels, 1976, pp. 353–354, emphasis added)*

This is a powerful statement of *materialist psychology and psychological change*. It reveals social conditions as underlying extant consciousness and also as underlying an alternative consciousness. Engels states that capitalism has already undermined division of labor, and it has thus prepared the infrastructure for the collective expropriation of production. This is the dynamic of the capitalist mode of production. In order to expand and realize itself, capitalism is led to develop new higher forms of itself that, inadvertently, contain crucial elements of an alternative mode of production which supersedes capitalism. Capitalism contains the seeds of its own undoing and the seeds of overcoming its own problems. This is the internal, dialectical development of any system. It grounds the future as an outgrowth of the present, in the *aufhebung* of present conditions. The future is not a metaphysical ideal unrelated to the present and artificially and externally imposed on the present.

It is up to the proletariat to expropriate what the capitalists have prepared and to develop its social-collective character. This is the essence of revolutionary liberation. It will expand our consciousness accordingly. Consciousness does not change spontaneously or wishfully. It changes in accordance with propitious conditions – which is the Darwinian model of animal behavior raised to the human, conscious, social level. This scope of social-psychological change is impossible if these conditions are lacking.

The historical-materialist theory of changed social consciousness is programmatic, didactic, prescriptive, and necessary. It is not simply an open possibility that people decide upon for themselves. Marx and Engels prescribe what people must do in order to develop viable, concrete alternative social conditions and consciousness. We must eliminate private property; we must collectively own, control, and plan (coordinate) our society; we must eliminate social classes and fixed divisions of labor. All this is necessary to expand our mental faculties and understand our social world and ourselves. This is why Marx called his theory of alternative society "scientific socialism."[6] It is the same approach that we take to solving any problem. When people become sick, experts identify the cause as polluted water, and they tell the people: "You must stop polluting the water, and you must boil and filter the water in order to become healthy." This is objective, programmatic, didactic, and prescriptive. Anything other than analyzing and following objective, scientific study of conditions will preclude healthy individuals; for example, engaging in narratives where people express their personal feelings and wishes about possible actions to take are counterproductive because they fail to apprehend the scientific causes and solution to their disorders.

Because the Marxian, environmental, macro cultural approach is misunderstood as impeding consciousness and psychological and social change, we devote the remainder of this section on Marxist consciousness to explaining how this approach promotes and sustains the greatest change in society and consciousness – greater than any other psychological approach. This process can be summarized in ten points.

a) Identify the concrete political-economic conditions that cause social-psychological problems in existing society.

These causal conditions include private property, market economic exchange and the social relations that underlie it, money, wage labor, and the capitalist class structure.

b) Scientifically deduce concrete negations of these causes in an alternative mode of production.

These include eliminating private property, market economic exchange, money, wage labor, and the capitalist class as a political structure. These conditions must be replaced by opposite conditions – collective, communal, democratic ownership and control of social conditions, the mode of production, and the means of production.

c) Identify propitious conditions in existing society that prepare for, enable, and support the alternative mode of production.

"With all the miseries it imposes upon the proletariat, the present system simultaneously engenders the *material conditions* and the *social forms* necessary for an economical reconstruction of society" (Marx, 1865). According to Marx and Engels, these preconditions consist of technical developments in the way the forces of production have been organized. Marx argues that capitalist productive forces have been integrated, coordinated, administered, and planned by capitalists in the form of transnational corporations, global governing bodies such as the United Nations and World Trade Organization, interlocking boards of directors of major corporations, and monopolization of industries in a few gigantic (vertically and horizontally) corporations. This is an enormous, powerful, viable, technical infrastructure for underpinning a socialist, collectivistic, communal mode of production. The proletariat must appropriate it in their political struggle for transforming society.

d) Points a, b, and c are the material conditions for a new social consciousness that apprehends (1) the nature of existing society and (2) fulfilling social relations that Engels describes in his statement.

The conditioned conditionality of consciousness means that it takes its guide from material and social conditions. Consciousness does not freely decide the form it will have. Social conditionality is advantageous because it endows social consciousness with a supportive social and material infrastructure that can enrich it in a viable manner. Marx and Engels (1932/1968, Part 1) state this as follows:

> Things have now come to such a pass that the individuals must appropriate the existing totality of productive forces, not only to achieve self-activity, but, also, merely to safeguard their very existence. This appropriation is first determined by the object to be appropriated, the productive forces, which have been developed to a totality and which only exist within a universal intercourse. From this aspect alone, therefore, *this appropriation must have a universal character corresponding to the productive forces and the intercourse.*
>
> The appropriation of these forces is itself nothing more than the development of the individual capacities corresponding to the material instruments of production. The appropriation of a totality of instruments of production is, for this very reason, the development of a totality of capacities in the individuals themselves.

Grounding individual capacities in the material instruments and mode of production affords enormous expansion and emancipation of those capacities. The vastness and socialization of capitalist productive forces culminates in the development of a totality of capacities in individuals. Consciousness does not expand on its own simply because it wishes to; it expands by appropriating expansive social conditions that "stretch" it in the act of appropriating them. Capitalist means of production have broken down localism and nationalism of work and consciousness and have universalized both.

Graziano (2016) insightfully observes that waves of globalization and international governing bodies in the past two centuries have contributed to weakening the sovereignty of nation states. They have lost their capacity to provide national identity, meaning, and well-being to the bulk of the populace. This breakdown opens the possibility of a universal, global consciousness.

New, fulfilling social consciousness is a function of conditions:

- It depends upon the existence of conditions (e.g., socialized means of production). In *The Poverty of Philosophy*, Marx discusses a condition where "productive forces are not yet sufficiently developed in the bosom of the bourgeoisie itself to enable us to catch a glimpse of the material conditions necessary for the emancipation of the proletariat and for the formation of a new society" (1847/2008, p. 186).
- It is made necessary by those conditions.
- It is made possible by them.
- It is organized and directed by those conditions.
- It is circumscribed by those conditions.

New consciousness is reciprocally required for apprehending and consummating conditions. Conditions afford action but they cannot substitute for action. Class consciousness is necessary to appropriate the mode and means of production and transform them to socialism. In "The principles of communism," Engels says: "Mechanical and chemical processes are not enough to bring industrial and agricultural production up to the level we have described; the capacities of the men who make use of these processes must undergo a corresponding development" (in Marx and Engels, 1976, p. 353). Furthermore, "Men will be so much changed that the last forms of the old social relations will also be able to fall away" (ibid., 351). The authors are saying that culturally engendered subjective changes are necessary for changing social relations.

e) Marx and Engels identify an additional conditionality of new social consciousness. This is the position that people occupy in society.

In "Contribution to Hegel's philosophy of law," Marx says, "Revolutionary energy and consciousness of its own power do not suffice" (in Marx and Engels, 1975, p. 185).

Marx and Engels (1932/1968) state that the requisite social position is one that is deprived of ownership and control and that has no sources of fulfillment or success other than revolutionizing the social system:

a class is called forth, which has to bear all the burdens of society without enjoying its advantages, which, ousted from society, is forced into the most decided antagonism to all other classes; a class which forms the majority of all members of society, and from which emanates the consciousness of the necessity of a fundamental revolution, the communist consciousness, which may, of course, arise among the other classes too through the contemplation of the situation of this class.

They also write:

> The *positive* possibility of a German emancipation … lies in the formulation of a class with *radical chains*, a class of civil society which is not a class of civil society, an estate which is the dissolution of all estates, a sphere which has a universal character by its universal suffering and claims no *particular right* because no *particular wrong*, but *wrong generally*, is perpetuated against it; which can invoke no *historical*, but only *human*, title; which does not stand in any one-sided antithesis to the consequences but in all-round antithesis to the premises of German statehood; a sphere, finally, which cannot emancipate itself without emancipating itself from all other spheres of society and thereby emancipating all other spheres of society, which, in a word, is the *complete loss* of man and hence can win itself only through the *complete re-winning of man*. This dissolution of society as a particular estate is the *proletariat*.
>
> *(Marx and Engels, 1975, p. 186, emphasis added; see also Llorente, 2013)*

Marx looks for, and finds, universalizing conditions that lead groups of people who occupy them to develop a universal social consciousness and a universal emancipatory potential that can eradicate all the particular problems for the vast majority of the population. Marx says that emancipation for a country depends upon the activity of a particular class within that country. The country as a whole cannot emancipate itself because it consists of an oppressive ruling that resists emancipation. The proletariat, not "the people as a whole," is the engine of liberation for the majority of the population. Marx says that the chains that imprison the proletariat are *radical chains*, which means they have radical possibilities for liberation. Lukács identifies an important element of this process. He says that the extreme alienation of commodified labor objectifies the proletariat as a distinct entity; this enables it to see itself as a class that can only rely on itself; i.e., on the association of its members. According to Engster (2016, p. 81):

> A proletariat separated from "every direct link with nature" can thus recognize within itself … and can hence make itself – its own subjectivity – into an object of appropriation by a collective social totality. Here the commodity-formed alienation and reification are not only condemned by Lukács, they are also the condition for a "revolutionary leap."

Alienation is thus a "radical chain."

For the first time in human history, existing (capitalist) society has prepared the universal possibility of universal emancipation. Importantly, Marx conceives of this as a *concrete universal* in the sense that the universal is a concrete social class in concrete social conditions.

It is not an abstraction like "humanity." Humanity is universal but not in Marx's concrete terms. It has no potential for actually uniting people in concrete, common action to produce a universal society without social classes. The same is true for "woman." Women are half the people in the world; however, they have no concrete unity or possibility of unity. "Woman" includes capitalist women, Nazi women, etc., who cannot form the social basis of socialist society. The same is true for other generalities such as Latina, Indian, and black. For example, the wealthiest black person in Charleston, South Carolina, in 1860 was Maria Weston, who owned 14 slaves and property valued at more than $40,000 at a time when the average white man earned about $100 a year. It is well known that African slave traders, who hunted down fellow black people and sold them to white slave traders, were black. There is nothing about being black that prevents this. However, proletariat prevents this kind of exploitation. A worker who acquires capital and hires other workers to expropriate their surplus value is by definition no longer a worker. A capitalist or slave-owning proletariat is an oxymoron, whereas a capitalist or slave-owning woman or black person or homosexual is perfectly consistent. Consequently, "Womanhood is powerful" and "Black lives matter" are not progressive slogans because they include support for capitalist, reactionary members of these categories. They are not structural, class concepts with specific class interests. "Opposing the richest 1 percent" is also not a social class concept because it includes tennis players with capitalists and mandates opposition to both. Any category that encompasses tennis players and capitalists is not a structural, class concept with class interests.[7]

Marx emphasizes the dialectical relationship between oppression and emancipation. The depth and nature of oppression dialectically produce the highest opportunities for liberation.

The importance of oppressive social conditions for revolutionary consciousness leads to the deduction that individuals who do not occupy this particular oppressive social position (role) are *unlikely* to derive the impetus and support that it offers for a universalizing, revolutionary consciousness. This includes individuals at the top of the social hierarchy as well as individuals who are outside the labor force and do not work or live as proletarians. Marx and Engels, along with Mao and Fanon, called them "lumpen proletariat" (Franklin, n.d.) Many of the lumpen are former laborers who were expelled from their jobs; however, many have been dispossessed in other ways. Marx and Engels say they come from many classes for diverse reasons. Being outside wage labor, they are not exploited by the capitalist system as a source of surplus value and profit. Accordingly, their hardships do not necessarily lead to proletarian social consciousness of capitalist exploitation. Another conditionality that minimizes proletarian class consciousness for marginalized lumpen proletarians is that they are not situated in the socialized means of capitalist production that provides laborers with potential class consciousness and class unity.

Other forms of marginalization present similar obstacles to revolutionary proletarian consciousness. Many victims of discrimination fit this analysis. For instance, discrimination against sexual orientation is not a matter of capitalist economic exploitation of a laboring class.

Marx, Engels, and Mao recognize that certain individuals outside the proletariat may become involved in the revolutionary struggle for socialism. However, this is not a mass phenomenon because transforming capitalism is not essential for, as one example, their sexual freedom.[8]

f) Social conditions are necessary but not sufficient for social consciousness.

The socialized means of production do not automatically produce class consciousness among the proletariat; neither does the oppressed social position of the proletariat automatically generate clear class consciousness of this oppression and its required supersession. Marx and Engels insist that consciousness has to *acquire* an understanding of conditions. This is enabled by working-class organizations. These organizations should not simply work for improved working conditions within the status quo, but must also instruct workers about their social position and develop their class consciousness about what kind of social transformation is necessary for genuine liberation. This is a clear example of the fact that social consciousness is not a mechanical reflection of the means of production on a passive consciousness. This is why the populace must read Marx's works where they can discover the understanding and supersession of their exploitation. Mechanistic, conscious reflection of reality would obviate the need for all this. I contend that capitalist antipathy to unions is driven by the fear of socialist class consciousness that can be generated by unions as much as by the restrictions that unions impose upon capitalist profit (by demanding better working conditions, including ecological aspects).

g) The enrichment of social consciousness that working-class organizations develop is not a purely intellectual act; it is a revolutionary political act that transforms conditions.

This revolutionary, transformative political action is a necessary condition for generating transformative social consciousness.

> Both for the production on a mass scale of this communist consciousness, and for the success of the cause itself, the alteration of men on a mass scale is, necessary, an alteration which can only take place in a practical movement, a revolution; this revolution is necessary, therefore, not only because the ruling class cannot be overthrown in any other way, but also because *the class overthrowing it can only in a revolution succeed in ridding itself of all the muck of ages and become fitted to found society anew.*
>
> (Marx and Engels, 1932/1968, Part 1)

h) This revolutionary transformation of the political economy and social consciousness of existing society must be reflected in all concepts about social phenomena.

New concepts are necessary to apprehend the new social content of social phenomena. New social concepts will highlight the historical transition that brought about the new social phenomena, which are the referents of concepts. In the Introduction to this book, we discussed Marx's reconception of labor as a social act that is alienated in capitalist society, but which transitions to a fulfilling act of self-determination under socialism. All of this is embodied in labor as a cultural-historical, dialectical materialist concept. This cultural-historical content of concepts is necessary for reinforcing the new social content and preventing regression to the oppressive social content. If concepts are conceptualized abstractly, as we discussed in the Introduction, this deprives them of this progressive social function to promote an alternative social system that is necessary for genuine emancipation.

Marx and Engels provide an important example of this in the case of community. Under socialism, community takes on a new, fulfilling, liberating form that must be distinguished from communities in class societies. A new concept of community must include its actual historical development to the liberating form. This will reinforce that form and prevent it from being dissolved in a contentless abstraction. Marx and Engels (1932/1968) write:

> Only in community [with others has each] individual the means of cultivating his gifts in all directions; only in the community, therefore, is personal freedom possible. In the previous substitutes for the community, in the State, etc. personal freedom has existed only for the individuals who developed within the relationships of the ruling class, and only insofar as they were individuals of this class. The illusory community, in which individuals have up till now combined, always took on an independent existence in relation to them, and was at the same time, since it was the combination of one class over against another, not only a completely illusory community, but a new fetter as well. In a real community the individuals obtain their freedom in and through their association.

The concept and reality of genuine community must include its political form and leadership, namely, revolutionary proletarian community: "With the community of revolutionary proletarians who take their conditions of existence and those of all members of society under their control, it is as individuals that the individuals participate in it" (ibid.).

This cultural-historical-political articulation of community should be used to guide all cultural and psychological phenomena. It must also form the core of demands for social and psychological change. When we demand community, cooperation, democracy, justice, respect, fulfilling labor, etc., we must emphasize the socialist form that these shall take. We must rid them of their current cultural-political forms. Unfortunately, social activists do not do this. They utilize concepts that contain the current cultural-political form. Members of cooperatives and alternative social movements continue to use democracy in its bourgeois form of "one person, one vote." They do this implicitly as they use these concepts abstractly without specifying any cultural-political form, which leaves the existing form intact. If they used concrete terms to denote these concepts, they would speak of bourgeois cooperation, bourgeois democracy, bourgeois justice, etc. This would sensitize them to the cultural-political form and would facilitate their revolutionizing the form to a socialist one.

i) The conditioned conditionality of change limits its achievements.

Because change emanates from existing conditions, the latter carry through into their alternative. The alternative is not divorced from the conditions that call for and afford it. Marx explains that socialism is initially tainted by its capitalist heritage and can never completely break with it. The first stage of socialism cannot, therefore, be fully emancipatory. It is only a later stage of socialism, founded on post-capitalist socialism, that can free itself from the capitalist legacy that remains in the immediate post-capitalist stage of socialism. Socialism is not an ideal that can be fully implemented on the basis of what people wish for.

This *dialectic of social conditions* refutes three alternative notions of them: 1) conditions preclude change; 2) conditions are inherently oppressive, so emancipation must circumvent and transcend their limitations; 3) individual-interpersonal-abstract processes exist that can provide liberation without transforming the social system. For example, liberation is pinned on respecting people's "humanity," "agency," "diversity," "solidarity," and "democracy." There is little analysis of extant conditions and little analysis of how to fundamentally negate them into their dialectical opposite – e.g., socialism. This is why contemporary movements rarely lead toward socialism or any substantive emancipatory change.

j) Individual issues are not directly germane to the culturally conditional, conditioned nature of social-psychological formation and transformation.

Critics of Marxism claim that it neglects social and psychological change. This leads to condemning Marxism as static, reified, and mechanistic. And this leads to searching for individual and abstract acts that can effect social and psychological change apart from cultural restrictions. These mechanisms include agency, voice, resistance, resilience, solidarity, respect, diversity, indigenous customs, personal meanings, and psychoanalytic defense mechanisms such as sublimation.

However, we have explained that this critique and its alternatives are specious. Marx explains social-psychological formation and transformation in socio-economic-political conditions/processes. He identifies social and material conditions that prepare for material, social, and psychological transformation. He brilliantly explains how the rulers of society prepare the conditions for change (for their own supersession). Capitalism's contradictions not only destroy it, they also recreate it; they generate its successor. It is the capitalists who socialize, centralize, rationally plan, and universalize the means of production; they produce a class of people whose social position makes them need to transform the mode of production and endows them with the possibility of massive class unity and class consciousness for doing so. (This is the pattern in all societies. For example, feudal rulers established merchants who then grew into a bourgeois class that developed capitalism out of its feudal preconditions.) This is a dialectical *aufhebung* that supersedes the present in a new future that it conditions.

The social conditions that condition social and psychological change provide the necessity, possibility, directionality, viability, and limits of liberation. They provide for the greatest, most complete, most viable liberation of consciousness because consciousness will expand to comprehend and master and transform the entire concrete infrastructure of society. The organization of social conditions in a social cone also provides for the most effective form of social change because focusing upon the base of society generates simultaneous, consistent, unifying change along all the multiple radiuses from it to the panoply of social domains. This is far more effective than working on each domain and individual separately. Marxist historical materialism provides for the most comprehensive, deep, concrete, viable, and effective social and psychological change.

Processes, factors, and mechanisms that are extrinsic to social conditions are not necessary for emancipation; neither are they helpful for emancipation. On the contrary, factors such as intraindividual psychobiological mechanisms and personal mechanisms minimize the social conditioning of behavior/consciousness. This minimizes the necessity and possibility of apprehending and transforming those social conditions. It raises false hopes about emancipation through those factors (e.g., agency, autonomy, femininity, sublimation, ethnicity). It leads people to forsake Marxism for these facile, personal, and interpersonal pseudo solutions. Thus, liberalism is not a step towards socialism; it is a displacement of socialism by bourgeois ideals. This leaves people trapped in existing social conditions and consciousness, incapable of changing them.

Social conditions are neither formed nor transformed on the individual-interpersonal level. They are formed on the macro cultural level that is grounded in the material practices of production. This is what needs to be comprehended by social science, and it must be apprehended by emancipatory politics. As we have explained, the more deeply we comprehend oppression, the more deeply we comprehend the need for and possibility of emancipation. The more superficially we comprehend oppression, the more superficial will be our understanding of the need for and possibility of social-psychological transformation.

Individualistic critics of Marxism – e.g., postmodernists, social constructionists, liberals, neoliberals, micro cultural psychologists – are rightly concerned about social autocracy that governs the activity of individuals without their consent or input. However, they do not understand the reason for this problem or its solution. They attribute social autocracy to culture itself. They raise autocracy to the abstract level of a universal, inherent characteristic of culture – culture in general, not a particular cultural system. With culture synonymous with autocracy, the solution is, logically, to repulse culture and rely upon individual processes of activity – agency, will, personal meanings, voice, resistance, negotiation. A correct understanding of, and solution to, autocracy is to move it to the concrete level of culture, as characteristic of a particular cultural organization/system. This makes autocracy comprehensible in terms of concrete cultural factors; it also affords the possibility to eradicate autocracy by transforming the autocratic cultural factors into democratic ones. The solution is to change one concrete culture into a better culture, not to repulse all culture by individual processes. There is neither any scientific nor any practical reason to postulate Individual processes of psychological formation or social formation. Individual processes can neither comprehend nor solve social problems because they ignore the emergent social processes and objectifications that are essential to forming and transforming them.

III. Extending Marx's analysis of social consciousness to psychology

Marxist psychology extends Marx and Engels' historical-materialist analysis of social consciousness to psychological phenomena. Marxist psychology includes a comprehensive psychological theory of each phenomenon that integrates Marx's analysis of consciousness with distinctive features revealed by psychological research by non-Marxist psychologists. A distinctive methodology must be devised to research this novel complex of elements.

Marxist psychology maintains the political and scientific interconnection that Marx and Engels articulated in historical materialism. The scientific understanding of psychology must lead to social improvement, and it does so by illuminating and critiquing the concrete totality of the social cone and its productive base that is crystallized in every psychological phenomenon. Conversely, social understanding and critique illuminates the empirical and theoretical characteristics of psychology.

Marxist psychology supersedes noting associations between psychological phenomena and the social cone. Marxist psychology *theorizes* or *problematizes* psychological phenomena. It develops comprehensive theories about the origins, content, and organization of psychological phenomena.

Marxist psychology realizes Marx and Engels' statement:

> the history of *industry* and the established *objective* existence of industry are the open book of *man's essential powers*, the perceptibly existing human *psychology*. … A psychology for which this book, the part of history existing in the most perceptible and accessible form, remains a closed book, cannot become a genuine comprehensive *real* science.

> *(1975, p. 303)*

This psychology will be scientific and revolutionary/emancipatory.

For example, Marxist psychology addresses the psychological fact that in 2015, only 4 percent of Detroit public school eighth graders were proficient in math and only 7 percent were proficient in reading. Sixty-seven percent of all American public-school eighth graders were *not* proficient in math or reading. The figure rises to over 80 percent for black students (Higgins, 2015). Only 37 percent of American twelfth graders were academically prepared for college math and reading in 2015, down from 39 percent in 2013 (Brody, 2016). The Marxist psychological explanation moves in two directions:

- It looks "outward" to explore how this cognitive phenomenon is related to the political economy; i.e., why the political economy does not need or demand high cognitive skills from the majority of the populace. It explores the demographic distribution of reading and math competencies to identify the social class(es) that harbors low competence and high competence. It explains how the low class is trained for the de-industrial, deskilled, low-wage economy. It elucidates the politics of social-educational policies that institutionalize this class interest. This outward look is what Marxian historical materialism directs.
- Marxist psychology also looks "inward" to psychological phenomena. It develops a psychological theory of cognition that explains all of its specific characteristics (reasoning, memory, intelligence) in relation to the panoply of other psychological phenomena (emotions, self-concept, development). It explains how and why psychology is organized by the "outward" cultural factors and the ontogenetic and phylogenetic developmental processes of cognition.

This is where Marxist psychology needs assistance from established psychological disciplines that theorize and research cultural-psychological phenomena. I propose that the discipline of cultural psychology is the best psychological school for advancing Marxist psychology.

Cultural psychology develops Marxist psychology by:

1. Contributing a *cultural theory of psychology* that enriches Marxist historical-materialist social philosophy.
2. *Applying* this theory to particular psychological phenomena such as emotions, memory, mental illness, child development, perception, the body, sexuality, personal experience, personal meanings, agency/will, socialization of cultural and class psychology, and the role that biological processes play in cultural psychology and Marxist psychology.
3. Developing a *methodology* for researching cultural origins, organization, socialization, operation, administration, and social function of psychological phenomena. This is relevant to researching class aspects of psychology.
4. Conducting empirical *research* to confirm or correct Marxist Psychological theories.

5. Developing interpersonal *interventions* that enrich psychology by cultural-environmental-political support and stimulation.

6. Developing social *policies* for transforming the cultural environment in ways that will comprehensively stimulate and support psychological fulfillment and enrichment. This is directly applicable to Marxist political-economic reorganization. Policies will derive from sound theoretical and empirical research.

7. Drawing Marxism into psychological issues, and accommodating them to it. This makes psychology Marxist, as it makes Marxism psychological.

Advancing Marxist psychology via cultural psychology

Cultural psychology consists of three threads or approaches:

1. A Marxist thread that relates psychology to macro cultural factors, and to the mode of production. This approach encompasses all three levels of the left side of Figure 1.2. This is the cultural-historical psychology of Vygotsky, Luria, and Leontiev. These scholars focused most of their work on relating psychology to macro cultural factors. The acknowledged the mode of production and historical materialism; however, they did not develop their relationship to psychology and macro cultural factors in any detail. This is why Marxist psychology is necessary.

2. A thread that relates psychology to macro cultural factors in Figure 1.2, but does not extend psychology and cultural factors to the mode of production. I call this "macro cultural psychology." Its most important contributors have been psychological anthropologists in the 1980s and 1990s – e.g., Shweder, Kleinman, Lutz, Rosaldo, D'Andrade, Geertz, Scheper-Hughes, Obeyeskere. Sociologists and historians have contributed to this macro cultural psychological approach by emphasizing the sociological and historical basis and organization of psychological issues such as emotions, the body, cognition, memory, self-concept, and mental illness (see Bericat, 2016). The French school of the 1930s known as Mentalities is a noteworthy contribution.

3. The third thread of cultural psychology is what I call "micro cultural psychology." It arose during the 1990s in the US. It follows the subjectivism and individualism of postmodernism and social constructionism and neoliberalism. It prioritizes individual agency, negotiation, creativity, choice, responsibility, self-organization, and freedom over structural, macro cultural factors in forming human action. Culture is simply "out there" as a "toolkit" for individuals to perceive, interpret, select, and reject to suit their own personal needs as they wish.

Micro cultural psychologists have brought mainstream psychology's focus on individual mechanisms of psychology and denial of cultural structures into the heart cultural psychology (Ratner, 2012b, 2015a, 2015b, 2016). They are "Contras" of cultural psychology who decimate it from within. We do not discuss this approach here.

Nor do we discuss cross-cultural psychology which is incongruent with macro cultural psychology and Marxist psychology. Cross-cultural psychology takes some interest in macro cultural factors in relation to psychology; however, its macro variables are transcultural, fragmented, abstract, ahistorical, and apolitical – e.g., "collectivism." Moreover, cross-cultural psychologists utilize positivistic methodology that elicits superficial, purely quantitative, behavioral responses. This obscures concrete cultural content that macro cultural psychology and Marxist psychology elucidate in extended, qualitative responses (Ratner and Hui, 2003; Ratner, 1997, 2012b).

The macro and Marxist approaches to cultural psychology are uniquely qualified to construct a Marxist psychology. They are uniquely qualified to act as a coupler, or conduit, of Marxism and psychology. They are well grounded in the field of psychology, and they have already developed a sophisticated cultural analysis of many psychological phenomena. This can be seamlessly integrated with the Marxist sociopolitical framework. It simply involves broadening culture to include the social cone and political economy. The macro cultural psychological developments can then flow into Marxism and vice versa.

This synergy between macro cultural psychology and Marxism rests on their common conceptualizing, framing, and formatting of psychology as a cultural-historical phenomenon. Marxist psychology is obviously a particular form of cultural psychology that emphasizes culture as a conical system rooted in a mode of production. This can be incorporated into non-Marxist cultural psychology and vice versa. No other psychological school has this fundamental cultural compatibility with Marxism.

In the following, we document the homology of Marxism with macro cultural psychology and Marxist cultural psychology. Thereafter, we indicate several ways that macro cultural psychology and Marxist cultural psychology expand and deepen Marxism to initiate a Marxist psychology that can be developed in the future.

Homology between Marxism and Marxist psychologists

Marx (1843) expresses the cultural nature of human psychology thusly: "Man is the world of man – state, society." In the third of his "Economic and Philosophical Manuscripts," he says, "though man is a unique individual ... he is an individual communal being – he is equally the whole, the ideal whole, the subjective existence of society" (in Marx and Engels, 1975, p. 298). "My *general* consciousness is only the *theoretical* shape of that of which the *living* shape is the *real* community" (ibid.). "The *sense* caught up in crude practical need has only a *restricted* sense. ... The care-burdened, poverty-stricken man has no *sense* for the finest play" (ibid., p. 302). Similarly, "Pleasure is subsumed under capital, and the pleasure-taking individual under the capital-accumulating individual" (ibid., p. 316).

Vygotsky similarly maintains that "Higher mental functions [are] the product of the historical development of humanity" (1998, p. 34).

> The structures of higher mental functions represent a cast of collective social relations between people. These [mental] structures are nothing other than a transfer into the personality of an inward relation of *a social order that constitutes the basis of the social structure of the human personality.*
>
> *(Ibid., pp. 169–170, emphasis added)*

"Each person is to some degree a measure of the society, or rather class, to which he belongs, for the whole totality of social relationships is reflected in him" (Vygotsky, 1997a, p. 317). Vygotsky describes the depth of the social conditioning of psychology: "The various internal contradictions which are to be found in different social systems find their expression both in the type of personality and in the structure of human psychology in that historical period" (1994b, p. 176).

Luria expresses the Marxist character of cultural-historical psychology:

> The "cultural" aspect of Vygotsky's theory involved the socially structured ways in which society organizes the kinds of tasks that the growing child faces and the kinds of tools, both mental and physical, that the young child is provided to master those tasks.
>
> [...] It is through this interiorization of *historically determined and culturally organized ways of operating on information that the social nature of people comes to be their psychological nature as well.*
>
> *(1979, emphasis added)*

Vygotsky subscribes to Marx's social model depicted in Figure 1.2. He states in *The Psychology of Art* (1925/1971) that:

> the relationship between art and the economic conditions generating it turns out to be extremely complex. This does not mean that social conditions do not completely determine the character and the effect of a work of art; it merely shows that they determine it indirectly.

By indirect determination, he means the mediation of the mode of production by the complex of macro cultural factors at various levels in the social cone. These are mediations *of* economic conditions; they are not negations and evasions of cultural organization of psychology.

In his article "Activity and consciousness," Leontiev (2009, p. 411) says:

> Despite all its diversity, all its special features, the activity [*Tatigkeit*] of the human individual is a system that obeys the system of relations of society. Outside these relations human activity does not exist. How it exists is determined by the forms and means of material and spiritual communication

that are generated by the development of production and that cannot be realised except in the activity of specific individuals. It stands to reason that the activity of every individual depends on his place in society, on his conditions of life.

Leontiev affirms Marx's emphasis on social conditions conditioning consciousness.

Vygotsky and Luria's cross-cultural research in Uzbekistan additionally demonstrates how cultural-historical psychology adopted Marxism's emphasis on the mode of production as the ultimate organizer of human psychology. Gielen and Jeshmaridian (1999, p. 281) tell us

> Vygotsky prepared and, in 1931 and 1932, Luria organized two psychological expeditions to Soviet Central Asia to validate Vygotsky's Marxist hypothesis about the close connection between the political-economic and the social-cognitive dimensions of human existence. Vygotsky predicted that the ongoing change from the "feudalistic" conditions prevailing in the traditional villages of Uzbekistan and Kirgizia to the more modern, scientific, and collective forms of agricultural production in the kolkhozes would induce former peasants to think in less "primitive" and more modern, "scientific," and logical ways about cognitive and social issues and problems.

Bourdieu provides a sociocultural account of mind that echoes Marx's emphasis on the conditionality and conditioning of psychology by social conditions. This deserves to be included in Marxist cultural psychology.

> The social order is progressively inscribed in people's minds. Social divisions become principles of division, organizing the image of the social world. Objective limits become a sense of limits, a practical anticipation of objective limits acquired by experience of objective limits, a "sense of one's place" which leads one to exclude oneself from the goods, persons, places and so forth from which one is excluded.
>
> *(Bourdieu, 1984, p. 471)*

> To reconstruct what has been pulled apart [different practices performed in different fields] ... one must return to the practice-unifying and practice-generating principle, i.e., the class habitus, the internalised form of the class condition and of the conditionings it entails.
>
> *(Ibid., p. 101)*

Bourdieu articulates Marx's conical social theory in *Distinctions* (ibid.). He explains how the knowledge and use of cultural artifacts, adorning and carrying the body, and the taste which people develop for culture (everything from food, clothing, and lifestyle to preferences in painting and music) are all centered upon, organized by, reflect, and reproduce the political economic core of society. Bourdieu goes so far as to label diverse behaviors as forms of capitalist economic capital. He identifies cultural capital, educational capital, linguistic capital, body capital, and social capital as correlates of economic capital. This terminology draws seemingly extraneous activities (such as eating, art consumption, museum visits) into the orbit of the political economy.

Contemporary sociological research in the Bourdieu genre documents how diverse cultural domains socialize cultural competencies that reflect and reproduce core political-economic demands. DeLuca and Andrews (2016) document this in the upper-middle-class Valley View Swim and Tennis Club. Although the club was ostensibly an institution devoted to the practice and development of physical skills, Valley View represents a site for the complex interplay of economic, social, cultural, and physical capitals complicit in the preservation and reproduction of members' upper-middle-class habitus. The authors discuss the findings of ethnographic fieldwork focused on the acquisition, transmission, and conversion of economic, social, cultural, and physical capital in and through the involvement of member families in somatic activities.

Social-psychological research illustrates Marx's point about religion mystifying consciousness (Ratner and El-Badwi, 2011). Clinicians have observed that extreme religiosity generates severe guilt. A syndrome has been coined, known as "scrupulosity." Scrupulosity is an obsessive concern with one's own sins and compulsive performance of religious devotion. Steketee *et al.* (1991) explain that the more religious a patient is, the more likely he or she is to complain of religious obsessions. Scrupulosity can affect any devoutly religious denomination (Inozu *et al.*, 2012; Yoriulmaz *et al.*, 2010).

Scrupulosity generates distress through its normal religious rituals, and when scrupulosity becomes intensified, it can lead to severe obsessive-compulsive symptoms. Sica *et al.* (2002) and Abramowitz *et al.* (2004) found a higher incidence of obsessive-compulsive disorder among people who were exposed to devout religion. Okasha *et al.* (1994, p. 191) report that "The role of religious upbringing has been evident in the phenomenology of OCD in Egypt, which is similar to the outcomes of studies in Jerusalem."[9]

Homology between macro cultural psychologists, Marxist cultural psychologists, and Marxists

Macro cultural psychologists are not Marxists, yet they conceive psychology as a cultural phenomenon. This framing and formatting allows for integrating macro cultural psychology into Marxist cultural psychology and Marxist psychology. Macro cultural psychology includes the upper two levels of Figure 1.2. It is straightforward to couple these to the base level in the mode of production emphasized by Marxists.

Macro cultural psychology was pioneered by Enlightenment historians and philosophers such as Vico and, later, Herder and Dilthey and the German human sciences movement.

Vygotsky, Luria, and Leontiev drew upon this work to gain insight into cultural aspects of human psychology, which they incorporated into their Marxist cultural psychology. In his autobiography, Luria (1979, Chapter 1) states:

> Dissatisfied with the competing arguments over mental elements, I looked for alternatives in the books of scholars who were critical of laboratory-based psychology. Here I was influenced by the work of the German neo-Kantians, men like Rickert, Windelband, and Dilthey. Dilthey was especially interesting because he was concerned with the real motives that energize people and the ideals and principles that guide their lives. He introduced me to the term *reale Psychologie* in which man would be studied as a unified, dynamic system. He contended that a real understanding of human nature was the foundation for what he referred to as the Geisteswissenschaften or "social sciences." This psychology was not the psychology of the textbooks but a practical psychology based on an understanding of people as they live and behave in the world. It was a psychology that described human values but made no attempt to explain them in terms of their inner mechanisms, on the grounds that it was impossible to achieve a physiological analysis of human behavior.

Marx similarly draws on Vico's work: "Vico says human history differs from natural history in this, that we have made the former, but not the latter" (1867/1961, p. 372, fn. 3).

Macro cultural psychology is strong in explaining and demonstrating the cultural character and formation (socialization) of psychology. According to psychological anthropologist Richard Shweder, "Cultural psychology is the study of the way cultural traditions and social practices regulate, express, transform, and permute the human psyche, resulting less in psychic unity for humankind than in ethnic divergences in mind, self, and emotion" (1990, p. 1). "In the language of cultural psychology there are no pure psychological laws, just as there are no unreconstructed or unmediated stimulus events. … Cultural psychology signals an end to the purely psychological in psychology" (ibid., p. 24).

In 1958, anthropologist Gregory Bateson defines cultural ethos as "the expression of a culturally standardized system of organization of the instincts and emotions of individuals" (in Kleinman and Good, 1985, p. 108). Similarly, psychological anthropologist Lutz (1988, p. 5) tries

> to demonstrate how emotional meaning is fundamentally structured by particular cultural systems and particular social and material environments. … The concepts of emotion can more profitably be viewed as serving complex communicative, moral, and cultural purposes rather than simply as labels for internal states whose nature or essence is presumed to be universal. … Emotion is culturally defined, socially enacted, and personally articulated.

Harry Daniels, a Vygotskyian educator, similarly states, "the way in which the social relations of institutions are regulated has cognitive and affective consequences for those who live and work inside them" (2012, p. 44). In the same way, Basil Bernstein, a Vygotskyian educational sociologist, emphasizes

> the process where a given distribution of power and principles of control are translated into specialized principles of communication differentially, and often unequally, distributed to social groups/classes ... and how ... these shape the formation of consciousness of members of these groups/classes.
>
> *(Quoted in ibid., p. 44)*

Language is thus a cultural mediation of the social structure that transmits the latter to people's psychology. The mediation by language is not an individual, personal escape from society. People's experience with things is mediated by cultural mediations such as speech.

Bartlett extends this model to memory.

> Nearly all important human reactions, and most unimportant ones as well, have a social frame or background into which they must fit. When we realize that human response can be directly conditioned by group properties, we see at once that the psychological facts of social life do more than provide a background for individual action. ... We have got to admit that the specific bias, appetitive, instinctive, ideal, or whatever else it is, in the group, awakens in the individuals too an active tendency to note, retain, and construct specifically along certain directions.
>
> *(1932/1967, p. 241)*

> The essentially social character of the determination remains an ultimate fact.
>
> *(Ibid., p. 254)*

> A persistent framework of institutions and customs acts as a schematic basis for constructive memory.
>
> *(Ibid., p. 255)*

> Social organization gives a persistent framework into which all detailed recall must fit, and it very powerfully influences both the manner and the matter of recall. Moreover, this persistent framework helps to provide those schemata which are a basis for *the imaginative reconstruction called memory*. ... This means that the group itself, as an organized unit, has to be treated as a veritable condition of human reaction.
>
> *(Ibid., p. 296)*

Bartlett shatters the myth of cultural determination being mechanistic and reified. He states that sociocultural structures such as institutions and customs contain a particular style of activity that includes perception, emotions, etc. These subjective elements of cultural factors generate corresponding interests, tendencies to perceive, retain, and construct/interpret information in cultural members. There is nothing passive, static, inert, or lifeless about cultural factors and culturally organized subjectivity of individual cultural members. Subjects engage in substantive rearrangement of stimulus material – e.g., stories – in order to make them meaningful in memory. Bartlett calls this "effort after meaning." Subjects produce a logical arrangement of material according to cultural standards. (Bourdieu has exactly the same conception of culturally organized "habituses.")

Cultural research on emotions (by historians, anthropologists, psychologists, and sociologists) is congruent with, and useful for, Marxist psychology. Historian Reddy defines the concept of "emotional regime" as "the set of normative emotions and the official rituals, practices, and 'emotives' that express and inculcate them; a necessary underpinning of any stable political regime" (2001, p. 129). Emotion is a political phenomenon that is constituted by official, administered, political acts which make it a "regime."

For example, Reddy argues that "the making of romantic love lies in the Gregorian Reform" (cited in Bonneuil, 2016, p. 254). It began in the mid-eleventh century and was established in 1122. This aristocratic romantic love was a personal reaction against Gregorian reforms which imposed strict emotional and behavioral controls on people. The reforms a) transformed the feudalism-vassalage system controlled by the princes into a system dominated by the Roman Church, b) fixed the rules of intimate conduct for aristocratic men and women, c) thereby redefining social and emotional identities. "The Roman Church had successfully imposed its values on kings, establishing its 'emotional norms' while channeling violence to enforce justice, prohibit private wars and plundering, and defend the weak (as well as itself)" (ibid., p. 255).

The Church employed emotions to regulate interpersonal relations. It did so in draconian, coercive, administered ways.

> In its enterprise to increase the cost of access to the opposite sex, the Church instilled other emotions: terror and shame, which serve as counter-emotions to desire-as-appetite. Guilt in particular is defined as the emotion felt by someone having transgressed a moral imperative. In taking this course, the Church launched an emotional arms race. Excommunication, as part of the Church's formidable repressive machinery, could apply to individuals but also to the territory where a transgressor was living until his or her submission and repentance. Christian love was sanctioned by priestly approval and presented as a step toward salvation. *The Church worked tirelessly to discipline consciences, enforcing submission* to parents, husband, wife, and priest, encouraging ignorance of sexuality, and idealizing a mode of marital life: Keeping bodily appetites under strict control was necessary in order to engage in the constant prayer and meditation that permitted the development of spiritual affects, especially love of God for his own sake. Constant prayer

and meditation were also the best way of maintaining strict control of bodily appetites, urgings, and imaginings.

(Ibid., p. 260, emphasis added)

Bonneuil explains how emotions were culturally organized by the Church apparatus. Emotions became codified in moral percepts. This was inducement to feel in certain ways, and not other ways, in order to be moral/good people. Infusing emotions with cultural values led to curtailing violence that was associated with negative emotions such as anger and hatred: "Moralizing emotions or building morals on strategically selected emotions and counter-emotions allowed the Church to subordinate physical violence to its own hegemony" (ibid., p. 269). Moralizing emotions = emotionalizing morals. Emotions were thus utilized to carry forth cultural-political moral behaviors.

All of the elements of propagating emotional control are political in the sense of being formed in the Church by the Church leaders to promote their political objectives. Emotional control was embedded in moral concepts that were equally political. All of this was imposed on the kings and citizens through power politics. It was not invented by individual people searching for personal meaning.

Bonneuil explains the rise of courtly (aristocratic) love in this context. It was a reaction against the strict, coercive, repressive emotional regime of the Gregorian Church. (Bonneuil does not indicate cultural reasons, forces, factors, organizations, or politics behind this reaction.) Romantic love was an illicit, spiritual pairing of an aristocratic married woman with a knight or troubadour. However, this was a very limited revision that remained beholden to the other strictures of Gregorian personal relations which remained intact: the lack of sexual contact, interpersonal distance, imaginary ideals of one's partner, worship at a distance (see Ratner, 2000, 2012b, p. 69).

> Courtly love imitates the religious doctrine of intimate relationships in many respects: rejection of desire-as-appetite, devotion to the object of worship, suffering as a means of redemption and identification of the righteous, and self-sacrifice in the ceaseless fight to overcome trials and ordeals as the pious do. The key difference is that the object of worship is no longer God but the lady. A single element of the social and emotional configuration has been modified: substituting the lady for God as the object of love: *Fin'amors* permitted aristocrats to surreptitiously reformulate the longing for association as a feeling with a spiritual status equal to that of the spiritual emotions of the Church's ascetic heroes.
>
> *(Bonneuil, 2016, p. 262)*

> Courtly love corresponds to the smallest and least unacceptable deviation from the Gregorian emotional regime.
>
> *(Ibid., p. 263)*

This cultural analysis was performed by a non-Marxist cultural historian, yet it is completely congruent with Marx's discussion of society and consciousness. Consciousness and psychology are raised to the macro cultural level where they are infused with politics and economics. Bonneuil's account of aristocratic love validates Marxism in that he explains how its emotional revolution only managed to revise one minor point of the Gregorian emotional regime. This echoes Marx's conditionality of consciousness on social conditions. Aristocratic love was bound by Gregorian conditions and the social roles of knights and aristocratic women. It was not a free invention of individuals. Fuller emotional and sexual freedom would have required transforming the social and religious conditions under which people lived. This was performed by the capitalist revolutions later on in history.

This mutual sharing and enrichment among Marxism, Marxist cultural psychology, and macro cultural psychology may additionally be seen in the relating of psychology to work.

Marx and Engels (1975, p. 303) state that:

> the history of *industry* and the established *objective* existence of industry that are the open book of *man's essential powers*, the perceptibly existing human *psychology*. … A psychology for which this book, the part of history existing in the most perceptible and accessible form, remains a closed book, cannot become a genuine comprehensive *real* science.

Marxist psychologist Vygotsky (1987, p. 132) similarly says:

> The tasks that are posed for the maturing adolescent by the social environment – tasks that are associated with his entry into the cultural, professional, and social life of the adult world – are an essential functional factor in the formation of concepts.

A non-Marxist, macro cultural psychological explanation of occupational psychology is provided by Dewey:

> Occupations … furnish the working classifications and definitions of value; they control the desire processes. Moreover, they decide the sets of objects and relations that are important, and thereby provide the content or material of attention, and the qualities that are interestingly significant. The directions given to mental life thereby extend to emotional and intellectual characteristics. So fundamental and pervasive is the group of occupational activities that it affords the scheme or pattern of the structural organization of mental traits. Occupations integrate special [psychological] elements into a functioning whole.
>
> *(Cited in Ratner, 2006, p. 88)*

All three statements are aligned in a continuous sequence from Marxism through Marxist cultural psychology to macro cultural psychology.

Dewey insightfully observes the processes and mechanisms of cultural organization of psychology in the activity and field of production. It adds specificity to Marx's formulations about this relationship. Dewey's formulation is important for articulating that the cultural organizing of subjectivity is not mechanistic, reified, or passive.

These examples demonstrate that macro cultural psychology is readily integrated into the historical-materialist model in Figure 1.2. Because both frame psychological phenomena in cultural terms, it is a straightforward matter to expand macro culture to include the mode of production and, conversely, to expand the mode of production to include distinctive features of religion, the family, and schooling into its rubric. This is depicted in Figure 1.1 as coupling the core level of society with the upper two levels of psychology and cultural factors. In addition, the complex interaction of macro cultural factors and psychology that cultural psychologists have elucidated – e.g., the encoding of emotions in morals and social relations – can be extended to reveal ways that the mode of production promulgates psychological phenomena (e.g., in consumerism, the news) and the ways that psychology reflects production. This enriches and is enriched by historical materialism. Marxism illuminates the power relations by which social classes impose their political interests on cultural and psychological factors. Marxism explains why emotions cannot free themselves from macro cultural factors, as we discussed in the case of aristocratic romantic love.

Cultural psychology identifies specific processes and mechanisms by which culture organizes and operates psychology.

An important cultural-psychological theory of this is External Mind Theory. This explains how psychology originates within and is organized by external factors such as cultural factors (Clark and Chalmers, 1998). Wilson (2010, p. 180) writes in this vein:

> While much fruitful work has focused on how culture influences the contents of cognition, here I argue that culture can in addition exercise a profound effect on the *how* of cognition—the mechanisms by which cognitive tasks get done. I argue that much of the fundamental processes of daily cognitive activity involve the operation of *cognitive tools* that are not genetically determined but instead are invented and culturally transmitted. Further, these cognitive inventions become "firmware," constituting a re-engineering of the individual's cognitive architecture. ... Cognitive tools result in reorganization of the neural system.

This is only possible because "sufficient neural plasticity exists so that acquired cognitive tools can indeed re-engineer the system" (ibid., p. 181). Neural plasticity is demonstrated by the fact that "two cognitive strategies may recruit the same brain areas (e.g., motor areas, visual representation areas)" (ibid., p. 186). This disproves modularity of psychological processes in specialized/localized cortical centers (discussed in the previous point).

Cultural psychologists have developed a theory of cultural learning that also underpins the entire enterprise of Marxist psychology in which psychology is culturally formed and performed. Tomasello explains: "children learn from pedagogy not just episodic facts but the generic structure of their cultural worlds. … Human children do not just culturally learn useful instrumental activities and information, they conform to the normative expectations of the cultural group" (2016, p. 643, emphasis added). Legare and Harris demonstrate that "children everywhere draw on a *repertoire of cultural learning strategies that optimize their acquisition of the specific practices, beliefs, and values of their communities*" (2016, p. 633, emphasis added). Cultural learning strategies involve learning *from people about social behavior* such as social norms and intentions. This is entirely different from an animal learning from the environment about natural phenomena – e.g., gearing food-finding to conditions. Cultural learning involves high-fidelity imitation that is necessary for acquiring detailed cultural knowledge and acting in culturally appropriate ways. Cultural learning includes children's seeking out information about the cultural environment through *inquiring* of caretakers. Cultural learning includes modeling and scaffolding by caretakers to transmit necessary cultural information. As Tomasello (2016, p. 644) puts it,

> human children are not just individuals attempting to learn more effective ways of doing things, but they are in addition individuals who are being pressed by the culture to learn and behave in normatively specified ways— and they have a tendency to conform to these normative expectations.

Once they have acquired cultural information about normative behavior, young children enforce social norms on other children (ibid., p. 645). Finally, cultural learning includes children regarding physical objects and artifacts *teleologically* or instrumentally; i.e., as having social use and purpose. Children are thus not simply "little scientists"; they are little anthropologists who "deploy a repertoire of strategies for reproducing and deciphering the distinctive set of phenomena that make up a culture" (Lagere and Harris, 2016, p. 636). Language is a central mechanism for this process. (Cultural learning strategies are behavioral adaptations to the novel human environment, culture. They epitomize Darwinism. Nonhuman primates who do not live in sophisticated, human-type, cultural environments do not display these elements of cultural learning. See Bailey, 2003, for additional information about cultural learning.)

Cultural psychologists have produced a powerful developmental theory and learning theory that specifically addresses the cultural processes of human leaning, the cultural requirements for these strategies, the cultural uses of them, the cultural pressures for them, and their cultural sensitivities. This is useful and necessary for explaining how human subjects become cultural creatures who adopt cultural forms of subjectivity and behavior. No other conception of learning or social interaction achieves this level of cultural dedication and specificity.

Cultural learning strategies underlie Marx's description of commodity exchange:

In order that these objects may enter into relation with each other as commodities, *their guardians [owners] must place themselves in relation to one another, as persons whose will resides in those objects*, and must behave in such a way that each does not appropriate the commodity of the other, and part with his own, except by means of an act done by mutual consent. They must therefore, mutually recognise in each other the rights of private proprietors. This juridical relation ... is a relation between two wills, and is but the reflex of the real economic relation between the two. It is this economic relation that determines the subject-matter comprised in each such juridical act.

(1867/1961, p. 84, emphasis added)

Biological processes in psychological functioning

We have said that the human organism had to change in order to develop cultural capacities and competencies. Human biology had to recede as a determination in order for culture to emerge. Culture is not an external variable that is conjoined to the biological determinants of animal behavior. Vygotsky and other cultural psychologists have made an important contribution to understanding this process – a process that is central to the Marxian emphasis on the cultural formation of consciousness and senses. The organic integration of consciousness and social conditions requires subordinating non-cultural factors to cultural factors, or replacing the former with the latter.

Non-cultural factors include idiosyncratic, personal issues such as experiences, motives, and desires as well as biological mechanisms that are presumed to determine the form and content of psychological phenomena. Purging or subordinating these factors in human psychology is both a scientific and a political issue. It is scientifically important for explaining, describing, and predicting human psychology. And it is politically important for illuminating the full society that is crystalized in human psychology so that it can be evaluated, and improved.

A variety of scholars, from biologists to anthropologists to sociologists to psychologists, have explained the process and basis of culture vis-à-vis biological determinants (see Ratner, 1991, chapters 1 and 5, and the bulk of Ratner's work on cultural psychology). Some of their key points include the fact that human psychology/behavior is mediated by cultural symbols (concepts, representations) that represent the nature of things. Psychology is not a direct, immediate response to stimuli (which it primarily is for animals). Language is a key symbolic mediation of things, as Vygotsky emphasizes and as "symbolic interactionism" emphasizes.

Geertz, a leading pioneer of cultural psychology from the perspective of anthropology, observes that it is

only because human behavior is so loosely determined by intrinsic sources of information that external [cultural] sources are so vital. ... We live in an "information gap." Between what our body tells us and what we have to know in order to function, there is a vacuum we must fill ourselves, and we fill it with information (or misinformation) provided by our culture ... we are incomplete or unfinished animals who complete or finish ourselves through culture – and not through culture in general but through highly particular forms of it.

(Cited in Ratner, 1991, p. 16; for further discussion
see Ratner, 1991, chapters 1 and 5)

This is a cultural theory of human nature and human behavior. It explains why culture is so powerful an influence on psychology and how it powerfully organizes psychology. This is a major contribution to Marxist psychology, which has not hitherto explained these questions. Geertz explains that culture is powerful because biological functions have lost the determining role for people that they have in relation to animals. Biological functions have either been subordinated to cultural processes or else they have completely dropped out of psychological determination. Instincts are a good example of a biological mechanism that strictly determines animal behavior but which has dropped away in human behavior, enabling us to socially construct varied social interactions, dispositions, perceptions, reasoning processes, and sexuality.

Vygotsky and Luria make this point: "The new cultural techniques acquired at school turn out to be so strong that they suppress the older, primitive methods" (1930/1993, p. 180). And Vygotsky (1987, p. 132) says

> In contrast to the maturation of instincts or innate tendencies, the motive force that ... sets in action the maturational mechanism of behavior impelling it forward along the path of further development is located not inside but outside the adolescent. The tasks that are posed for the maturing adolescent by the social environment – tasks that are associated with his entry into the cultural, professional, and social life of the adult world – are an essential functional factor in the formation of concepts.

Vygotsky replaces innate tendencies with the social environment that demands, stimulates, and supports the formation of concepts. This is Darwinism par excellence – used by Marx.

> In the process of evolution, man invented tools and created a cultural industrial environment, but this industrial environment altered man himself; it called forth complex cultural forms of behavior that took the place of the primitive ones. ... Behavior becomes social and cultural, not only in its contents, but also in its *mechanisms*, in its means.
>
> The child is born to an already existing cultural-industrial environment. ... The pre-existent social cultural environment stimulates in the child those necessary forms of adaptation which were created long ago in the adults surrounding him.

(Vygotsky and Luria, 1930/1993, pp. 170–171)

Vygotsky analogizes the replacement of primitive, natural behavioral mechanisms by cultural mechanisms to Darwinian evolution, which Marx and Engels found so useful for understanding historical changes in behavior as the resultant of changing conditions:

> The history of the cultural development of the child must be considered as analogous to the living process of biological evolution, to how new species of animals developed gradually, how in the process of the struggle for existence, the old species became extinct, how catastrophically adaptation of the living organisms to nature proceeded. ... Introduced into the history of child development at the same time is the concept of conflict, that is, contradiction or clash between the natural and the historical, the primitive and the cultural, the organic and the social. All cultural behavior of the child develops on a base of its primitive forms, but this growth often involves conflict: the old form is forced out, is sometimes completely disrupted. ... When Wundt called development of speech in the one-year-old precocious development, he had in mind specifically the great contradiction and genetic *lack of correspondence between the organically primitive apparatus of the youngster and the complex apparatus of cultural behavior.*
>
> *(Vygotsky, 1997c, pp. 221–222, emphasis added)*

Cultural psychologists' general conception of biology as subordinated to culture and organized by culture leads seamlessly to its concretization by particular social systems. This explains and describes cultural features of bodily processes – what Mauss (1935/1973) calls "techniques of the body." It makes the body a window into culture, and a potential social critic and social activist.

Nobody expressed this better than Foucault in his concepts of biopower and biopolitics. These denote the practice of modern states to regulate their subjects through "an explosion of numerous and diverse techniques for achieving the subjugations of bodies and the control of populations" (Foucault, 1978, p. 140). Although Foucault was not a cultural psychologist *per se*, his work on culture and psychology *should* be considered as valuable contribution to cultural psychology, just as Bourdieu's work is. For instance:

> By bio-power I mean a number of phenomena that seem to me to be quite significant, namely, the set of mechanisms through which the basic biological features of the human species became the object of a political strategy, of a general strategy of power.
>
> *(Foucault, 2007, p. 1)*

This bio-power was without question an indispensable element in the development of capitalism; the latter would not have been possible without the controlled insertion of bodies into the machinery of production and the adjustment of the phenomena of population to economic processes. But this was not all it required; it also needed the growth of both these factors, their reinforcement as well as their availability and docility; it had to have methods of power capable of optimizing forces, aptitudes, and life in general without at the same time making them more difficult to govern. If the development of the great instruments of the state, as institutions of power, ensured the maintenance of production relations, the rudiments of anatomo- and bio-politics, created in the eighteenth century as techniques of power present at every level of the social body and utilized by very diverse institutions (the family and the army, schools and the police, individual medicine and the administration of collective bodies), operated in the sphere of economic processes, their development, and the forces working to sustain them. They also acted as factors of segregation and social hierarchization, exerting their influence on the respective forces of both these movements, guaranteeing relations of domination and effects of hegemony. The adjustment of the accumulation of men to that of capital, the joining of the growth of human groups to the expansion of productive forces and the differential allocation of profit, were made possible in part by the exercise of bio-power in its many forms and modes of application. The investment of the body, its valorization, and the distributive management of its forces were at the time indispensable.

(Foucault, 1978, pp. 140–141)[10]

Foucault demonstrates how the cultural framing of biology and psychology (aptitudes, competencies, habits) performed by cultural psychologists can be seamlessly fitted to the Marxist conception of the social cone that is grounded in a mode of production. Foucault explains powerful mechanisms of socializing psychological processes that are employed by the mode of production. This is a major expansion of Marxism and materialism into the discipline of psychology. It required a cultural reformatting of biology and psychology that is facilitated by cultural psychology. This new cultural theory of the body/biology is the theoretical framework for Foucault's insights. It explains how they are viable and plausible; because biology has the open, flexible, plastic character that cultural psychologists have elucidated. It dispenses with objections to Foucault that might be levelled by psychobiologists – i.e., that Foucault and Mauss make no sense because biology is the source of our psychology/behavior/agency/uniqueness. Cultural psychologists and Foucault and Mauss refute these notions and explain how the body is a manifestation of culture.

Macro cultural psychology and personal meaning

An important issue in cultural psychology that contributes to Marxist psychology is the nature of personal experience and meanings vis-à-vis cultural organization of behavior. Many psychologists and non-academics reject cultural psychology and Marxism on the grounds that it ignores personal experience and meanings. In fact, cultural psychology provides a logical, coherent explanation of personal meanings that is consistent with macro cultural influences on psychology.

Leontiev (2009, pp. 416–417) acknowledges personal meanings that comprise personal life.

> Whereas external sensuousness associates objective meanings with the reality of the objective world in the subject's consciousness, the personal meaning associates them with the reality of his own life in this world, with its motivations. It is the personal meaning that gives human consciousness its partiality.

Leontiev goes on to explain that personal meanings about one's own life are not free inventions. They draw on social values and concepts to interpret personal events (such as family psychological abuse).

> In contrast to society, the individual has no special language of his own with meanings that he has evolved himself. His comprehension of reality can take place only by means of the "ready-made" meanings he assimilates from without – the knowledge, concepts, and views he receives through intercourse, in the various forms of individual and mass communication.
>
> *(Ibid., p. 417)*

Leontiev subsumes even the most arcane psychological processes within a cultural framework:

> although a scientific psychology must never lose sight of man's inner world, the study of this inner world cannot be divorced from a study of his activity and does not constitute any special trend of scientific psychological investigation.
>
> *(Ibid., p. 419)*

> When the products of socio-historical practice, idealised in meanings, become part of the mental reflection of the world by the individual subject, they acquire new systemic qualities. … Meanings lead a double life. They are produced by society and have their history in the development of language, in the history of the development of forms of social consciousness; they express the movement of science and its means of cognition, and also the ideological notions of society – religious, philosophical and political. In this objective existence of theirs, *meanings obey the socio-historical laws and at the same time the inner logic of their development.*
>
> [...] In this second life of theirs, meanings are individualized and "subjectivized" only in the sense that their movement in the system of social relations is not *directly contained* in them; they enter into another system of

relationships, another movement. But the remarkable thing is that, in doing so, they do not lose their socio-historical nature, their objectivity.

(Ibid., p. 411)

This is an important formulation of personal experience and behaviors that grounds them not in individual choice but in social conditions. Leontiev argues that personal experience is a variant of cultural factors, not independent of them. Personal experience reflects particular interactions *with* cultural factors, and internalizations of them. For instance, a distraught person will protect herself by drawing on consumerist values and practices or on conservative, self-centered, individualistic values and practices. She does not invent these. She *personalizes* them in the sense of using them for her personal needs, which are simply particular forms of cultural-psychological needs that are generated by distinctive positions in society. Using cultural factors to solve personal needs additionally brings them into those needs, which enhances their cultural content.

Personalized cultural psychology, or encultured personal psychology, enables us to observe the effects of cultural factors on people via their psychological functions. This is an important development in Marxist Psychology, contributed by cultural psychology.

Marxist psychology, Vygotsky, and "will"

Vygotsky and Luria expand Leontiev's comments on personal experience to "will." They explain that individual will is not the product of the individual; rather, it is a social phenomenon that the individual is expressing. According to Vygotsky and Luria (1930/1993, p. 188):

> Traditional psychology attempted to explain voluntary behavior as the activity of the will, and considered it to be a typical example of willful behavior. Needless to say, in essence this does not appear to be an explanation because the appearance of "will" also requires an explanation and does not appear to be a final, independent factor.

The authors deny the prevalent assumption that voluntary = individual will. They assert an opposite equation: voluntary = cultural. Culture is the basis of, the content of, and the mechanisms of voluntary will. It is only the cultured organism that possesses will. Vygotsky and Luria speak of "artificial, voluntary, cultural attention" (ibid.). Voluntary = cultural = artificial. Luria states:

> There is no hope of finding the sources of free action in the lofty realms of the mind or in the depths of the brain. The idealist approach of the phenomenologists is as hopeless as the positive approach of the naturalists. To discover the sources of free action it is necessary to go outside the limits of the organism, not into the intimate sphere of the mind, but into the

objective forms of social life; it is necessary to seek *the sources of human consciousness and freedom in the social history of humanity.* To find the soul it is necessary to lose it.

(Retrieved from: https://www.marxists.org/ archive/luria/index.htm, emphasis added)[11]

This is obvious in the case of consumerism: consumer craving for products is merely the expression of consumer psychology that has been inculcated by consumer capitalism. Similarly, when a religious devotee has food or dress preferences, this is an expression of the religious role that the individual is performing. It is not an authentic, personal, agentive desire based upon rational thinking and emancipatory politics.

The fascinating mind or fascinating society?

We have seen that Marxist psychology reformulates the mind as a cultural element. Even illusions and personal experience/meanings are cultural elements. This leads to the unorthodox conclusion that it is not the mind *per se* that is fascinating in terms of what it can do; rather, it is social systems that are fascinating for what they can do to the human mind and what they make the mind do. It is the social system that generates magnificent creativity and development. The social system is the root of illusions and confusions and compulsions and self-destructive acts. It is the social system that enables individuals to have diverse, complex experiences from their different social positions. The individual mind does not create these on its own. Of course, the mind is active subjectivity that does do these things; however, it does not invent them out of itself. It takes its lead, inspiration, affordances, need for, direction, and mechanisms from society. Vygotsky and Luria (1930/1993, p. 105) state this clearly in their discussion of

> the cultural development of human memory. External development takes the place of inner development. ... The historical development of human memory can basically and primarily be summed up as the development and perfection of those auxiliary means that social humans have worked out in the process of their cultural life.

Horkheimer (1993, p. 119) expresses this point succinctly:

> Rather than a foundational science, psychology becomes instead an indispensable auxiliary science for history. Its content is influenced by this transformation of function. In the context of this theory, its object loses its unitary quality. Psychology no longer has to do with human beings [individual psyches] as such. Rather, it must differentiate within each epoch the total spiritual powers available within individuals.

Vygotsky says the same thing at the end of Chapter 4 of *Thinking and Speech*:

> verbal thinking is not a natural but a socio-historical form of behavior. It is
> therefore characterized by a whole series of *features and laws* that do not apply
> to natural forms of thinking and speech. The most important point, however,
> is that this recognition of the historical natural nature of verbal thinking
> requires that in analyzing it we apply the same methodological theses that
> historical materialism applies to the other historical phenomena of human
> society.
>
> *(1987, p. 120)*

The science of psychology thus enters the fascinating complexity of society.
Understanding religious psychology enters the fascinating politics and power relations
of the Church, how it embedded its social-political interests in moral percepts and in
emotions and cognitions and perceptions, its struggles with kings and politicians, its
internal struggles and machinations for imposing its will on segments of the
population, and its reflecting of material relations of production in its moral and
psychological dictums. This uplifts the social consciousness of psychologists and their
followers, and it primes them for political action for social reform.

Methodology: cultural qualitative methodology

Macro cultural psychology, and Marxist cultural psychology, contribute to Marxist
psychology by developing methodology that identifies the historical materialist
basis, organization, content, administration, socialization, politics, and function of
lived psychological phenomena. Personal psychology is revealed as implicitly
embodying cultural psychology. Strictly personal issues such as a particular fondness
for opera that one's father liked are not germane to Marxist Psychology – or to
scientific Psychology in general, which, like all science, established general
principles of phenomena.

Marxist psychological methodology emphasizes oppressive social forces that
dissemble oppressive reality in order to deter comprehension and rebellion. This
has momentous consequences for psychological research. It means that research
cannot take people's self-consciousness as indicating their full psychology.
Subjective responses about the origins, content, mechanisms, and function of
psychology are generally mistaken. Consequently, these features can only be
apprehended from an external, objective, interpretative, reconstructed point of
view. This is why Vygotsky (1997a, pp. 325–326) says:

> *Not a single science is possible* without separating direct experience from
> knowledge. … If in psychology, appearance and being were the same, then
> *everybody would be a scientist-psychologist* and science would be impossible. It is
> *one thing* to live, to experience, and *another* to analyze.
>
> […] No science can be confined to the subjective, to *appearances*.

Objectivist, external methodology is mandated by the factual, cultural-political character of psychological phenomena. In conditions where people are aware of the social-political character of their psychological phenomena, subjective responses to questions may, perhaps, be an adequate methodology.

Silva (2015) presents an external, objective, interpretative, ethnographic methodology that is necessary for explaining, describing, and predicting the psychology of neoliberal subjects – i.e., people living in neoliberal, capitalist society.

Silva describes one man, Cory, who has been living paycheck to paycheck since he was 16, has given up setting goals and lives moment to moment. He says: "If I had goals then there could be a lot to let that down. So I am floating. Whatever happens next, happens, and I will deal with it when it happens" (ibid., p. 15).

Silva explains the objective social basis of this response: "The men and women I spoke with cope with their disappointments in the labor market by actively fostering a kind of flexibility within themselves, bending with the constant disruptions and disappointments in the labor market" (ibid., p. 95). The concrete social conditions require people to adjust to them in this manner. Failure would result in increased frustration and losing a job. The response does not emanate from a separate, personal, autonomous realm of agency. On the contrary, agency adjusts itself to survive in a particular environment – just as Vygotsky and Darwin said about all behavior.

Neoliberal social conditions on psychology include the template through which individuals interpret their experience, themselves, and their society.

> Just as neoliberalism teaches young people that they are solely responsible for their economic fortunes, the "mood economy" [what Bourdieu might call "emotional capital"] renders them responsible for their emotional fates. … The mood economy dovetails neoliberalism by privatizing happiness [and success].
> *(Ibid., p. 21)*

Silva's subjects interpret their misfortunes and their opportunities for advancement in terms of individual, psychological processes. Misfortune is due to inadequate personality traits such as laziness, drug dependency, weakness, macho aggressiveness that got them into trouble. Advancement is possible through cultivating appropriate individual, psychological traits such as motivation, persistence, strength, flexibility, and rejecting drug dependency. Individuals do not view their misfortune or success (or that of other people) in terms of social structural factors such as job opportunities, job policies that encourage job outsourcing, wage levels, class structure, or political economy: "Rob feels redeemed because he has managed to successfully defeat the temperament he inherited from his father and to grow into a morally worthy person, despite his inability to find a full-time job or keep a [romantic] relationship going" (ibid., p. 22).

Silva explains how neoliberal economics sets the parameters and the content for meaning-making: "Neoliberalism, then, reigns not only as an abstract and removed set of discourses and practices in the economic sphere, but also as a lived system of meanings and values in the emotional sphere" (ibid., p. 98).

This isomorphism is systematically cultivated and socialized through administered social institutions. "This model is ubiquitous in their everyday interactions, propagated through school psychologists, family services, the service economy, self-help literature, online support groups, addiction recovery groups, medical trials, or even talk shows such as *Oprah*" (ibid., p. 21).

This cultural formation of psychology makes the subjects "acquiescing neoliberal subjects" (ibid., p. 109) of psychological oppression.

This is a model for Marxist psychological methodology. It identifies the social basis, content, socialization, and function of psychology in the mode of production and its radiating social factors such as ideology. Individuals experience these factors; however, they are not fully informed about them and the way that they shape their psychological reactions. A sociologically and politically informed researcher must bring this knowledge to people to help them understand their experiences.

IV. Bringing it all back home: integrating non-Marxist psychological theories into Marxist psychology

Although macro cultural psychology is not Marxist, it has the unusual character of being compatible with Marxism, engaging in reciprocal enrichment with it, and contributing to Marxist psychology. There is nothing incompatible or antithetical between these. This is unusual because every other psychological theory contains elements that are incompatible with the thorough cultural basis, organization, administration, socialization, and operation of psychological phenomena that is central to Marxist psychology. This is why Vygotsky, Luria, and Leontiev reject other theories such as psychoanalysis, behaviorism, personalism-subjectivism, psychobiology, and cognitivism.

It is important to discuss the relationship of Marxist psychology to incompatible psychological approaches. We reject a relationship of eclecticism or interactionism that juxtaposes various approaches together. This is the common way of treating qualitative and quantitative methodologies as a toolkit to be used at the researcher's discretion. Eclecticism-interactionism violates the fundamental principle of science, which is logical coherence. This is known as the law of parsimony. It holds that the plethora of empirical and theoretical issues be commonly explained by a few core, consistent principles. Eclecticism-interactionism postulates multiple contradictory principles that are invoked to explain different issues. Vygotsky explains this failure as follows:

> It is this feeling of a system, the sense of a common style, the understanding that each particular statement is linked with and dependent upon the central idea of the whole system of which it forms a part, which is absent in the essentially eclectic attempts at combining the parts of two or more systems that are heterogeneous and diverse in scientific origin and composition. Such are, for instance, the synthesis of behaviorism and Freudian theory in the

American literature; Freudian theory without Freud in the systems of Adler and Jung; the reflexological Freudian theory of Bekhterev and Zalkind; finally, the attempts to combine Freudian theory and Marxism. So many examples from the area of the problem of the subconscious alone! In all these attempts the tail of one system is taken and placed against the head of another and the space between them is filled with the trunk of a third. ... What the eclectics do, is to reply to a question raised by Marxist philosophy with an answer prompted by Freudian metapsychology.

(1997a, p. 259)

The system of Marxism is defined as being monistic, materialistic, dialectic, etc. Then the monism, materialism, etc. of Freud's system is established; the superimposed concepts coincide and the systems are declared to have fused. Very flagrant, sharp contradictions which strike the eye are removed in a very elementary way: they are simply excluded from the system, are declared to be exaggerations, etc. Thus, Freudian theory, is de-sexualized as pan-sexualism; this obviously does not square with Marx's philosophy. No problem, we are told – we will accept Freudian theory without the doctrine of sexuality. But this doctrine forms the very nerve, soul, center of the whole system. Can we accept a system without its center? After all, Freudian theory without the doctrine of the sexual nature of the unconscious is like Christianity without Christ or Buddhism with Allah.

(Ibid., p. 261)

The identity of the two systems is declared by a simple formal-logical superposition of the characteristics – without a single analysis of Freud's basic concepts, without critically weighing and elucidating his assumptions and starting points, without a critical examination of the genesis of his ideas, even without simply inquiring how he himself conceives of the philosophical foundations of his system.

(Ibid., p. 262)

Instead of combining incompatible systems together, we must first elucidate the essential incompatibility of systems such as Freudianism and Marxism; then we can extract particular elements of the non-Marxist system from that system, purge them of their incompatible features – i.e., their deformities – and integrate them within Marxism to refurbish (retrofit) them and realize their potential truth (as Hegel said). Our discussion of personal meanings and personal experience and emotions and labor and community have followed this path. This is exactly what Marx did with the capitalist means of production: he recognized their potential usefulness for socialism, so he expropriated them from capitalist ownership and principles of the capitalist mode of production and incorporated them within the socialist mode of production, imbuing them with its features.

This expropriating and refurbishing of concepts is what all scholars do in order to construct coherent conceptual systems. Vygotsky's non-Marxist followers have done this to his concepts: they have ignored, denied, and distorted the Marxist system of Vygotsky's concepts, and they have infused them with bourgeois features – such as reducing them to individual or interpersonal phenomena, or to abstractions, which we have documented in the Introduction to this book. Of course, this deforms them rather than realizing their truth; however, the refurbishing *process* is the same.

Let us illustrate this important issue with Freudo-Marxism.

Luria (1979, Chapter 1) was initially attracted to psychoanalysis but eventually rejected it as incompatible with Marxist cultural psychology:

> I plunged into psychoanalytic research. To begin with, I established a small psychoanalytic circle. I even ordered stationary with "Kazan Psychoanalytic Association" printed in Russian and German on the letterhead. I then sent news of the formation of this group to Freud himself, and was both surprised and pleased when I received a letter in return addressed to me as "Dear Mr. President." Freud wrote how glad he was to learn that a psychoanalytic circle had been founded in such a remote eastern town of Russia. This letter, written in a Gothic German script, as well as another letter authorizing the Russian translation of one of his smaller books, are still in my files.
>
> In later years, I published some papers based on psychoanalytic ideas and even wrote a draft of a book on an objective approach to psychoanalysis, which was never published. But I finally concluded that it was an error to assume that one can deduce human behavior from the biological "depths" of mind, excluding its social "heights."

Vygotsky was also initially open to psychoanalytic ideas. He joined the Psychoanalytic Society, and with Luria he co-authored the introduction to the Russian translation of Freud's *Beyond the Pleasure Principle*. This early work, published in 1925, was a youthful exuberance at encountering some novel psychological ideas. Vygotsky and Luria quickly corrected their overestimation of Freud's scientific and political contribution as they developed their antithetical cultural-historical psychology.

Luria tells us: "Vygotsky was strongly opposed to Freud's 'depth psychology' with its overemphasis on man's biological nature. Instead he proposed a psychology from the 'heights' of man's socially organized experiences, which, he maintained, determines the structure of human conscious activity" (1979, Chapter 3).

In *The Psychology of Art*, Vygotsky (1925/1971) explains the antithesis between Freud and cultural psychology (and culture in general):

> social psychologists like McDougall, Le Bon, Freud, et al., regard the social psyche as secondary, originating from the psyche of the individual. They assume that there is a special individual psyche and that from the interaction

of individual psyches or psychologies there arises a collective psyche or psychology common to all individuals Thus, social psychology is regarded as the psychology of a collective individual, in the same way that a crowd is made up of single individuals, even though it has a supra-individual psychology. We see that non-Marxist social psychology has a primitive empirical approach to the social entity, regarding it as a crowd, a collective entity, a relation between individuals or persons. Society is taken to be an association of people, and it is regarded as an accessory activity of one individual. These psychologists do not admit that somewhere, in a remote and intimate corner of his thought, his feelings, etc., the psyche of an individual is social and socially conditioned.

According to Vygotsky,

> Psychoanalysis displays not dynamic, but highly static, conservative, anti-dialectic and anti-historical tendencies. It directly reduces the higher mental processes – both personal and collective ones – to primitive, primordial, essentially prehistorical, prehuman roots, leaving no room for history. The same key unlocks the creativity of a Dostoyevsky and the totem and taboo of primordial tribes; the Christian church, communism, the primitive horde – in psychoanalysis everything is reduced to the same source. That such tendencies are present in psychoanalysis is apparent from all the works of this school which deal with problems of culture, sociology and history. We can see that here it does not continue, but contradicts, the methodology of Marxism.
>
> *(1997a, p. 263)*

> This does by no means imply, of course, that Marxists should not study the unconscious because Freud's basic concepts contradict dialectical materialism. On the contrary, precisely because the area elaborated by psychoanalysis is elaborated with inadequate means it must be conquered for Marxism.
>
> *(Ibid., p. 265)*

This last sentence captures my point about expropriating psychological issues from non-Marxist systems and incorporating them into Marxism in a refurbished form. (It also applies to political movements. Most movements are anti-Marxist; their useful elements must therefore be extracted from their political theory and reframed within Marxist theory. This makes them extensions of Marxism to important new issues. This is true of the co-op movement, populism, ethnic movements, and gender movements.

Freud's psychophysics

The antithesis between Freudianism and Marxist cultural psychology is rooted in Freud's psychophysical basis of the psyche, which he adopted from Fechner.

Fechner was a physicist who applied physical principles to psychological phenomena such as drives, instincts, sensations, and even thoughts. Freud attended Fechner's lectures and thoroughly studied his work. Freud quotes Fechner in many of his works. Fechner's concept of mental energy, his "topographical" concept of the mind (the partitioning of mind into unconscious, preconscious and conscious regions), his principles of pleasure-unpleasure, the ideas of constancy and of repetition all find their way with little modification into Freud's grand scheme. Freud's theory of drives was a psychophysical concept about tension and drive level and homeostasis and conservation of energy that obeyed psychophysical laws: physiological needs, when unmet, create anxiety and a negative state of tension. When a need is satisfied, the drive tension is reduced, giving pleasure as the organism returns to a state of homeostasis. Indeed, Freud's entire conception of psychic forces having quantitative features derives from Fechner, as was his idea of the pleasure principle; and Freud's theory of hysteria directly reflects Fechner's psychophysics (Sulloway, 1992, pp. 66–67).

In his 1912 lecture on "Anxiety and instinctual life" (Freud, 1965, p. 106), Freud claims that the conservative nature of instincts to restore earlier states is the reason that repressed experiences of childhood are reproduced in dreams and other reactions. In other words, repressed ideas linger in the unconscious and steer behavior because psychic instincts, like organic instincts, aim at preserving those originary ideas.

Freud propounded a non-psychological, non-cultural conception of the psyche, or mind. It cannot be integrated into Vygotsky's Marxist cultural psychology, as Vygotsky points out. Marxist philosopher Lichtman correctly states that "Freud's metapsychology, and particularly his instinct theory, cannot be integrated into a Marxist perspective. Such an attempt is futile because of the basic contradiction between the theories" (1982, p. 253).

Freud's incompatibility with Marxism is responsible for its numerous errors in conceptualizing, interpreting, and solving psychological problems.

Defense mechanisms lack empirical support

Holt concludes that "many – perhaps most – of the obscurities, fallacies, and internal contradictions of psychoanalytic theory are rather direct derivatives of its neurological inheritance" (1989, p. 129). Sulloway (1991, p. 245) echoes this evaluation:

> many of Freud's most essential psychoanalytic concepts were based upon erroneous and now outmoded assumptions from nineteenth-century biology. ... Bad biology ultimately spawned bad psychology. Freud erected his psychoanalytic edifice on a kind of intellectual quicksand, a circumstance that consequently doomed many of his most important theoretical conclusions from the outset.

Sulloway (1992) argues that Freud remained a "crypto-biologist" to the end of his career.

I would invert Sulloway's causal arrow that bad biology produced bad psychology. It is really because Freud had a fallacious understanding of psychology that he turned to biology to legitimate this understanding. A good psychologist with a strong cultural orientation would never turn to psychophysics for explanatory constructs. Biological determinism legitimizes bad psychology; it does not produce it.

Baumeister et al. (1998) empirically rebut defense mechanisms. Holmes reviewed research on these mechanisms and concludes that "at the present time there is no controlled laboratory evidence supporting the concept of repression" (1990, p. 96).

Freud's cases

Freud's extra-cultural, psychophysical, ego mechanisms displace the social content of psychology. This led Freud (and his followers) to misinterpret all of his famous cases.

Freud's study of Daniel Schreber is a case in point. Freud never met Schreber, but in 1911 he wrote an analysis of him based on Schreber's book *Memoirs of My Nervous Illness*. Freud concludes that Schreber's paranoia had been a defense against homosexual love for his father. Moreover, Schreber's experiences of persecution by god were a disguised displacement of his fear of his father, which was a reaction formation against his love for his father.

Schatzman (1973) demonstrates that Freud's interpretation inverted the true source of Schreber's fear. It was his father's brutal mistreatment of him. Schatzman has found child-rearing pamphlets written by Moritz Schreber, Daniel Schreber's father, which stressed the necessity of taming the rebellious savage beast in the child and turning him into a productive citizen. Many of the techniques recommended by Moritz Schreber were mirrored in Daniel's psychotic experiences. For example, one of the "miracles" described by Daniel Schreber was that of chest compression, of tightening and tightening. This can be seen as analogous to one of Moritz Schreber's techniques of an elaborate contraption which confined the child's body, forcing him to have correct posture at the dinner table. Similarly, Daniel's "freezing miracle" might mirror Moritz Schreber's recommendation of placing the infant in a bath of ice cubes beginning at age three months. Yet again, Daniel experienced a hallucination of a "hierarchy of powers in the realm of god," which recapitulates his father's stated insistence on a parent setting up a hierarchy by which he applies his power upon the nurse to apply hers upon the baby.

Fear in the Schreber household recapitulated the fearful, authoritarian relation between father and son throughout Germanic society at the time. Yet Freud ignored all of this social reality; indeed, he mystified and obscured it with his specious psychological explanation. This is the political function of Freud's psychologistic theory. In contrast, cultural-historical-psychology a) elucidates the social relation between father and son and then b) traces this to macro cultural factors, which are critiqued and challenged.

This analysis applies to all of Freud's case studies. He misconstrued all the fears of his female patients as resting upon their natural, Oedipal, libidinous love for their fathers or other significant, but then denying this socially tabooed love via unconscious defense mechanisms that converted love into fear/hatred, hysteria, etc. Feminist critics have thoroughly demonstrated that the women's fear and hatred of their fathers was genuine, not a defense mechanism, and it was a direct reaction to the fathers' authoritarian treatment of them. This individual situation reflected a broad social pattern of parent–child relations. And this family pattern reflected and reinforced broader authoritarian political-economic social relations in work.

Ramas (1990) dubs Freud's analysis of Dora "romantic fiction" because he inverts obvious social influences that generated Dora's symptoms into arcane, unsubstantiated, unverifiable (unfalsifiable), fictitious unconscious causes. For instance, Dora's parents were friends with another couple, Herr K. and Frau K. Herr K. attempted to seduce Dora, while Frau K. was having an affair with Dora's father! Dora, justifiably, was upset at both men, which *may* have had something to do with her sexual frigidity and general distress. Yet despite the fact that Dora had rebuffed Herr K. and slapped him, Freud contorts this into its opposite – that she loved him and that "you are afraid of Herr K. [because] you are afraid of the temptation you feel to yield to him" (cited in Ramas, 1990, p. 167). As with Schreber, Freud pretends that Dora's hysteria was due to her own tabooed sexual desire (for Herr K.) that was disguised by psychophysical defense mechanisms. The real social problem is expunged from consideration. Fromm (1942) expresses this evaluation of Freud: "Freud's observations are of great importance, but he gave an erroneous explanation. … He mistook the causal relation between erogenous zones and character traits for the reverse of what they really are."

Lichtman (1982, pp. 131–173) gives an exhaustive Marxist critique of Freud's misinterpretation of Dora. He states that

> Freud could not grasp the [social] significance of his own discovery because his basic social assumptions led him to reify his insights and to attribute either biology, physics, or universal anthropology what was, in fact, the precipitate of bourgeois social relations.
>
> *(Ibid., p. 131)*

Historian David Stannard concludes that: "psychohistory does not work and cannot work. The psychoanalytic approach to history is irredeemably one of logical perversity scientific unsoundness, and cultural naivete" (1980, p. 156). Freud's psychoanalytical biography of Leonardo da Vinci is "dazzlingly dismissive of the most elementary canons of evidence, logic, and, most of all, imaginative restraint" (ibid., p. 3; see also Crews, 1993, 1994, and Wolpe and Rachman, 1960).

In contrast, Laing and Esterson (1970) have demonstrated that psychological symptoms are straightforward, direct, transparent reflections of debilitating social interactions imposed by parents on patients – as was true for Schreber and Dora. This opens the door to tracing this general family pattern to underlying, broad social forces. This parallels Silva's perceptive analysis of the cultural psychology of oppressed Americans, which traced their psychology to neoliberal values and practices. Objective analyses of mental illness confirm the cultural-psychological perspective that culminates in Marxist psychology.

Fromm (1942) explains how Freud's characterological findings become fruitful for social psychology by reversing Freud's explanation of them.

> As long as we assume, for instance, that the anal character, as it is typical of the European lower middle class, is caused by certain early experiences in connection with defecation, we have hardly any data that lead us to understand why a specific class should have an anal social character. However, if we understand it as one form of relatedness to others, rooted in the character structure and resulting from the experiences with the outside world, we have a key for understanding why the whole mode of life of the lower middle class, its narrowness, isolation, and hostility, made for the development of this kind of character structure.

Freud's "case studies" contort and obfuscate the social reality of psychology. Freud initiated this mystifying process by contorting children's fear of their parents (and other adults) into love. This contortion of emotions inexorably led to contorting the social relations that generated them. The positive emotion implies that the parent–child relation was good, which is why the children really loved their parents. Depriving the patients of any reasonable social cause of their disorder inexorably leads to ascribing the disorder to the patients' own psychic operations. This is akin to saying that the reason for unemployment and poverty lies not in socioeconomic policy (which is benevolent) but, rather, in the deficient motivation of the poor.

Freud's conservative politics

Freud's incompatibility with Marx is additionally evidenced in Freud's political ideas about solving social-psychological problems; i.e., changing society and psychology. Freud's politics are ignorant and conservative, based on his erroneous, naturalistic, universalistic psychic instincts.

His *Civilization and Its Discontents* (1930/2015) ends with:

> the fateful question whether and to what extent human cultural development will succeed in mastering the disturbance of communal life by the human instinct of aggression and self-destruction. … It may be expected that the other of the two heavenly forces, Eternal Eros will make an effort to assert himself in the struggle with his equally immortal adversary. But who can foresee with what success and with what result?

Even if civilization masters aggression, the result is unhappy and unfulfilling: "What a potent obstacle to civilization aggressiveness must be if the defense against it can cause as much unhappiness as aggressiveness itself!"

Freud used this thought to reject the communistic social-psychological transformation that Marx propounded:

> I am able to recognize that the psychological premises on which the [communist] system is based are an untenable illusion. In abolishing private property we deprive the human love of aggression of one of its instruments, certainly a strong one, though certainly not the strongest; but we have in no way altered the differences in power and influence which are misused by aggressiveness, nor have we altered anything in its nature. Aggressiveness was not created by property. It reigned almost without limit in primitive times, when property was still very scanty, and it already shows itself in the nursery almost before property has given up its primal, anal form; it forms the basis of every relation of affection and love among people (with the single exception, perhaps, of the mother's relation to her male child). If we do away with personal rights over material wealth, there still remains prerogative in the field of sexual relationships, which is bound to become the source of the strongest dislike and the most violent hostility among men who in other respects are on an equal footing. If we were to remove this factor, too, by allowing complete freedom of sexual life and thus abolishing the family, the germ-cell of civilization, we cannot, it is true, easily foresee what new paths the development of civilization could take; but one thing we can expect, and that is that this indestructible feature of human nature will follow it there.
>
> *(Ibid., p. 87)*

Freud is saying that aggression is a fixed, innate tendency that is independent of social conditions. Any change in conditions that is designed to curtail aggression must fail because aggression will simply express itself in another condition. Freud can only pin his hope on the "heavenly force," eternal Eros and love: "And in the development of mankind as a whole, just as in individuals, love alone acts as the civilizing factor in the sense that it brings a change from egoism to altruism" (1921/2012, p. 32). This is a pitiful, ignorant, quasi-religious conception of history and politics. It is diametrically opposed to Marxism.[12]

Reconciling the irreconcilable

It is impossible to conjoin irreconcilables. The only resolution is to transform one in line with the other. This is not a matter of compromise in which both are adjusted toward each other while retaining their essence, for there is no common ground between irreconcilable essences. Adjustment requires destroying the essential irreconcilability of one element to make it consonant with the other.

Eclecticism is a myth because it cannot preserve the essential characters of its antagonistic elements while unifying them. It is usually the inferior element that transforms the superior element. Marxists who attempt to utilize non-Marxist constructs inevitably become used by them. In Freudo-Marxism, psychoanalysis transforms Marxism more often than the reverse. Marxist Freudians inevitably devolve into Freudian Marxists. The modifier and modified become reversed – the Marxism that modifies Freud becomes modified by it and transformed into an offshoot of Freudianism. The same fate befalls Marxist Lacanians; they become Lacanian Marxists. Hybrid Marxism impedes genuine Marxist psychology. (This is also true in the political economic sphere: socialist efforts to utilize capitalist practices – as in China – inevitably culminate in socialist capitalists devolving into capitalist socialists.) It is therefore necessary for Marxism to conquer non-Marxist and anti-Marxist elements, or they will conquer Marxism.

One strategy that psychoanalysts utilize for claiming a congruence between Freud and Vygotsky is to reduce both their theories to simple, abstract considerations. One such strategy is to emphasize that both theories recognize the importance of interpersonal interactions between parents and children for generating psychological functions. This is misleading because it strips away profoundly different concrete details.

Pavón-Cuéllar (2015) utilizes this abstract line of thinking to equate Freud's and Marx's interest in social-psychological illusions. He says that both emphasized illusions of consciousness that masked reality and that this allies their approaches. He equates the following statements by Marx and Engels, and Freud:

> Consciousness can never be anything else than conscious existence, and the existence of men is their actual life-process. If in all ideology men and their circumstances appear upside-down as in a camera obscura, this phenomenon arises just as much from their historical life-process as the inversion of objects on the retina does from their physical life-process.
>
> *(Marx and Engels, 1932/1968)*

> There are two differences between me and the superstitious person: first, he projects the motive to the outside, while *I look for it in myself*; second, he explains the accident by an event which *I trace to a thought* [emphasis added].
>
> [...] I believe that a large portion of the mythological conception of the world which reaches far into the most modern religions *is nothing but psychology projected into the outer world*.
>
> *(Freud, 1914, pp. 308–309)*

Pavón-Cuéllar (2015, p. 57) seeks to combine Freud and Marx into a hybrid Freudo-Marxism. He equates these explanations of illusion:

> In both conceptions, metaphysics is reduced to a psychology that is not only illusory and distinct from the real or exterior world, but implies a psychically

produced or projected truth that remits us to the human mind, to psychic factors and constellations of the unconscious.

Pavón-Cuéllar contends that Marx and Freud shared a meta-psychology: "metaphysics, mythology and religion, which Marx and Freud conceive in ways that are both consonant and complementary" (ibid.).

Pavón-Cuéllar's reasoning is faulty. It is true that Marx and Freud were concerned with illusions; however, this abstract concern is meaningless on its own because it ignores concrete details (as Vygotsky says eclectics always do). The details are quite opposite. And this invalidates Pavón-Cuéllar's conclusion that they are consonant.

We have analyzed Marx's explanation of religion as reflecting oppressed, mystified social life. Illusions are objective. Marx does not attribute mystified consciousness to subjective, unconscious, psychic projections as Freud does (and Pavón-Cuéllar condones). Marx does not accept the Freudian conceptual world of a psychically produced or projected truth that remits us to the human mind, to psychic factors and constellations of the unconscious. Nor should anyone accept it because it is false, as objective analysis of Freud's cases proves and as Laing and Estersom (1970) confirm.

Pavón-Cuéllar does not simply declare consonance between Marx and Freud where it does not exist; he seeks to produce it. He does so by distorting Marx to make him fit Freud's model of illusions. This is the result of all eclectic attempts to combine antithetical viewpoints with Marxism. Pavón-Cuéllar's integration moves in the direction that is the reverse of what it should be. He does not reframe psychoanalytic notions of illusions in cultural-historical, materialist terms. Instead, Marxist Freudianism has devolved into Freudian Marxism; Marxism has been captured by psychoanalysis and has lost its Marxism.[13]

This error occurs in psychological anthropology as well. Robert LeVine, a psychoanalytic cultural psychologist, attempts to embed psychoanalytic processes within the cultural environment. Writing in the journal *Human Development*, he says, "Psychoanalysis is designed to be the study of an ongoing developmental process, viz. the growth and resolution of a transference neurosis over several years in adulthood" (LeVine, 1971, p. 105). This reduces culture from an organizing source of psychology to an external context in which intra-individual, universal, psychoanalytic mechanisms play themselves out.

The proper integration of psychoanalysis, Marxism, and Vygotskyian cultural psychology

The typical subordination of Marxism and cultural psychology to psychoanalysis (and other non-cultural approaches) must be reversed. As Vygotsky states, "precisely because the area elaborated by psychoanalysis is elaborated with inadequate means it must be conquered for Marxism." This is the theoretical accompaniment of the transformations that must occur throughout society: labor, community, self-concept, thinking, sexuality, love, religion must all be conquered for Marxism/ socialism. Marxist social theory and psychology elucidate the need for this transformation, its possibility, and the form it must take. This is why social theory must be conquered for Marxism.

A few scholars have managed to conquer psychoanalysis for Marxism instead of the reverse.

Darmon (2016, p. 124) explains

> the Bourdieusian approach to psychoanalysis is better understood as a sociologization of psychoanalysis – an annexation of psychoanalytic constructs through the sociological treatment of certain of its concepts – rather than as a complementary or integrated merging of psychoanalytic and sociological concepts.

Fanon takes this approach to psychoanalysis with regard to understanding colonized Algerian people. Derek Hook explains that

> in his use of a psychoanalytic interpretative approach, Fanon points out that such "pathologies of affect", even once "wired through" the sexual realms, through unconscious processes, are *ultimately derived from inequalities present in wider social structures* and cannot as such be reduced to the internal psychical workings of individual subjects.
>
> *(2004, p. 117)*

> The basis of the racial neurosis of the black subject lies, for Fanon, *in the infantile trauma caused by the black child's exposure to the racist values of the oppressive colonial* environment.
>
> *(Ibid., p. 120)*

This contrasts with Freud's basis of neurosis in individual relationships with a parent – e.g., son loving his mother.

Similarly,

> Fanon's version of the "European collective unconscious" "is purely and simply the sum of prejudices, myths, collective attitudes of a given group" (1986, 188). Fanon's attempt, as McCulloch (1983) puts it, "is to transform this concept of the collective unconscious from an ahistorical mechanism located in inherited cerebral matter to a historically specific psychic structure that is open to continuous social reinforcement" (71).
>
> *(Ibid., p. 126)*

Fanon describes the cultural neurosis of the colonial subject as being forced to choose the alien identity of the colonist as his own:

> As I begin to recognize that the Negro is the symbol of sin, I catch myself hating the Negro. But then I recognize that I am a Negro ... this [is a] neurotic situation in which I am compelled to choose an unhealthy, conflictual situation fed on fantasies [that are] hostile and inhuman.
>
> *(Cited in Hook, 2004, p. 128)*

The process of identity formation is neurotic, conflictual, ambiguous, hateful, sinful, immoral, and fed on hostile fantasies; however, each of these neurotic elements is cultural. They are not individual or interpersonal or psychophysical elements.

Fanon explores the sexual ambiguity of the colonist in relation to the colonized. This sexual ambiguity is not the product of a natural, universal, unconscious process that on its own psychophysics twists colonial hatred of the colonized into its opposite and generates a sexual admiration of this despised subject. On the contrary, this sexual ambiguity and complexity is a straightforward recapitulation of cultural roles, myths, and symbols about black sexuality that the colonists imposed on people with dark skin. Oppressed Algerians were used for physical labor power; hence, the colonists regarded them as primarily physical and sexual. This imposed cultural role generated a certain admiration and also jealousy from the colonists that contained a fear of black sexual prowess: "the raping black man" (ibid., p. 132). Fear of the black man also justified/rationalized whites' aggressive suspicion and oppression of them that was based upon political-economic needs, not psychological needs.

Hook's analysis of Fanon's psychoanalysis reveals it to be congruent with Vygotskyian Marxist psychology. Active, conflicting, disturbing, hateful, ambiguous, emotional, fantasy, identity, and sexual processes are emphasized as cultural processes that are stripped of Freudian, individual, imaginary, naturalistic, psychophysical, universal qualities. Cultural psychology and Marxist psychology are enriched by incorporating these vibrant subjective processes and then extending cultural analyses to explain, describe, predict, and transform them. This is precisely how Martín-Baró addresses fatalism (Ratner, 2011, 2014, 2015b, 2017; Clark, 1965/1989). This "psychopolitics" (Fanon's term cited in Hook, 2004), as opposed to psychophysics, sharpens the critique of colonialism to include its pernicious psychological effects. Psychoanalytic postulates blunt social critique by turning critique against individual victims, as Freud did.

Hook (ibid., p. 135) concludes that Fanon

> borrows concepts from psychoanalysis but puts them to use within the frame of a very precise historical and political context. As I suggested in relation to Freud, it would seem that Fanon's use of Jungian ideas departs so strongly from their original conceptualisation that they become totally different concepts.

This epitomizes conquering psychoanalytic concepts by Marxist psychology for an emancipatory psychological science.

Notes

1 Science and politics are intertwined in *every* social science theory, methodology, and intervention. Social science is always inspired by political values and reinforces them. Interestingly, emancipatory politics leads to the deepest social science, while conservative politics leads to superficial, ideological social science.

2 Marx and Engels reject the specific mechanisms of natural selection that Darwin identifies. They emphasize that human evolution is consciously made by human changes in production. In addition, naturalistic struggle for survival is not an analogy for human social life.

> The essential difference between human and animal society is that animals are at most *gatherers* whilst men are *producers*. This single but cardinal distinction alone makes it impossible simply to transfer the laws of animal societies to human societies. … At a certain stage, therefore, human production reaches a level where not only essential necessities but also luxuries are produced, even if, for the time being, they are only produced for a minority. Hence the struggle for existence – if we allow this category as valid here for a moment – transforms itself into a struggle for enjoyments, a struggle no longer for the mere means of existence but for the means of development, *socially produced means of development*, and at this stage the categories of the animal kingdom are no longer applicable. But if, as has now come about, production in its capitalist form produces a far greater abundance of the means of existence and development than capitalist society can consume, because capitalist society keeps the great mass of the real producers artificially removed from the means of existence and development; if this society is forced, by the law of its own existence, continually to increase production already too great for it, and, therefore, periodically every ten years, reaches a point where it itself destroys a mass not only of products but of productive forces, what sense is there still left in the talk about the "struggle for existence?" The struggle for existence can then only consist in the producing class taking away the control of production and distribution from the class hitherto entrusted with it but now no longer capable of it; that, however, is the Socialist revolution.
>
> *(Engels' letter to Lavrov, 1875, emphasis added)*

Marx's environmentalism may be called intentional (or teleological) environmentalism in that the environment which is necessary for stimulating and supporting particular behavior is consciously produced; it is not the product of natural laws that are suffered, as in Darwinian environmentalism.

3 Laing and Esterson (1970) demonstrate the truth of this in patients diagnosed with mental disorders. Their ethnographies of schizophrenogenic families found that it was parents' contradictory messages to their children that generated the latter's confusion. Maya Abbott's parents would whisper among themselves about her, which she partially overheard, but then denied their actions to her. She thus developed the belief that mysterious voices were talking about her although she could never locate them. She felt confused and disoriented about these unfounded voices. Of course, it was her parents who were the source of her disorientation, but psychiatrists blamed Maya's distorted psychological processes for her delusion.

4   A non-systemic set of individual social elements cannot be apprehended and transformed comprehensively and thoroughly. It would be impossible to reorganize every single disparate social element in the same way at the same time. Only piecemeal reforms could be enacted. This is why fragmentary theories composed of individual mechanisms are favored by the status quo.

5   Civil rights are supportive of the capitalist political economy in that they simply enable marginalized people to join the capitalist system. They allow the system to apportion marginalized people within the class hierarchy. Most of the integrated people will be allotted to the lower class, which makes up the majority of the social pyramid. A relative few will occupy the middle strata, and a tiny fraction will occupy the upper echelons. There is nothing liberating about integration into an exploitive class system. It only appears to be liberating if one focuses upon the small fraction that enters the middle and upper echelons. And it appears liberating if one simply compares groups within strata of the social hierarchy; for instance, if comparison is made between middle-class women and middle-class men, or black working women and white working women. This *lateral comparison* reveals increasing parity and the appearance of liberation and justice. This lateral comparison does not look up the social hierarchy to compare wealth/income with the elite, ruling class. If this kind of *vertical comparison* is made, it is obvious that equality and liberation vanish. Disparities of social class are increasing. Indeed, as women's wages have gained greater parity with men's, the wages of both women and men have fallen in relation to capitalists' wealth and power. The vertical class comparison is rarely presented because it strikes at the exploitive heart of capitalism. The powers that be want the populace to be preoccupied with lateral comparisons in order to distract from vertical comparisons. They want women to focus on wage disparities with men; they want blacks to struggle against whites for parity. This is because these internecine struggles ignore the root of exploitation and the major manifestation of exploitation in the political-economic system, depicted in Figure 1.2. (Similarly, gendering violence by attributing it to masculinity shunts – lateralizes – the problem and solution away from capitalist violence to masculinity vs. femininity. The problem is attributed to misogyny, hatred of women, derogation of women, male sexual inadequacy. Interestingly, black violence against black people is recognized as having political-economic roots, not black hatred or black sexual inadequacy or black shame.)

Women are exploited by capitalists (including women capitalists), not by male workers. Consequently, wage parity with males is not a measure of decreased exploitation. Women are *increasingly* exploited by capitalists, as measured by women's productivity gains, capitalist profits as a rising percentage of GDP, and wages as a declining percentage of GDP. This falsifies the claim that gender parity, fairness, justice, and respect constitute liberation.

This holds true for diversity. Diversity involves another lateral comparison that does not affect the vertical pyramid of class structure. Diversity simply replaces white males, for example, with black women of the same social strata. Diversity does not add more working-class people to the upper class. That kind of diversity is never considered. Diversity does not raise the class position of blacks. As a class, they have made no upward progress for the past 60 years (Michaels, 2008).

The women's movement, in general, has not specifically opposed neoliberal capitalism, its insatiable mode of production, its rapacious foreign policy, its increasing exploitation of the populace. Indeed, women have become willing neoliberal subjects fighting for success within capitalist parameters. Their success is taken as proof that "the system works for the people." The women's movement has contributed to the carceral state of increased surveillance and imprisonment. The movement has demanded more crime-fighting measures and harsher, vindictive penalties for gender crimes. It has not produced a Marxist analysis of gender crimes that is rooted in the capitalist political economy. Neither has it worked out a socialist alternative to dealing with these crimes and preventing them now and in the future.

Feminism generally contracts broad issues of capitalism into narrow conflicts between genders. For instance, sexual harassment is construed as a problem of masculinity where men seek to conquer women and do not respect women's autonomy concerning personal space and sexual decision-making. The feminist solution is to a) punish men and b) make men more respectful of women's decision-making by continually asking their agreement to pursue love-making.

A Marxist perspective on sexual harassment looks at *sexuality* as a form of capitalist practice that encompasses women and men. It does not limit the problem to a single gender or see it as one that can be solved by gender sensitivity or punishment. Sexual harassment is a problem of capitalist sexuality, not simply male sexuality. Capitalist sexuality can only be corrected by transforming capitalism. This draws men and women into a common struggle against a common enemy. It does not pit women against men, in a "divide and conquer" strategy that capitalists endorse. (The fact that capitalists – and their political representatives – endorse the gendering of harassment and its correction is proof positive that this strategy ignores the true causes and solutions, which involve the capitalist mode of production. Capitalists provide the best indicators of which political ideas are conservative and ineffective and which are radical and effective.)

Marxism recognizes sexual harassment as spawned by the rampant commodification, sensationalizing, objectifying, and depersonalizing of sexuality in general. This is what desensitizes men – and women – to personal considerations of sex; it is what makes sex into a sport for men and women that is an intoxicating game of enticement, flirtation, seduction, objectification, sensational arousal, hedonistic egoism, lacking in personal interest and commitment (see Taylor, 2014).

Harassment is a female phenomenon as well as a male phenomenon. "According to a 2011 CDC [Center for Disease Control] report, an estimated 4,403,010 female victims of sexual violence had a female only perpetrator" (cited in www. femalesexoffenders.org/resources). "The 2000 AAUW [American Association of University Women] data indicate that 57.2 percent of all students report a male offender and 42.4 percent a female offender" (ibid.). According to the CDC, "More women (58 percent) than men (42 percent) are perpetrators of all forms of child maltreatment" (ibid.). "One in six adult men reported being sexually molested as children, and ... nearly 40 percent of the perpetrators were female" (ibid.). "There is an alarmingly high rate of sexual abuse by females in the backgrounds of rapists, sex offenders, and sexually aggressive men – 59 percent (Petrovich and Templer, 1984), 66 percent (Groth, 1979) and 80 percent (Briere and Smiljanich, 1993)" (ibid.). Feminists are silent about this. They confine harassment to masculinity, thereby exempting the broad capitalist system from critique and reform. Yet a full consideration of the phenomenon proves that harassment is a broader issue of capitalism that encompasses both genders.

The women's movement, as all civil rights movements, welcomes marginalized people into the capitalist exploitive system to become victims of exploitation. By proclaiming this an act of liberation, anti-discrimination mystifies what liberation is. Anti-discrimination is a laudable movement to the limited extent that it benefits a relatively small number of capitalist-friendly, marginalized individuals. However, it falls far short of liberation for its own members, to say nothing of outsiders.

Women's increased participation in the US labor force from 1950 to 2000 was accompanied by men's reduced participation. This recapitulates capitalist competition. Marcuse highlights the weaknesses of contemporary social reform movements: "The radical consciousness is also false consciousness inasmuch as it refuses to develop the Marxian categories corresponding and comprehending the changes in the structure of capitalism" (2015, p. 19).

6   The complimentary relation between objective, necessary, possible, and propitious was articulated by Hegel (1969, pp. 549–550) in his inimitable phraseology:

> what is really possible can no longer be otherwise; under the particular conditions and circumstances something else cannot follow. Real possibility and necessity are therefore only *seemingly* different; the identity [of possibility and necessity] is already *presupposed* and lies at their base. [...] Real possibility does become necessity.

7   Unfortunately, progressive political movements today emphasize particular rights and emancipation against particular wrongs. Marx (1844) castigates this in his essay *On the Jewish Question*:

> liberty as a right of man is not founded upon the relations between man and man, but rather upon the separation of man from man. It is the right of such separation; the right of the *circumscribed* individual withdrawn into himself. The practical application of the right of liberty is the right of private property. The right of property is the right to enjoy one's fortune and to dispose of it as one wills. ... It is the right of self-interest.

This is the essence of contemporary movements for respect of diversity. Each marginalized group demands tolerance for its behavior. Diversity is difference. Its etymology is the Latin "*divortere*," which means to go in different ways, to part, divide, divorce, and be disimilar. This sense is maintained in the contemporary use of diversity as autonomy for different groups and individuals. This is why Marx criticized it as bourgeois individualism. Diversity abdicates concern with a coherent social system. It prevents one because differences are emphasized. This is the case with gender rights, sexual orientation rights, ethnic rights, religious rights, dietary rights, obesity rights, speech rights, abortion rights, clothing rights (see Ratner, 2016b, pp. 76–79). Religious rights, for example, grant religious groups freedom to discriminate against women and homosexuals and freedom to refuse to obey civil laws (such as providing birth control and abortions in religious hospitals) and activities such as reading certain books and attending school or work on certain dates. These fragmenting diversity rights seek autonomy for special interests. They are not inputs into a common, coherent social system that is organized to meet the common interests of the population. Instead, the social good consists of individual rights to pursue individual interests, as Adam Smith proposed. Diversity is often presented as unity in the sense that we all respect each other instead of disavowing one another. However, this is misleading. We really respect each other's *differences* from ourselves; i.e., the freedom to do whatever each one wishes. Genuine unity requires common interests that supersede individual differences. Diversity posits no particular common interest. Diversity is bourgeois unity – it is unity that is shot through with individualism, privacy, fragmentation, and conflict. It is false unity, like bourgeois society is false society – that is now collapsing.

The right to express one's sexual identity typifies this individualistic separation. It is a right for individual autonomy to choose any gender and orientation one wishes. It has nothing to do with working for a socialist mode of production that will solve deep-seated, general, social problems. Philosopher Judith Butler champions this individualism. She discusses gender assignment, which

> forms a very intense predicament for those who want to contest the terms of that assignment, or to engage in practices of self-assignment that refute or revise (deviate from) assignment given by others and prior to the formation of my will. The formation of the will in the sphere of gender might be understood as taking up the task of self-assignment, and we might understand the linguistic register of autonomy here.
>
> *(Cited in Ahmed, 2016, p. 486)*

Recent demands for ethnic diversity in universities illustrate the individualistic, ethnocentric, separatist nature of the demands: "it's very important to me to have professors who look like me and who I feel that I can relate to," say black students at Stanford University (www.democracynow.org/2016/4/14/whos_teaching_us_stanford_students_demand). Increasing the number of black professors and students is motivated by the need to validate students' own physical appearance. They cannot relate well to people who are not just like them physically. This means that black Stanford students relate better to black, arch-conservative, war criminal, Stanford professor Condi Rice, who *looks* like them, than they can to white, progressive Noam Chomsky who does not *look* like them. Ironically, when white people use this same argument, that they do not feel comfortable with blacks or Muslims because they look different and suspicious, this is condemned as intolerant racism. Elite Stanford intellectuals cannot see that they duplicate this form of racism in their demands for diversity. Here we see how a concern with race *per se* supports the status quo, whereas a concern with politics would lead to learning about anti-capitalism from Chomsky.

The emphasis on special interests is a false consciousness that weakens class consciousness. Members of the working population lose sight of the fact that they are a universal class that bears the exploitation of capital and is capable of eradicating this exploitation for the population in general by expropriating the means and mode of production. This is exactly why diverse interests are encouraged by the powers that be; that is, diversity distracts from common, central problems in the mode of production that must be eradicated by concerted, unified political action to transform it.

Diversity is cultural *laissez faire*. It accepts whatever beliefs and practices a group adopts as its self-definition. This is cultural subjectivism; it is not based upon a rigorous, objective analysis of social-psychological problems and their logical, objective solution that will improve the lives of the populace in general (Ratner, 2017).

Diversity is identity politics in the sense that it confines itself to valuing people for their identity as members of social groups. It values minorities, women, homosexuals, and cultural and religious groups simply for their humanity, not for the social-political-economic content of their *praxis*. This is expressed in statements like "we need a Muslim on this committee," "we need women in Congress," "we need black executives." This validates people for their group membership or identity, nothing more. Validation of existing identity (and tradition) displaces structural transformation of the social structure (e.g., the class structure). Validation of identity is the new populist definition of social change. However, a Muslim perspective, or a woman's perspective, or a homosexual's perspective, or a young person's perspective, or an Indian's perspective (or tradition) is not a socialist praxis, or even an anti-capitalist praxis. This conservatism is why diversity is socially acceptable, whereas socialism is not (Ratner, 2016b, pp. 69–164).

8   Indeed, capitalist countries, and the capitalist ruling class, are currently accepting of sexual diversity and denounce discrimination against it. This proves that sexual diversity is entirely compatible with capitalism; it is not anti-capitalist. A transgender man is still a capitalist subject; his sexuality does nothing to oppose capitalist values or to generate socialist values as Marx defined them. This is true of all human rights or civil rights. Rights for women, ethnic minorities, and religious groups do not threaten capitalism.

Marcuse (2015, p. 33) provides some explanation of the cultural-political character of these cultural movements:

> After the tent had already collapsed of the student movement, after the weakening of the opposition which was strongest in the Sixties and began to decline '69–'70, the disillusion, the disappointment was so strong that they had to find a way out in other forms of non-conformity, or, of course, alleged non-conformity, because in reality this is a very highly developed conformity. Any absenteeism from political life … is escapist and is conformist.

9   Of course, not every devout believer develops psychological disorders – just as not all smokers develop lung cancer. The reason is that each individual is exposed to a combination of cultural factors, and some mitigate the effects of a debilitating factor. And different people are exposed to different intensities of the factor. This combination of social experiences accounts for individual psychological differences (Ratner, 1991, pp. 34–36; Gladwell, 2008; Howe, 1990, 1999). Competing cultural factors do not negate the deleterious character of a single factor or the need to alter it. The fact that it debilitates a large number of people is sufficient need to alter it. If a certain food sickened 1 percent of the population, this would generate strong calls for banning it, despite the fact that not everyone was sickened by it.

10   It follows that sexual orientation is a cultural phenomenon, like all other psychological functions. It cannot be biologically determined because no psychological function is. Defenders of the biologistic basis of homosexuality contradict their own rejection of other biologistic claims that assert that women are biologically inferior to men.

11   Bourdieu (1993, p. 716) extends this critique to interpersonal relations and the family:

> One should be careful not to see the family as the ultimate cause of the distress it seems to cause. … Behind the story of the most "personal" difficulties and of apparently strictly subjective tensions and contradictions are often expressed the deepest structures of the social world and their contradictions.

12   Marcuse invokes sublimation within a Marxist framework as a cultural-political mechanism for circumventing social repression and generating alternatives to it. Sublimation, as proposed by Freud, is a psychophysical mechanism that mechanically releases socially repressed libidinous (erotic) energy in a disguised, socially acceptable form. One form may be "higher," "civilized" acts such as art, science, philosophy, or medicine.

Marcuse regards this sublimation as "a great refusal" of the individual to succumb to social repression. He says,

> sublimation is enforced by the power of society, but the unhappy consciousness of this power already breaks through alienation. To be sure all sublimation accepts the social barrier to instinctual gratification, but it also transgresses this barrier. ... In its most accomplished modes, such as in the artistic *oeuvre*, sublimation becomes the cognitive power which defeats suppression while bowing to it.
>
> *(Marcuse, 1964, p. 76)*

Marcuse's proposal is fatally flawed. In the first place, most important artworks and philosophical works recapitulate society rather than transcend or revolutionize it. (Freud conceived of sublimation as a socially acceptable disguise of antisocial Eros.) Sociologists of art as well as Marxist critiques of philosophy pinpoint this conservatism. For example, Hauser (1968, pp. 118–119) says that

> Dickens accepts the presuppositions of the prevailing capitalistic system without question. He knows only the burdens and grievances of the petty bourgeoisie, and fights only against evils which can be remedied without shaking the foundations of bourgeois society. ... The demands of the working class only frighten him. ... He viewed socialistic agitation as nothing but demagogy.

An additional flaw in Marcuse's proposal is that it casts high culture, social resistance and transcendence as individual, psychobiological acts, not as social acts. Sublimation is an ego defense mechanism of the individual psyche. It mechanically produces behavior on the basis of psychophysical mechanisms that release libidinal energy in measured amounts. Social stimulation and support and values are discounted. Sublimation does not admit political confrontation and transformation of status quo institutions. Indeed, it dissipates these by dissipating the repression that would generate social confrontation and transformation. Nor does sublimated social refusal entail a class analysis, a class position, a social critique, or a socialist negation of capitalism.

Fortunately, Marcuse returns to Marxism in other passages. He says,

> *If* the development of consciousness and the unconscious leads to making us see the things which we do not see or are not allowed to see, *then*, art *would* work as part of the liberating power of the negative and would help to free the mutilated unconscious and the mutilated consciousness which solidify the repressive establishment.
>
> *(2015, p. 84, emphasis added)*

Art only becomes a great refusal under certain transformative social and psychological activities. In its current form, the unconscious is mutilated; it is not a counter-social force for liberation.

The same is true for Marcuse's use of Eros. He accepts Freud's construct as containing inherent, unifying, harmonizing, loving tendencies. These psychobiological, universal tendencies offer a basis for negating competitive, selfish, destructive tendencies of the social system. Political action must conform to the inherent form and content of Eros in order to implement liberation (ibid., p. 24; Marcuse, 1970, pp. 1–26). In reality, people cannot find emancipation by looking inward to Eros. On the contrary, it is the capitalist political economy that provides the necessity and the possibility of social-psychological cooperation. And this possibility is only realized by a proletariat that occupies a particular social position, and becomes aware of its objective existence in the political economy, through class-oriented political struggle. Marcuse appreciates these points that contradict the romantic, desperate appeal to Eros.

13   I evaluate Pavón-Cuéllar's analysis as an example of this line of thinking in Freudo-Marxism. I am not claiming that this is *his* entire position on the subject.

References

Abramowitz, J. S., Deacon, B. J., Woods, C. M., and Tolin, D. F. (2004). Association between Protestant religiosity and obsessive–compulsive symptoms and cognitions. *Depression and Anxiety*, 20 (2): 70–76.

Ahmed, S. (2016). Interview with Judith Butler. *Sexualities*, 19 (4), 482–492.

Angell, M. (2016). Why be a parent? *New York Review of Books*, November 10, pp. 8–10.

Bader, E. J. (2015). As public funding of universities dwindles, faculty are unionizing. *Truthout*, December 20. Available at: www.truth-out.org/news/item/34102-as-public-funding-of-universities-dwindles-faculty-are-unionizing (accessed December 1, 2016).

Bailey, R. (2003). Learning to be human: Teaching, culture and human cognitive evolution. *London Review of Education*, 1 (3), 177–190.

Bartlett, F. C. (1967). *Remembering: A study in experimental and social psychology*. New York: Cambridge University Press. (Original work published 1932).

Baumeister, R., Dale, K., and Sommer, K. (1998). Freudian defense mechanisms and empirical findings in modern social psychology: Reaction formation, projection, displacement, undoing, isolation, sublimation, and denial. *Journal of Personality*, 66 (6), 1081–1124.

Bericat, E. (2016). The sociology of emotions: Four decades of progress. *Current Sociology*, 64 (3), 491–513.

Bonneuil, N. (2016). Arrival of courtly love: Moving in the emotional space. *History and Theory*, 55 (2), 253–269.

Bourdieu, P. (1984). *Distinctions: A social critique of the judgment of taste*. Cambridge, MA: Harvard University Press.

Bourdieu, P. (Ed.) (1993). *La misère du monde*. Paris: Seuil. (Translated as *The weight of the world: Social suffering in contemporary society*. Stanford, CA: Stanford University Press.)

Brody, L. (2016). Just 37% of US high school seniors prepared for college math and reading, test shows, *Wall Street Journal*, April 27, p. A2.

Brown, W. (2015). *Undoing the demos: Neoliberalism's stealth revolution*. New York: Zone Books.

Clark, A., and Chalmers, J. (1998). The extended mind. *Analysis*, 58 (1), 7–19.

Clark, K. B. (1989). *Dark ghetto: Dilemmas of social power*. Hanover, NH: Wesleyan University Press. (Original work published 1965).

Crews, F. C. (1993). The unknown Freud. *The New York Review of Books*, 40 (19), 55–66.

Crews, F. C. (1994). The revenge of the repressed. *The New York Review of Books*, 41 (19), 49–58.

Daniels, H. (2012). *Vygotsky and sociology*. London: Routledge.

Darmon, M. (2016). Bourdieu and psychoanalysis: An empirical and textual study of a pas de deux. *The Sociological Review*, 64 (1), 110–128.

DeLuca, J., and Andrews, D. L. (2016). Exercising privilege: The cyclical reproduction of capital through swim club membership. *Sociological Inquiry*, 86 (3), 301–323.

Engels, F. (1875) Letter to Lavrov, November 12. Available at: https://www.marxists.org/archive/marx/works/1875/letters/75_11_12.htm (accessed December 1, 2016).

Engster, F. (2016). Subjectivity and its crisis: Commodity mediation and the economic constitution of objectivity and subjectivity. *History of the Human Sciences*, 29 (2), 77–95.

Foucault, M. (1978). *The history of sexuality*. New York: Pantheon.

Foucault, M. (2007). *Security, territory, and population*. New York: Palgrave Macmillan.

Franklin, B. (n.d.). The lumpenproletariat and the revolutionary youth movement. *Encyclopedia of anti-revisionism on-line*. Available at: https://www.marxists.org/history/erol/ncm-1/red-papers-2/franklin.htm (accessed December 1, 2016).

Freud, S. (1914). *Psychopathology of everyday life*. New York: MacMilllan.

Freud, S. (1965). *New introductory lectures on psychoanalysis*. New York: Norton.

Freud, S. (2012). *Group psychology and the analysis of the ego*, trans. J. Strachey. Greensboro, NC: Empire Books. (Original work published 1921).

Freud, S. (2015). *Civilization and its discontents*, ed. T. Dufresne, trans. G. C. Richter. Peterborough, Ontario: Broadview Press. (Original work published 1930).

Fromm, E. (1942). Character and social process. Appendix to *Escape from Freedom*. Available at: https://www.marxists.org/archive/fromm/works/1942/character.htm (accessed December 1, 2016).

Gielen, G., and Jeshmaridian, S. (1999). Lev Vygotsky: The man and the era. *International Journal of Group Tensions*, 28 (3–4), 273–301. Available at: http://lchc.ucsd.edu/mca/Paper/Vytogsky-the_man_and_the_era.pdf (accessed December 1, 2016).

Gladwell, M. (2008). *Outliers: The story of success*. New York: Little, Brown.

Graziano, M. (2016). The long crisis of the nation-state and the rise of religions to the public stage. *Philosophy and Social Criticism*, 42 (4–5), 351–356.

Hauser, A. (1968). *The social history of art. Volume 4: Naturalism, impressionism, the film age*. London: Routledge & Kegan Paul.

Hegel, G. (1965). *The logic of Hegel*. New York: Oxford University Press. (Original work published 1817).

Hegel, G. (1969). *Science of logic*. New York: Humanities Press.

Higgins, L. (2015). Michigan's black students lag behind the nation. *Detroit Free Press*, December 10. Available at: www.freep.com/story/news/local/michigan/2015/12/10/michigans-black-students-academic-performance/77099294/ (accessed November 20, 2016).

Holmes, D. (1990). The evidence for repression: An examination of 60 years of research. In J. Singer (Ed.), *Repression and dissociation* (pp. 85–102). Chicago: University of Chicago Press.

Holt, R. (1989). A review of some of Freud's biological assumptions and their influence on his theories. In R. Holt (Ed.), *Freud reappraised* (pp. 114–140). New York: Guilford Press.

Hook, D. (Ed.) (2004). Fanon and the psychoanalysis of racism. In *Critical psychology* (pp. 114–137). Lansdowne, South Africa: Juta Academic Publishing.

Horkheimer, M. (1993). *In between philosophy and social science*. Boston: MIT Press.

Howe, M. (1990). *The origins of exceptional abilities*. Oxford: Blackwell.

Howe, M. (1999). *The psychology of high abilities*. New York: New York University Press.

Inozu, M., Clark, D., and Karanci, A. (2012). Scrupulosity in Islam: A comparison of highly religious Turkish and Canadian samples. *Behavior Therapy*, 43 (1), 190–202.

Kleinman, A., and Good, B. (1985). *Culture and depression: Studies in the anthropology and cross-cultural psychiatry of affect and disorder*. Berkeley, CA: University of California Press.

Kosok, M. (1972). The formalization of Hegel's dialectical logic. In A. MacIntyre (Ed.), *Hegel: A collection of critical essays* (pp. 237–288). New York: Doubleday Anchor.

Laing, R. D., and Esterson, A. (1970). *Sanity, madness and the family: Families of schizophrenics*. New York: Pelican.

Legare, C., and Harris, P. (2016). The ontogeny of cultural learning. *Child Development*, 87 (3), 633–642.

Leontiev, A. (2009). *The development of mind: Selected papers of A. N. Leontiev*. Available at: www.marxists.org/admin/books/activity-theory/leontyev/development-mind.pdf (accessed December 1, 2016).

LeVine, R. (1971). The psychoanalytic study of lives in natural social settings. *Human Development*, 14 (2), 100–109.

Levitin, K. (1982). *One is not born a personality*. Moscow: Progress Publishers.

Lichtman, R. (1982). *The production of desire: The integration of psychoanalysis into Marxist theory*. New York: Free Press.

Llorente, R. (2013). Marx's concept of "universal class": A rehabilitation. *Science and Society*, 77 (4), 536–560.

Lukács, G. (1970). *Lenin: A study on the unity of his thought*, trans. N. Jacobs. London: New Left Books. (Original work published 1924). Available at: https://www.marxists.org/archive/lukacs/works/1924/lenin/ch04.htm (accessed December 1, 2016).

Luria, A. (1979). *The making of mind: A personal account of Soviet psychology*. Cambridge, MA: Harvard University Press. Available at: https://www.marxists.org/archive/luria/works/1979/mind/ (accessed December 1, 2016).

Lutz, C. (1988). *Unnatural emotions*. Chicago: University of Chicago Press.

Marcuse, H. (1964). *One-dimensional man: Studies in the ideology of advanced industrial society*. Boston: Beacon Press.

Marcuse, H. (1968). *Negations: Essays in critical theory*. Boston: Beacon Press.

Marcuse, H. (1970). *Five lectures*. Boston: Beacon Press.

Marcuse, H. (2015). *Herbert Marcuse's 1974 Paris lectures at Vincennes University*. Charleston, SC: CreateSpace.

Marx, K. (1843). *A contribution to the critique of Hegel's philosophy of right*. Available at: https://www.marxists.org/archive/marx/works/1843/critique-hpr/intro.htm (accessed December 1, 2016).

Marx, K. (1844). On the Jewish question. Available at: https://www.marxists.org/archive/marx/works/1844/jewish-question/ (accessed December 1, 2016).

Marx, K. (1961). *Capital, Volume 1*. Moscow: Foreign Languages Press. (Original work published 1867).

Marx, K. (1962). *Capital, Volume 3*. Moscow: Foreign Languages Press. (Original work published 1894).

Marx, K. (1865). Value, price and profit. Speech to the First International Working Men's Association. Available at: https://www.marxists.org/archive/marx/works/1865/value-price-profit/ch03.htm (accessed December 1, 2016).

Marx, K. (1973). *Grundrisse: Foundations of the critique of political economy*. London: Penguin Books. (Original work published 1939).

Marx, K. (1977). *Capital, Volume 1*. New York: Vintage. (Original work published 1867).

Marx, K. (2008). *The poverty of philosophy*, trans. H. Quelch. New York: Cosmio. (Original work published 1847).

Marx, K. (2010). Letter to Lassalle, January 16, 1861. In *Karl Marx Frederick Engels Collected works: Volume 41* (pp. 245–247). New York: Lawrence & Wishart.

Marx, K., and Engels, F. (1968). *The German ideology*. Moscow: Progress Publishers. (Original work published 1932). Available at: https://www.marxists.org/archive/marx/works/1845/german-ideology/ (accessed December 1, 2016).

Marx, K., and Engels, F. (1975). *Karl Marx Frederick Engels Collected works: Volume 3*. New York: International Publishers.

Marx, K., and Engels, F. (1976). *Karl Marx Frederick Engels Collected works: Volume 6*. New York: International Publishers.

Massing, M. (2015). Reimagining journalism: The story of the one percent. *The New York Review of Books*, December 17. Available at: www.nybooks.com/articles/2015/12/17/reimagining-journalism-story-one-percent/ (accessed November 20, 2016).

Mauss, M. (1967). *The gift*. New York: Norton.

Mauss, M. (1973). Techniques of the body. *Economy and Society*, 2 (1), 271–293. (Original work published 1935).

Mayer, J. (2016). *Dark money: The hidden history of the billionaires behind the rise of the radical right*. New York: Doubleday.

Michaels, W. (2008). Against diversity. *New Left Review*, 52, July/August, 33–36.

Miller, J. (2016). Hedge funds underwrite political networks to privatize K-12 public education. *Alternet*, May 10. Available at: www.alternet.org/education/hedge-funds-underwrite-political-networks-privatize-k-12-public-education?akid=14245.152322.UB3hem&rd=1&src=newsletter1056168&t=10 (accessed December 1, 2016).

Okasha, A., Saad, A., Khalil, A. H., el Dawla, A. S., and Yehia, N. (1994). Phenomenology of obsessive-compulsive disorder: A transcultural study. *Comprehensive Psychiatry*, 35 (3), 191–197.

Pavón-Cuéllar , D. (2015). The metapsychology of capital. *Annual Review of Critical Psychology*, 12, 53–58.

Ramas, M. (1990). Freud's Dora, Dora's hysteria. In C. Bernheimer and C. Kahane (Eds.), *In Dora's case: Freud–hysteria–feminism* (pp. 149–180). New York: Columbia University Press.

Ratner, C. (1991). *Vygotsky's sociohistorical psychology and its contemporary applications*. New York: Plenum.

Ratner, C. (1997). *Cultural psychology and qualitative methodology: Theoretical and empirical considerations*. New York: Plenum.

Ratner, C. (2000). A cultural-psychological analysis of emotions. *Culture and Psychology*, 6 (1), 5–39.

Ratner, C. (2006). *Cultural psychology: A perspective on psychological functioning and social reform*. Mahwah, NJ: Lawrence Erlbaum.

Ratner, C. (2011). Macro cultural psychology, the psychology of oppression, and cultural-psychological enrichment. In P. Portes and S. Salas (Eds.), *Vygotsky in 21st century society: Advances in cultural historical theory and praxis with non-dominant communities* (pp. 87–112). New York: Peter Lang.

Ratner, C. (2012a). *Cultural psychology: Theory and method*. New York: Plenum.

Ratner, C. (2012b). *Macro cultural psychology: A political philosophy of mind*. Oxford: Oxford University Press.

Ratner, C. (2014). The psychology of oppression. In T. Teo (Ed.), *The encyclopedia of critical psychology*. New York: Springer.

Ratner, C. (2015a). Classic and revisionist sociocultural theory, and their analyses of expressive language: An empirical and theoretical assessment. *Language and Sociocultural Theory*, 2 (1), 51–83.

Ratner, C. (2015b). Recovering and advancing Martin-Baro's ideas about psychology, culture, and social transformation. *Theory and Critique of Psychology*, 6, 48–76. Available at: www.sonic.net/~cr2/Montero%20review.pdf (accessed November 20, 2016).

Ratner, C. (2016). Culture-centric vs. person-centered cultural psychology and political philosophy. *Language and Sociocultural Theory*, 3 (1), 11–25.

Ratner, C. (2017). The generalized pathology of our era: Comparing the biomedical explanation, the cultural-political explanation, and a liberal-humanistic-postmodernist perspective. The generalized pathology of our era. *International Critical Thought*, 7 (1).

Ratner, C., and Hui, L. (2003). Theoretical and methodological problems in cross-cultural psychology. *Journal for the Theory of Social Behavior*, 33 (1), 67–94.

Ratner, C., and El-Badwi, S. (2011). A cultural psychological theory of mental illness, supported by research in Saudi Arabia. *Journal of Social Distress and the Homeless*, 20 (3–4), 217–274. Available at: www.sonic.net/~cr2/cult%20psy%20mental%20illness.pdf (accessed December 1, 2016).

Reddy, W. M. (2001). *The navigation of feeling: A framework for the history of emotions.* Cambridge: Cambridge University Press.

Rubin, I. I. (1978). Abstract labour and value in Marx's system. *Capital and Class*, 2 (2), 109–139.

Schatzman, M. (1973). *Soul murder: Persecution in the family.* New York: Random House.

Shweder, R. (1990). Cultural psychology – what is it? In J. Stigler, R. Shweder, and G. Herdt (Eds.), *Cultural psychology: Essays on comparative human development* (pp. 1–43). New York: Cambridge University Press.

Sica, C., Novara, C., and Sanavio, E. (2002). Religiousness and obsessive-compulsive cognitions and symptoms in an Italian population. *Behaviour Research and Therapy*, 40 (7), 813–823.

Silva, J. (2015). *Coming up short: Working-class adulthood in an age of uncertainty.* New York: Oxford University Press.

Stannard, D. (1980). *Shrinking history: On Freud and the failure of psychohistory.* New York: Oxford University Press.

Steketee, G., Quay, S., and White, K. (1991). Religion and OCD patients. *Journal of Anxiety Disorders*, 5 (4), 359–367.

Sulloway, F. (1991). Reassessing Freud's case histories: The social construction of psychoanalysis. *Isis*, 82 (2), 245–275.

Sulloway, F. (1992). *Freud, biologist of the mind: Beyond the psychoanalytic legend.* Cambridge, MA: Harvard University Press.

Taylor, K. (2014). She can play that game, too. *New York Times*, July 14, p. ST1.

Tomasello, M. (2016). Cultural learning redux. *Child Development*, 87 (3), 643–653.

Vygotsky, L. S. (1971). *The Psychology of Art.* Cambridge, MA: The MIT Press. (Original work published 1925). Available at: https://www.marxists.org/archive/vygotsky/works/1925/preface.htm (accessed December, 1, 2016).

Vygotsky, L. S. (1987). *The collected works of L. S. Vygotsky. Volume 1: Problems of general psychology*, ed. R. W. Rieber and A. S. Carton, trans. N. Minick. New York: Plenum.

Vygotsky, L. S. (1994a). The problem of the environment. In R. van der Veer and J. Valsiner (Eds.), *The Vygotsky reader* (pp. 338–354). Oxford: Blackwell.

Vygotsky, L. S. (1994b). The socialist alteration of man. In R. van der Veer and J. Valsiner (Eds.), *The Vygotsky reader* (pp. 175–184). Oxford: Blackwell.

Vygotsky, L. S. (1997a). *The collected works of L. S. Vygotsky. Volume 3: Problems of the theory and history of psychology*, ed. R. W. Rieber and J. Wollock, trans. R. van der Veer. New York: Plenum.

Vygotsky, L. S. (1997b). *Educational psychology*, trans. R. Silverman. Boca Raton, FL: St. Lucie Press. (Original work published 1926).

Vygotsky, L. S. (1997c). Cultivation of higher forms of behavior. In *The collected works of L. S. Vygotsky, Volume 4* (pp. 221–230). New York: Plenum.

Vygotsky, L. S. (1998). *The collected works of L. S. Vygotsky. Volume 5: Child psychology*, ed. R. W. Rieber, trans. M. J. Hall. New York: Plenum.

Vygotsky, L. S., and Luria, A. (1925). Introduction to the Russian translation of Freud's *Beyond the Pleasure Principle*. Available at: https://www.marxists.org/archive/vygotsky/works/reader/p010.pdf (accessed December 1, 2016).

Vygotsky, L. S., and Luria, A. (1993). *Studies on the history of behavior: Ape, primitive, and child.* Hillsdale, NJ: Lawrence Erlbaum. (Original work published 1930).

Wilson, M. (2010). The re-tooled mind: How culture re-engineers cognition. *Social Cognitive and Affective Neuroscience*, 5 (2–3), 180–187. Available at: www.ncbi.nlm.nih.gov/pmc/articles/PMC2894684/ (accessed December 1, 2016).

Wolpe, J., and Rachman, S. (1960). Psychoanalytic "evidence": A critique based on Freud's case of little Hans. *Journal of Nervous and Mental Disease*, 131 (2), 135–148.

Yoriulmaz, O., Gencoz, T., and Woody, S. (2010). Vulnerability factors in OCD symptoms: Cross-cultural comparisons between Turkish and Canadian samples. *Clinical Psychology and Psychotherapy*, 17 (2), 110–121.

2

MARXIST METHODOLOGICAL FOUNDATIONS IN VYGOTSKY'S WORK

Lígia Márcia Martins

This chapter seeks to identify the visceral existing correlation between the conditions of historical-cultural theory – which has as its main proponents Vygotsky (1896–1934) and Leontiev (1903–1979) – and the Marxist methodological upholstery; that is, the scientific method on which Marx (1818–1883) based his critique of the political economy.

With this work, we aim to advance the challenge to the unilateral interpretation of Vygotsky's work put forward by the international movement of idealism, imported by Brazil since the 1990s, in which it seeks to separate Vygotsky's work from its Marxist roots, effectively reinterpreting, re-editing and censoring what Vygotsky wrote and attempting to submit his theory to the dominating neoliberal interests (Duarte, 2001). We therefore assume a political commitment to clarifying the radical basis of the methodological movement that has built the trajectory adopted by Marxist psychology, suppression of which hides the significant advances that historical-cultural theory has brought to the field of study.

In search of a psychological Marxist science

As a starting point for our endeavor, we focus on the historical moment in which Vygotsky committed himself to the struggle for the construction of a legitimately Marxist psychology, simultaneously criticizing the trajectory taken by Russian psychology from this point. According to Vygotsky, the latter confined itself to mechanistic approaches and attempted to strictly formalize the link between psychology and Marxism without interrogating Marx's philosophy in a way that would allow the creation of a true scientific psychology; that is, without submitting psychology to the suppositions underlying the Marxian method. It was necessary, therefore, to identify the central elements of historical and dialectical materialism that would come to guide the epistemology and methodology of psychology.

Thus, the process of constructing Marxist psychology was not understood by Vygotsky as mere juxtaposition of adjectives and citation of fragments of the Marxist theory, mechanically connected to the concept of psyche; rather, for this endeavor, he thought it fundamental to submit the founding categories of traditional psychology to the same methodological process Marx used in the study of the categories of classic economy. In the Marxist case study of economical categories of the bourgeoisie society, those were developed until the essential contradictions emerged and interdependencies and interrelations were demonstrated, the unique configuration of which was able to lead to a higher form of production mode. In this way, through the study of categorical dispositions that conformed to its essence, Marx distinguished society from the capital of the precedents of social organization, revealing its origins, its general laws, and its transience.

Regarding this movement, in relation to psychology, Vygotsky affirms that it should write its own *Capital* and that, as in Marxian study of bourgeoisie society, this would imply developing psychological categories, taking account of their interdependencies and fundamental contradictions and reaching to identify the essence of the process which allowed the formation, in a unique psyche, of the human conscience. In this sense, historical-cultural psychology finds in the development of the superior human psychological functioning, the founding prerogative of the human psyche, distinguishing it from the animal psyche and revealing the general principles of its functionality which allows humans to become intelligible and to act over it.

Therefore, analyzing a phenomenon through the lens of Marx presupposes the domain of radical critique, through which the exposition of bourgeoisie society revealed its dialectics. The historical-cultural psychological task is, in this sense, a simple mechanical application of the Marxian theory to the understanding of psychology; beyond that, it presupposes that the study of psyche is submitted to the methodological movement of categorical development proposed by Marx. To do this, it is necessary to comprehend the process of categorical deduction described by the German thinker, rooted in methodological premises of historical and dialectical materialism.

Historical and dialectical materialism in the roots of Marxist psychology

According to the methodological foundations of historical dialectical materialism, the appropriation of reality as it is directly manifest does not offer the conditions necessary for the analysis of its general laws; such an approach is only capable of reaching the specific details of reality through numerous iterations in a process of synthesis that progressively reconstructs reality, beginning from its most simple determinations, without losing sight of its internal contradictory logic.

Following this, the basis of Marxist psychology constructed by Vygotsky is the assumption that objective reality cannot be learned by human conscience as a mechanical copy, completely trusting of the subject's surroundings. The capacity to master and capture reality is made possible by a system of mental processes, reached, in turn, by vital human activity – the social work – which acts as a mediator of relations between human beings and nature. In this way, the human psyche is constituted by a multifunctional system composed of cognitive-affective psychological functions that serve to create a subjective image of objective reality; the extent to which this corresponds to reality will depend on the educational trajectory and social positions throughout the individual's development (Martins, 2011).

Consistent with this idea of objective reality as a facsimile, and in contrast to the exposition of classical economics, for Marx, it is the abstract discernment of categorical elements that is responsible for the reproduction of the concrete in its multiple determinations in thought; having as a starting point the concrete as it is directly presented would imply analysis based on chaotic representation of the whole. So, the architectural structure of the gradual levels of conceptual development constructed in *Capital* comes from the highest levels of abstraction towards multi-determined concreteness, obeying the dialectical movement of progressive presentation of economic categories that overcomes the formal logical linearity approached in classic economy.

In light of this, in his work "The historical meaning of the crisis in psychology," Vygotsky (1999) points out the importance of regaining the fundamental premises of the Marxian method, which gravitates around identifying the configuration of bourgeois society in a more developed and diverse historical organization of production; this way, the categories that compose its structure enable comprehension of the production relations of all antecedent social organizations "out of the ruins and elements of which it built itself up, carrying within it partly still unconquered remnants, and part of which have developed full significance within it, etc." (Marx, 2011, p. 58).

Therefore, despite being presented as apparently anti-dilutive, that is, valid for all times, the abstract categories are "in the determination of their own abstraction, equally the product of historical relations, and have their full validation just for those relations" (Marx, 2011, p. 58). In this sense, even if the economic categories have their essence in previous social organization, "in all forms of societies, they are a determined product and their corresponding relations that establish the position and the influence of other productions and their respective relations" (Marx, 2011, p. 59).

Consequently, Marx reveals that although capitalist society is configured according to the economic categories of previous forms of social organization, his analysis always emphasizes the dominance of the current mode of production, which submits those prior categories to its own particular functionality. Therefore, an understanding of bourgeois society cannot lose sight of its specificity in which capital subjugates other categorical relations.

Accordingly, in his analysis relating to the crisis in psychology, Vygotsky (1999, p. 206) recovers those Marxian assertions as 'possible methodological paths' for the development of this science. In the same way they identify bourgeois social organization as a superior form of production mode, they recognize human consciousness as a superior form of psyche; despite corresponding categories in other forms of animal psyche, this reaches new heights compared to previous forms of psyche due to its specificity of making leaps according to laws that are biological but also, mainly, historical-social. Such specificity in the development of human psyche is made clear in the following quotation:

> we can say alongside Hegel that something is what it is, thanks to its quality and when it [is lost], no longer it is because the development of the conduct from animal to human being caused a new quality. *This is our main thesis.* This development is not limited in the simple complexity of relations between stimulus and reactions that we know in animal psychology. Neither has it gone through the quantitative and increased path and increment of its relations. There is in its center a dialectical leap that modifies the quality of its own relation between stimulus and reactions. We could formulate our main deduction by saying that human conduct is distinguished by the same qualitative peculiarity – compared to animal conduct that differs from the adaptation character and historical development of man, since the process of development of human psyche is part of the process of humanity's historical development.
>
> *(Vygotsky, 1995, p. 62, emphasis added)*

That is, just as Marxian theory sought to identify the functional laws of bourgeois social organization that characterize a more developed mode of production – overcoming the classic economic tendency of removing the historical differences and eternizing capital society – Marxist psychology committed itself to overcoming the linear and ahistorical analysis of psyche, identifying the specificities and characteristics of its more developed expression – human consciousness – and the historical-cultural laws that govern its development.

The historical development of psyche submitted to the Marxist categorical movement

Having delineated the fundamentals of the methodological path taken by Marxist psychology, it is necessary to gain a deeper understanding of categorical development based on the historical-dialectical logic in Marx's work. In this sense, it is necessary to rescue the double character of the presentation of Marxian theory; this exists in the simultaneous exposition and criticism of capital society, which comes from the fact that Marx sought to surpass the superficial conceptual articulation developed by classical economists with a new methodological justification. In this process, Marx reinvents and reverses, searching to identify internal conceptual bonds in articulation with the criticism in construction.

In a letter to Lassale, Marx points out that his work "is a *Critique of Economic Categories*, or, if you like, a critical exposé of the system of the bourgeois economy" (Marx, 1984, p. 270); in this statement, he already shows us that the criticism that will delineate the bourgeois economic system will become overloaded from its own exposition. Thereby, we have the simultaneous articulation of two important processes: Marx develops the classic economic categories, which expose the system's own insoluble limitations and contradictions according to its internal dynamics; from then on, he reorganizes and gives a new meaning to its fundamental concepts, developing the critique from the dialectical exposition. Therefore, the Marxian method of exposing categories of classic economic theory demonstrates its inconsistences, which features in his criticism and leads him to propose a new comprehension of general laws of bourgeois society in its movement and transience.

The same process can be observed in Vygotsky. Just as classic economy had approached the central categories of bourgeois society, traditional psychology approached its phenomena in an atomistic and unarticulated way until that historical moment. Consequently, Vygotsky exposes the methodological insufficiencies of traditional psychology, demonstrating the limitations of its dichotomies, its fragmentations, and its ahistorical attempts to comprehend psyche, which leads him to reorganize and give new meaning to fundamental concepts of this science. Therefore, the critical exposition elaborated by Vygotsky transformed into a new proposal for the study of the psyche, which conceives of it as cross-functional and to be examined in its totality. For Vygotsky (2000, p. 8),

> Psychology that aims to study the complex units … must move from the method of decomposing it into elements to a method of analysis that dismembers it into units. It is extremely important to find those properties that do not decompose and do prevail, that are inherent to a given totality as a unity, and to discover the units in which those properties are represented in an opposed aspect to try, through this analysis, to resolve the questions that are presented.

It is possible to identify in the quotation above the visceral correspondence to the Marxian method in Vygotsky's search for a unit analysis for psychology. Remaining on the apparent surface of classic economic categories leads to wrong conclusions about the functionality of the bourgeoisie, since according to the principles of his investigation, Marx aims to find the specific determinations of 'general capital' and to comprehend the internal tendencies of this abstract sphere. For this purpose, *Capital* begins by affirming, "the wealth of the societies in which the capitalistic production mode prevails appears as an immense accumulation of merchandise and individual merchandise as its elementary form" (Marx, 1995, p. 27).

Consequently, the author identifies within the merchandise of the work product the capacity of the bourgeoisie economy to grow, announcing it as a starting point of its exposition. This starting point is only justified by the fact that Marx's investigation is socially and historically founded and directed; all the steps taken by him are sustained by the prerogative that the path of the bourgeois economy is conditioned to a certain production mode and to a given historical form of wealth, escaping to a static and naturalistic character of the bourgeois way of thinking in which the categorical relations appear in external fashion, fragmented and, consequently, limited to its apparent manifestations. In *Capital*, it is the logical-historical contradictions inherent in this elementary and fundamental form of representation of the capitalistic society – the merchandise – that delineate the Marxian categorical development which will assist us in comprehending the general laws of function of this 'immense collection of merchandise' in its essence.

In explaining the scientific and methodological elements that underlie the choice of the path referred to above, Marx ensures that the economic sciences "cannot serve the microscope nor chemical reagents. The faculty of abstracting must substitute both" (Marx, 1995, p. 6). Therefore, abstraction being the tool by which the cellular form of economy is to be analyzed, to comprehend the capitalistic production mode and its correspondent production and circulation, it is necessary to observe from the categories more deeply, "under conditions that assure the pure passing of the process" (Marx, 1995, p. 6). Thus, Marx searches in the *cell* of the bourgeois society – the form of merchandise – for the construction of other economic fashions, once the minimum unit of analysis contains all the civilization trends of the researched phenomenon.

Marxist psychology follows these methodological steps in investigating a given historical and social form of psyche and, therefore, identifying the cell that constitutes the elementary and representative psychological processes of the human psyche. According to Vygotsky (2000), this minimum unit of analysis finds itself in word meaning, which contains the synthesis of all the upholstery of the process of conscious development.

> meaning is an inalienable part of the word as such, and thus it belongs to the language realm of language as much as the realm of thought. Without meaning, the word is not a word, but an empty sound. Separate from meaning, it is no longer belonging to the realm of language. That is why the meaning can be seen equally as a phenomenon of language and thought. We cannot talk about the meaning of the word taken separately. It is at the same time language and thought because it is a unit of the verbalized thought.
>
> *(Vygotsky, 2000, p. 10)*

According to Martins (2011), Vygotsky makes it clear that the development of superior psychological functioning is based on a dynamic system that assumes constant movement and reconstruction of cross functions. This movement is enabled by the use of signs which:

> operate transformations that exceed the specific scope of each function. The referred work does not complexify in a private way and so does not provoke just cross-functional transformations – it is not about the conversion, for example, from natural memory to logical memory, from natural attention into volunteer attention, from practical intelligence into abstract thinking, etc. The specific transformations of each function determine modifications

in the assembly of functions in which they take part; that is, the psyche as a whole.

(Martins, 2011, p. 58, author's translation)

So, the transformations reached over the course of the development of psyche are not given in each psychological function in an isolated way, but in the relations and cross functions that articulate new compositions as they reach new levels of development.

Once again, historical-cultural psychology demonstrates its intrinsic correlation with historical and dialectical materialism since, as in Marx's study of economic categories of bourgeois society, Vygotsky identifies that the study of each psychological function, from its simplest form of expression, when developed to its fundamental contradictions, results in other functions and finds in them its full development; and, in the same way, none of them can be comprehended in their essentiality without apprehension of those that have preceded them.

This same trajectory is delineated by Marx in his criticism of the classic economy. From the minimum unit of analysis of the bourgeois society – the merchandise – Marx demonstrates this same visceral correlation between each economic category, when subdivided in their essentiality. For example, by means of categorical deduction that obeys the interior structuring of the bourgeois society, the internal contradictions of the 'merchandise' category subdivides into 'value,' which presupposes the 'money' and derives in the 'capital.'

Through this methodological exposition, Marxian analysis was the only approach able to investigate and unravel these relations of interdependencies and changes between the economic categories, which were never revealed before, identifying from them the internal laws of the fundamental movement of the capitalist productive process.

In accordance with this approach, Vygotsky anchors his study of the history of development of superior functional processes in Marxian ideas, developing the psychological categories until he reveals their internal links so as to learn the general laws that fundament them. For that reason, he is a pioneer in the comprehension of the existing interdependency between the social and psychological levels, achieving what he termed the 'general genetic law of cultural development.' According to this law, any function in the child's cultural development appears at two levels: primarily at the social level (interpsychological category), afterwards in the psychological level within the child (intrapsychological category; Vygotsky, 1995). Therefore, Vygotsky's studies of human psyche conducted by historical and dialectical materialism put in terms of psychological science what already has been pointed out by Marx in the sixth thesis about Feuerbach; that is, human essence is not something abstract, interior to each isolated individual. It is, in his own reality, the combination of relations, social (Marx and Engels, 1984).

Maintaining the same methodological affiliation to Marxian premises, Vygotsky (2001) also dedicated himself to the study of the psychological process implied in the construction of knowledge. Linguistic signs provide complexity to the apprehension of the real in its internal, abstracted relations. This intellectual process enables the formation of generalization and logical operations of reasoning, such as: analysis/synthesis, comparison, generalization and abstraction.

The complex thinking should help the effectively abstracted thinking and this task subjugates itself, necessarily, to the internalization of the signs of the culture, the appropriation of products from abstract recodification work of concrete reality carried out by the individuals throughout history. This is a matter of irrevocable need for abstractions, theories, for the capture of the real in its appearance to give room to its essential apprehension. Only by means of theoretical, conceptual thinking can the object of consciousness be represented in its concreteness as a synthesis of multiple relationships and various determinations.

Final considerations

The development of Marxist psychology by Vygotsky does not consist in the search for a theory directed to the comprehension of human psyche in the works of Marx since, for Marxist theory, the object of study is ultimately the capitalist society. Therefore, the identification of Marxist methodological foundations of historical-cultural psychology must not be limited to the search for quotations in the author's work or in merely descriptive relations and juxtaposition between concepts.

Beyond that, we argue that the ascertainment of Marxist foundations of this psychology depends on strict analysis of the methodological movement that sustains his suppositions. In this sense, our aim in the present chapter is to demonstrate that, in the same way Marx adopted historical and dialectical materialism to perform his radical critique of the capitalist society and to discover its general laws of functioning, Vygotsky searched the Marxist path to find an analogous one which should be followed by Marxist psychology in the investigation of human psyche – resulting in the outlining of the specific methodological foundations for Marxist psychology.

In summary, in this endeavor, we see that Vygotsky studies the human psyche under the aegis of social-historic laws of development. He finds the minimum unit of psychic life in word meaning once the social character of consciousness formation is synthesized; unfolding psychic processes in their essence, he impounds their interdependencies and structural reorganization over the course of their development.

Therefore, the application of Marxist methodological principles revolutionized the study of human consciousness by demonstrating its specificity in a superior form of consciousness. In this process, it overcame the dualistic and fragmentary conceptions which atomized its development and, consequently, lost the complex view of the general principles that conducts it. In conclusion, taking consciousness as an object of historical and dialectical study has resulted in overcoming the limits of the logical-formal linearity towards the construction of a science able to understand the dialectical movement synthesized in the historical human being.

References

Duarte, N. (2001). *Vigotski e o aprender a aprender: críticas às apropriações neoliberais e pós-modernas da teoria vigotskiana* [Vygotsky and learning to learn: Criticism of the neoliberal and postmodern appropriations of Vygotskian theory]. Campinas: Autores Associados.

Martins, L. M. (2011). *O desenvolvimento do psiquismo e a educação escolar: contribuições à luz da psicologia histórico-cultural e da pedagogia histórico-crítica* [The development of psychology and school education: Contributions of historical-cultural psychology and historical-critical pedagogy]. Thesis in educational psychology, Department of Psychology, Universidade Estadual Paulista, Bauru campus.

Marx, K. (1984). Letter to Lassale, February 22, 1858. In Lawrence & Wishart (org.) *Karl Marx Frederick Engels collected works: Volume 40* (pp. 268–271). Moscow: Progress Publishers.

———. (1995). *Capital: A Critique of political economy – Book one: The process of production of capital.* Available at: https://www.marxists.org/archive/marx/works/1867-c1/ (accessed March 22, 2016).

———. (2011). *Grundrisse: manuscritos econômicos de 1857–1858: esboços da crítica da economia política* [Grundrisse: Economic manuscripts 1857–1858: Foundations of the critique of political economy]. São Paulo: Boitempo.

Marx, K., and Engels, F. (1984). *A ideologia alemã* [The German ideology], São Paulo: Moraes.

Vygotsky, L. S. (Vigotski) (1995). *Obras escogidas: Tomo III* [Selected works: Volume III]. Madrid: Visor.

———. (1999). O significado histórico da crise da psicologia: Uma investigação metodológica. [The historical meaning of the crisis in psychology: A methodological investigation]. In *Teoria e método em psicologia* (2nd ed.) trans. C. Berliner. São Paulo: Martins Fontes.

———. (2000). *A construção do pensamento e da linguagem* [Thought and language]. São Paulo: Martins Fontes.

———. (2001). *Obras escogidas: Tomo II* [Selected works: Volume II]. Madrid: Visor.

3

THE PROBLEM OF WORK, CONSCIOUSNESS, AND SIGN IN HUMAN DEVELOPMENT

Daniele Nunes Henrique Silva, Ilana Lemos de Paiva, and Lavínia Lopes Salomão Magiolino

Areas of psychology are keen to comprehend how man develops, how he learns, and what the explanatory mechanisms of his particular psyche are, compared to animal behavior. Influenced by Western philosophy, psychology focused its explanatory efforts on seeking to investigate the relationship of sense organs to environmental stimuli. This follows from the fact that many psychologists agree that humans' higher psychological functioning derives from the complex association they establish with nature.

Nevertheless, we still observe epistemological paradigms that dichotomize the nature/culture relation as a way of comprehending higher mental functioning, its origins, and its constitution on the phylogenetic and ontogenetic planes (see Damasio, 1994, 1999, 2003; Edelman, 1989, 2006; Tomasello, 1999, 2003; among others).

The relation of human consciousness to language, culture, and the use of instruments and signs run through the work of contemporary authors and acquires different emphases. We can see in Damasio (1999), for example, the omission of language in his explanation of consciousness and the highlighting of imagistic and signposting processes, rooted in the body, for marking states of mind. This is really a mechanistic and functionalist explanation of consciousness (Magiolino and Smolka, 2013). In Edelman (1989), brain morphology acquires relevance to the understanding of consciousness. In Tomasello (2003), the inclusion in culture, the use of instruments, and the dynamics of cooperation subsidized by language are highlighted in the different explanations of human and animal processes.

Such paradigms lead to discussions about the problem of consciousness in classic philosophy and psychology. In Vygotsky's time, this was a central concern, as can be seen in the following.

Discussions among idealists, influenced by J. Locke (1632–1704), E. B. Condillac (1715–1780), etc., and the mechanistic materialists, represented by the ideas of

R. Descartes (1596–1650), I. Kant (1724–1804), etc., influenced this question in nineteenth-century psychology. The problems of that period (which still reverberate today) were circumscribed by the notion of truth as the core of the Enlightenment, ideas about natural science versus human science, and different understandings of the *scientific mission* of the newly established psychology.

Idealistic psychology, represented by E. Spranger (1882–1963) and C. Ivanovich (1862–1936) among others, defended the idea that knowledge produced by men was constituted exclusively by impressions and associated ideas – from simple forms to more complex configurations. Although it was concerned with the explanatory basis of consciousness, idealistic psychology failed to develop a methodology that would meet the requirements of scientific research, taking refuge instead in spiritualist asylum.

In the adverse direction, the criticisms sustained by mechanistic conceptions pointed to the need for study of human behavior based on the natural sciences, based on the work of Pavlov (1849–1936) and Bejterev (1857–1927), among others. The scientific, natural approach sought to comprehend human psychic phenomena by extrapolating the elementary processes of superior functioning. Consciousness was impossible to access and was, therefore, neglected in these experiments.

In the formulations of Vygotsky (1997a,[1] 1997b), we follow his criticisms of these approaches on the basis that they subjugate or exclude the superior processes – and, therefore, consciousness – from the field of scientific psychology and methodological objectivity.

Thus, for Vygotsky, the reflexologists and reactologists, with whom he converses, interpret behavior and all its components as being limited to a sum of reflexes: "What is sensation? It is a reflex. What are language, gestures, mime? They are reflexes, too. And instincts, lapses, emotions? They are also reflexes" (2001, p. 61).

Vygotsky reported, at a very early age, that dualism as a way of analyzing and researching the human psyche could only be resolved through epistemological and methodological review. He firmly opposed the reductionism of reflexology in terms of theory and research. He wondered how it is possible to build a science on two fundamentally different kinds of being (Vygotsky, 1999, p. 362).[2] His response was the construction of a general psychology that had its foundation in historical and dialectical materialism.

In summary, we can affirm that throughout his work (1997a, 1997b, 1997c, 1998, 1999), Vygotsky questions the wounds of epistemological separatism. He urges researchers to move the problem of genesis of psyche from a naturalistic and/ or spiritualist base to a social and historical dimension.

In order to succeed in this task, he appeals to Marxist ideas, revolutionizing studies in this area as he no longer treats the phenomena of psyche in an isolated way, but as within a totality. He therefore defends a *social-psychological psychology*, able to work dialectically with subjectivity and objectivity (Sawaia and Silva, 2015).

The historical-cultural chain opens up a new way of understanding human relationships with the environment, revealing the fundamental role of history and culture in the formation of higher psychological functions – among which, language stands out by its status in the psyche and its role in the development of consciousness. Vygotsky discusses the origin of human thinking and its social constitution by mediation and symbolic processes, particularly influenced by the philosophical considerations of Marx.

Work in the constitution of the world of men: K. Marx and G. Lukács

In accordance with Marxist theory, the work category is one of the ontological fundaments in Vygotsky's work, presented as the central moment in the constitution of the world of men. It is worth remembering that Marx took a radical view of the historicity of human beings, defending the idea of man as a social animal. Vygotsky, following this principle, assumes that collective work is the genesis of conscious activity in the cultural structuring of men, and the explanation for the formation of a superior psyche derives from this.

This statement is illustrated in the quotation below from Marx's *Capital* (2002, pp. 211–212):

> The spider carries out operations reminiscent of a weaver and the boxes which bees build in the sky could disgrace the work of many architects. But even the worst architect differs from the most able bee from the very outset in that before he builds a box out of boards he has already constructed it in his head. At the end of the work process he obtains a result which already existed in his mind before he began to build. The architect not only changes the form given to him by nature, within the constraints imposed by nature, he also carries out a purpose of his own which defines the means and the character of the activity to which he must subordinate his will.
>
> *(Cited in Vygotsky, 1978, p. xiii)*

According to Marx and Engels (2009),

> men must be in a position to live in order to be able to "make history." But life involves before everything else eating and drinking, a habitation, clothing and many other things. The first historical act is thus the production of the means to satisfy these needs, the production of material life itself.[3]

For Abreu (2015), human survival depends on the production of material goods necessary to life, occurring through the intentional transformation of nature through work. In doing this, men not only produce the resources to live, but also develop their own consciousness from social relations. As established by Marx and Engels: "men, developing their material production and their material intercourse, alter, along with this their real existence, their thinking and the products of their thinking. Life is not determined by consciousness, but consciousness by life" (2009).[4]

Silva (2012), based on this premise, explains that man creates his livelihood and, indirectly, its materiality. Through work (social activity), his conditions of existence over the course of natural history become an essentially cultural story in which nature (constitutive of the biological condition of being) comes under the influence of culture.

Hence, it is important to highlight that *our actions in the world are intrinsically related to material conditions given by reality itself.* Thus, it is not the products of consciousness that constitute the foundations of the matrix of social reality, but the material relations that men establish among themselves that explain the ideas and institutions created by them. According to G. Lukács (1885–1971) – one of the most important theorists of modern Marxism – as ontological fundament of social being, the work category is the non-excluding foundation of all reproductive procedures. Simultaneously, it is only in the context of social reproduction that work can exist (Lukács, 1976).

Seen in these terms, it is important to rescue the Marxist concept of work, resumed by Lukács, in order to point out the ontological dimension of Marx's work that announces the historicity of human essence, as would be discussed by Vygotsky.

According to Lukács, the system of social reproduction is formed via concrete processes, determined historically, which are always contradictory and which construct man as a social being, ontologically distinct from nature yet maintaining an inalienable metabolic relationship with nature. It is in this context of concrete and historical processes that universal ontological categories of social being are brought into existence through work.

Therefore, social reproduction, as an ontological category, refers to private mediations that allow human beings to achieve even higher and more complex levels of sociability at each historical moment. This occurs at the same time as concrete forms of existence are configured and universal categories of social being are developed. In short, following Marx, Lukács applies the label of social reproduction to the system of categories formed by the sphere of specifications, which are real and historical moments of creation of being (Lukács, 1976; Lessa, 2004).

For Lukács, the world of men is a new substantiality, purely social, which has nothing to do with natural laws although it requires a never-ending organic exchange with nature (Lessa, 1995, p. 13).

Therefore, it is necessary to search in the social being for its specific logic, the ontological procedures which differentiate natural being from the social being and, within this, the specific categories that allow the development of more and more social totalities that distinguish themselves, step by step, from the original immediate relation of man with nature. In this process of elevation to complex and superior levels of sociability, which is the reproduction of the social being, the world of men is increasingly influenced by purely social categories.

For Marxist thinkers, the individualization process of men is only possible through history. Man, according to Lukácsian ontology, emerges as a general being, tribal animal, gregarious, as a result of complex production relations

(Hobsbawn, 2011). This peculiarity of work, "producing more than is necessary for the reproduction of the worker," is the "objective foundation" of the whole human history (Lessa, 1995).

In class society, especially capitalism, the more the worker appropriates the external world through his work, the more he is deprived of livelihood (Marx, 2004, p. 86). From this perspective, the worker begins to relate to the product of his work as a strange object.

Work is a *necessary organic product* (Lukács, 1976) and, concurrently, is constituted as an influence on the socialization process, requiring immediate development of systems that did not previously exist in nature. The diagram of praxis (ideation–action–evaluation) is only possible because of the existence of consciousness, as advocated by Vygotsky, having been created in the ontological dimension for the needs of work.

This ontological situation is not simply the continuation of the same, but also a continuation that builds itself in perennial and incessant change. The organ and the medium of such continuity, according to Lukács, is consciousness (Lessa, 1995, p. 34).

In this light, we can affirm that work is impossible without consciousness though after a determined time of historical development, it becomes consciously social, accomplishing the "full explanation of being-for-itself of mankind" (Lukács, 1976, p. 183) and overcoming its original muteness.[5] In this way, Lukács places the ontological genesis of language in work, as ability to create objective and subjective innovations, in so far as it retains the consciousness and makes communicable the achievements of mankind.

Following this line of argument, in Lukácsian ontology, language is indispensable for the continuity of reproduction of social being. Taking into consideration the need for social activity and the relationship between man and nature as well as relationships among people themselves, the symbolic experience fulfills the dual task of capturing and fixing the singular and the universal. The social function of language means that it soon becomes a universal social system as there is no aspect of human praxis that can be accomplished without mediation (Lessa, 1995).

Language is what allows previous ideation, being able to mediate relations of fundamental abstractions – what Vygotsky would explore as a specificity of superior psychological functioning. This way, it is possible to operate, in the consciousness field, with concreteness that is not presented to the human being in an immediate way but which is elementary to work activities and their derivations (art, philosophy, science, etc.).

In the social context, language is what mediates other systems of social reproduction, such as ideology, once it has its centrality in second order teleological input; in other words, human action modifies nature indirectly by the action of one human being over the other.

The problem of consciousness and language in Vygotsky and Bakhtin

As we explored above, for Marxist thinkers, work is the explanatory central category of the human species. Vygotsky is aware of that, and from that premise, he starts to comprehend consciousness and the superior psychological system. He avoids reducing those to subjective phenomena and/or mechanistic descriptions. His ideas seem really close to those elaborated by Lukács, but with some different emphasis, as follows.

For Vygotsky (1989), what defines work is nature's need for transformation. In fact, if the natural landscape did not show any challenge to perpetuation of the species, men would probably not need to create new forms of sociability and existence. It is inadequacy that generates the creation of new actions, resulting from the need to survive (Vygotsky, 2004).

In evolutionary terms, this means that through mediation, natural landscape could become a cultural construction. This qualitative leap in the course of evolution resulted in transformation of the organic into a social subject. According to A. Luria (1902–1977), that was only possible due to two factors: a) the use of instruments and b) the birth of language.

In fact, according to what we explore below, it is by the sign system and instruments, use of which allowed man to change the world, that social practices started to get more complex. The communication and technological advances that came out of the enhancement of instruments enabled new corporate arrangements which changed ways of thinking, feeling, and acting. That is, the use of signs and instruments marked, in the phylogenesis, the passage from Animal Man to Cultural Man, and that became the foundation for the mental understanding of superior order.

Engels (n.d., p. 272) affirms that

> First comes labor, after it, and then *side by side with it*, articulate speech— these were the two most essential stimuli under the influence of which the brain of the ape gradually changed into that of man, which for all its similarity to the former is far larger and more perfect.[6]

In order to treat those systems in more specific human terms, Vygotsky (1978) presents an approximation between sign and instrument, subordinating these to a more general concept: *the mediated activity and its role in the constitution of psyche*. In a different way from what happens in the rest of the animal world (e.g., the instinctive *tessitura* of the spider web in a previous quotation), conscious activity is mediated by instruments (tools), by psychological instruments (signs), and by human social relations.

The creation of the instrument enabled, in phylogenetic terms, the transformation of external activity. Here, we are referring to the emergence of cultural artifacts (such as the fishing rod, the hammer, etc.) that promoted a radical change in the way man used nature to produce his material goods.

The use of instrument – characterized by being external to man due to its direct action over nature – relates primarily to the activity level. However, Silva (2002) warns that this external *tool* is also a shared social sign that guides itself to the intrapsychic level, bringing in itself a whole history of signification, of cultural aspects of collective practices and men's use of these instruments. Therefore, "the axe is, at the same time, tool, for the domain of nature, and sign, word that designates the object itself, carrying the history of actions and its meaning, according to the interpersonal game of cultural constitution" (Silva, 2002, p. 35).

In this way, the study of the use of instruments (and the recurrent corporate dynamics) incites us to develop the role of language. There is an analogy between the development of forms of work and social practices and the use of instruments and production of signs that cannot be neglected in studies in the historical-cultural field – and so we assume difference from contemporary mechanistic and biological or neurobiological perspectives.

For Vygotsky, the emergence of language – the status of word as a sign – allowed man to operate through mental mechanisms that increased his potential to resolve problems. Language – understood as human product and production; something that makes it possible in social relation and goes beyond a mechanistic view of symbolization, decoding of signs and communication – constitutes thinking, emotion, perception, and memory. That is why we can affirm, based on Vygotsky, that without language, human consciousness would be impossible.

Vygotsky (2014, pp. 346–347) establishes that:

> Consciousness is reflected in a word as the sun in a drop of water. A word relates to consciousness as a living cell relates to a whole organism, as an atom relates to the universe. A word is a microcosm of human consciousness.[7]

According to Luria (1991), by starting to operate with signs, three essential changes emerge in men: a) the ability to differentiate between objects and preserve them in the memory; b) the capacity for abstraction and conceptual generalization; c) the possibility of transmitting and perpetuating information, allowing man to assimilate experience and dominate knowledge, which is historically produced and accumulated by mankind.

Language emerges as a way to comprehend the other and oneself and, at the same time, to act upon the world and upon oneself. The internalized word acts as a psychological instrument, as a sign, and constitutes thinking. In this process, language begins to guide actions and give form to the complex processes that constitute human consciousness. According to Vygotsky (1999), the study of the genesis of psychological processes shows that volitional operations involve the interpsychological dimension.

Here we can understand the role of articulate language for knowledge and consciousness. Language is, from the ontogenetic point of view, a way of establishing a bond between the child and those that surround him. Gradually, he starts to design his behavior by words that were somehow shared in his own social dynamics (Vygotsky, 1999). As we can see, for Vygotsky, the individual's consciousness implies empathy since one of the fundamental laws of the development of superior psychological functions emerges from an unfolding idea of functions in interpersonal relations and their synthesis in one person.

It is also remarkable that signs, which are perceived as having great significance in the history of cultural development, were initially a means of contact, a means to act upon others. When we consider their true origin as a form of contact, we can say that signs are, more broadly, a means of contact between certain mental functions of a social character. Transferred to the self, they also provide a means of combining functions within oneself, and we will be able to demonstrate that without signs and speech, the brain and the original connections could not form such complex relationships.

The problem of reaction (returning to Pavlov and the reflexologists) becomes critically re-elaborated, intrinsically connected to the problem of cross-functionality in psychological systems, sign and signification that is used in Vygotsky's elaboration in *Thought and Language*.

For Vygotsky, the word as a *microcosm of consciousness* is – as we see in Bakhtin (1895–1975) – a sign of the highest order. In addition, the sign is not something from the natural world that humans occupy, but something from human order in the social world. It is not a reflex, not just a mechanism of the natural organic order that serves to constitute the psyche and guide human action, but something that is formed through social relations and out of the historical and cultural spheres – it is a human production. Thus, human superior psychological functionality is not something that emerges from biological mechanisms, nor is it characterized by the complexity of the biological apparatus of the species; rather, it reflects the insertion of itself in history and human culture and the creation of instruments and signs that both affect and redesign this functionality.

Smolka (2004), in discussing the conditions and modes of production of signification, shows that in Vygotsky's conceptual development, we pass from representation (images formulation, organic sphere) to signification (production of signs and senses, cultural sphere). Smolka (2004, p. 42) helps us comprehend the question of the word/*verbum*:

> Sign, as what is produced and stabilized in interpersonal relationships, acts, resonates, reverberates in subjects. It has impregnation and reversibility as characteristics, that is, it affects the subjects in (and in the history of) relations. Moreover, the word as a sign by excellence is highlighted here as a purer and more sensitive way of social relation and, at the same time, semiotic material of interior life. Constituting a human specificity – allowing man not only to indicate, but to name, highlight and refer through language; and through language, he is able to direct, plan, (inter)regulate actions; also to know the world, to know (himself) and to become a subject; it allows man to lead and build reality. The emergence of *verbum* constitutes an event of irreversible nature.

In summary, we can affirm that Vygotsky, in his historical-cultural perspective, brings a series of elements to the comprehension of consciousness and specifically human mental functioning in a design that is not dichotomous, idealistic, or mechanistic. For him, the biological apparatus is redesigned; it is transformed in and through the process of immersion in history and culture, in and through the process of signification. However, his elaborations about signs are limited to their psychological and mediation role.

In M. Bakhtin-Volochinov (2002), we find elements that deepen and advance this discussion, as the Russian philologist starts to treat this psychological instrument proposed by Vygotsky – the sign – as an ideological fact that is deeply tangled in social relations of modes of production.

The sign, for Bakhtin-Volochinov, is shared in social contacts that are constituted in ways of thinking and acting in social settings. The link between the word and superstructure and infrastructure reflects relations of production and social struggles. It is important to emphasize that, according to this line of argument, an ideological product also combines with a determined reality, either natural or social, but it differs from other products because it reflects another reality that is exterior to it. In this sense, the phenomenon or ideological product implies a meaning and remit outside of itself.

In the process of comprehending the signification of language, for example, Bakhtin-Volochinov (2002) points to the difficulty and complexity of the problem and marks the importance of taking into consideration two concepts: theme and signification. The first one comprises not only the linguistic forms that make up part of the composition (words, shapes, sounds, etc.), but also the nonverbal elements of the situation because all elements of the situation are important to comprehend the enunciation. According to Bakhtin-Volochinov (2002, pp. 128–129): "The theme of an utterance is concrete—as concrete as the historical instant to which the utterance belongs. *Only an utterance taken in its full, concrete scope as an historical phenomenon possesses a theme.*"[8]

Signification is a trace of the union between interlocutors; it is only performed in the active and responsive process of comprehension. For Bakhtin-Volochinov (2002, p. 123),

> meaning does not reside in the word or in the soul of the speaker or in the soul of the listener. Meaning is the *effect of interaction between speaker and listener produced via the material of a particular sound complex*. It is like an electric spark. … Only the current of verbal intercourse endows a word with the light of meaning.[9]

He argues that "signs can arise only on an interindividual territory" (2002).[10] Signs emerge from the process of interaction between individual consciousnesses. Individual consciousness does not explain the ideological and social environment, nor is it constituted, at first, by eliminating itself from that. On the contrary, for Bakhtin-Volochinov, it is indeed a social-ideological fact; a phenomenon forged in this environment. In other words, consciousness acquires shape and existence in and through the signs created by a group organized in the course of its social relations. Word, gesture, image, sense, and meaning give shape to human consciousness. Without this semiotic material, which is ideological, there is only the simple organic and physiologic phenomenon, deprived of the senses that only signs are able to provide.

Bakhtin-Volochinov (2002, p. 49) establishes that

> *The reality of the inner psyche is the same reality as that of the sign.* Outside the material of signs there is no psyche; there are physiological processes, processes in the nervous system, but no subjective psyche as a special existential quality fundamentally distinct from both the physiological processes occurring within the organism and the reality encompassing the organism from outside. … [T]he subjective psyche is to be localized somewhere between the organism and the outside world, on the borderline separating these two spheres of reality. It is here that an encounter between the organism and the outside world takes place, but the encounter is not a physical one: *the organism and the outside meet here in the sign.* Psychic experience is the semiotic expression of the contact between the organism and the outside environment.[11]

For this author, all gesture or organic phenomenon – breathing, blood circulation, body movement, or interior language – can become material for expression and execution of psychic activity. After all, everything that can acquire a semiotic value has an ideological character.

It is in this sense that Bakhtin-Volochinov (2002, p. 38) argues:

> All manifestations of ideological creativity—all … nonverbal signs—are bathed by, suspended in, and cannot be entirely segregated or divorced from the element of speech.
> [...] Nonetheless, at the very same time, every single one of these ideological signs, though not supplantable by words, has support in and is accompanied by words, just as is the case with singing and its musical accompaniment.[12]

As we see in Vygotsky, the word, as the highest expression of a sign, is not limited by biological apparatus or mechanisms. Rather, it gives shape and material reality to human consciousness; it produces consciousness. Therefore, we understand the status and centrality of language, word, and sign in his work, something that is missing from idealist and mechanistic approaches.

In this way, Vygotsky and Bakhtin-Volochinov present an interconstitutive relation among work, language, and consciousness as key to explaining human specificity. For that reason, Vygotsky insists that man is fundamentally a historical-cultural being.

Final considerations

The historical-cultural perspective, proposed by Vygotsky and his collaborators, adhered to studying the most sophisticated psychological processes that are typical of human species: language, memory, emotion, among others. They assumed historical and dialectical materialism as a philosophical–methodological principle in order to leverage a theoretical project in a search to overcome the old psychology.

In this chapter, we have aimed to present the epistemological rupture that Vygotskian thinking represented in his time, and which still echoes today. By exposing the scientific project of the Belarusian psychologist, we plead that it cannot be disconnected from historical dialectical materialism, as some contemporary authors ignore (see Ratner and Silva in the Introduction to this book).

In order to trace Vygotsky's scientific project according to Marxist ideas, we appeal to the work category. In constructing our argument, the work of Lukács has been essential in establishing a link between authors, strengthening the thesis that human consciousness can only be understood through material and symbolic production that comes from human activity in the domain of nature.

If Vygotsky breaks with reductionists and mechanistic visions of his time, proposing a monistic, dialectical and materialistic psychology, it occurs because he managed – even in an unfinished way – to develop, theoretically, the role of sign in the formation of psyche. In other words: what we produce and dispute in the interpersonal context converts into something that constitutes us individually. His focus was on the signification process that emerges from social, dialectical, and contradictory relations and marks the dramatic process of the constitution of personality (Vygotsky, 1989).

However, in our opinion, the formulations presented by Vygotsky, concerning the questions around the central role of the sign, appear to gain more strength when they are combined with ideas developed by Bakhtin-Volochinov. There is here a promising theoretical meeting because Bakhtin-Volochinov, also supported by Marxist prerogatives, defends the ideological dimension of sign. We agree with Bakhtin-Volochinov (2002, pp. 98–99) when he states: "in actuality, we never say or hear words, we say and hear what is true or false, good or bad, important or unimportant, pleasant or unpleasant, and so on. Words are always filled with content and meaning drawn from behavior or ideology."[13]

In these terms, a sign cannot be conceived of merely as a physical response to an external stimulus, as the epistemic tradition of materialistic and mechanistic authors suggests; equally, it cannot be understood as something immaterial, as idealists would have it. As we see from Bakhtin-Volochinov and Vygotsky, *the sign is a human production*, a social–ideological fact that depends on the concrete, on the praxis of social relations.

Contemporary psychology should not neglect these theoretical precepts, because they allow us to understand that human consciousness cannot be separated from the history that we live in. It is history that teaches us what we are and what we can be.

Notes

1   See chapter 13.
2   Here, we deal exclusively with the *methodological* aspect of the question: Can there be one science about *two* fundamentally different kinds of being?
3   Quotation from Marx, K., and Engels, F. (1970). *The German ideology*. New York: International Publishers (original work published 1932): p. 48.
4   Ibid., p. 47.
5   According to Lukács, speech is a reflex, in social reproduction, and so it appears as an essential complex mediator to its continuity and, at the same time, it is a mediation that potentiates the nature of mankind that is no longer voiceless. It is referred to originating muteness because speech is absent from the natural world, overcome by mankind.
6   Quotation from Engels, F. (2007). On the part played by labor in the transition from ape to man. In M. Lock and Judith Farquar (Eds.), *Beyond the body proper* (pp. 25–29). Durham, NC: Duke University Press: p. 27, emphasis added.
7   Quotation from Vygotsky, L. S. (1986). *Thought and language*. Cambridge, MA: MIT Press: p. 256.
8   Quotation from Vološinov, V. N. (1986). *Marxism and the philosophy of language*, trans. L. Matejka and I. R. Titunik. Cambridge, MA: Havard University Press: p. 100, original emphasis.
9   Ibid., pp. 102–103, original emphasis.
10   Ibid., p. 12.
11   Ibid., p. 26, original emphasis.
12   Ibid., p. 15.
13   Ibid., p. 70.

References

Abreu, F. S. D. (2015). *Experiências linguísticas e sexuais não hegemônicas: um estudo das narrativas de surdos homossexuais* [Non-hegemic linguistic and sexual experiences: A study of gay deaf narratives]. Master's dissertation, Institute of Psychology, University of Brasil.

Bakhtin-Volochinov, M. (Vološinov). (2002). *Marxismo e filosofia da linguagem* [Marxism and the philosophy of language]. São Paulo: Hucitec.

Damasio, A. (1994). *Descartes' error: Emotion, reason and the human brain*. New York: G. P. Putnam.

Damasio, A. (1999). *The feeling of what happens: Body and emotion in the making of consciousness*, Orlando, FL: Harcourt, Inc.

Damasio, A. (2003). *Looking for Spinoza. Joy, sorrow and the feeling brain*. Orlando, FL: Harcourt, Inc.

Edelman, G. M. (1989). *The remembered present: A biological theory of consciousness*. New York: Basic Books.

Edelman, G. M. (2006). *Second nature: Brain science and human knowledge*. New Haven, CT: Yale University Press.

Engels, F. (n.d.). *Sobre o papel do trabalho na transformação do macaco em homem* [On the part played by labor in the transition from ape to man]. In K. Marx and F. Engels, *Obras Escolhidas* [Selected works]. Rio de Janeiro: Alfa-Ômega.

Hobsbawm, E. (2011). *How to change the world*. New Haven, CT: Yale University Press.

Lessa, S. (1995). *Sociabilidade e individuação* [Sociability and individuation]. Alagoas: Edufal.

Lessa, S. (2004). *Identidade e individuação* [Identity and individuation]. *Katálysis, 7*(9), 147–157.

Lukács, G. (1976). *Ontologia dell'essere sociale*, trans. Alberto Scarponi. 2 volumes. Rome: Riuniti.

Luria, A. R. (1991). A atividade consciente do homem e suas raízes histórico-sociais [Cognitive development: Its cultural and social foundations]. In *Curso de psicologia geral: Introdução evolucionista à psicologia*, Vol. 1, pp. 71–84. Rio de Janeiro: Civilização Brasileira.

Magiolino, L. L. S., and Smolka, A. L. B. (2013). How do emotions signify? Social relations and psychological functions in the dramatic constitution of subjects. *Mind, Culture, and Activity, 20*(1), 96–112.

Marx, K. (2002). *O capital: crítica da economia política – Livro primeiro: o processo de produção do Capital* [Capital: A critique of political economy. Volume 1: The process of production of capital]. Rio de Janeiro: Civilização Brasileira.

Marx, K. (2004). *Manuscritos econômico-filosóficos* [Economic and philosophic manuscripts]. São Paulo: Boitempo.

Marx, K., and Engels, F. (2009). *A ideologia alemã* [The German ideology]. São Paulo: Expressão Popular.

Sawaia, B. B., and Silva, D. N. H. (2015). Pelo reencantamento da psicologia: em busca da positividade epistemológica da imaginação e da emoção no desenvolvimento humano. [For the re-enchantment of psychology: In search of the epistemological positivity of imagination and emotion in human development]. *Cadernos Cedes, 35*(spe), 343–360. https://dx.doi.org/10.1590/CC0101-32622015V35ESPECIAL154115

Silva, D. N. H. (2002). *Como brincam as crianças surdas* [How deaf children play]. São Paulo: Plexus Editora.

Silva, D. N. H. (2012). *Imaginação, criança e escola* [Imagination, children and school]. São Paulo: Summus.

Smolka, A. L. B. (2004). Sobre significação e sentido: uma contribuição à proposta de rede de significações [About meaning and sense: A contribution to the proposed network of meanings]. In M. C. Rossetti-Ferreira, K. S. Amorim, A. P. S. Silva, and A. M. A. Carvalho (Orgs.), *Rede de significações e o estudo do desenvolvimento humano* [Net of meanings and the study of human development]. Vol. 1, pp. 35–49. Porto Alegre: Artes Médicas.

Tomasello, M. (1999) *The cultural origins of human cognition*. Cambridge, MA: Harvard University Press.

Tomasello, M. (2003) *Constructing a language: A usage-based theory of language acquisition*. Cambridge, MA: Harvard University Press.

Vygotski, L. S. (Vygotsky) (1978). *Mind in society: The development of higher psychological processes*. Cambridge, MA: Harvard University Press.

Vygotsky, L. S. (1989). Concrete human psychology. *Soviet Psychology, 27*(2), 53–77.

Vygotsky, L. S. (1997a). *The collected works of L. S. Vygotsky. Vol. 1: Problems of general psychology*. Robert W. Rieber and A. S. Carton (Eds.), trans. N. Minick. New York: Plenum.

Vygotsky, L. S. (1997b). Consciousness as a problem for the psychology of behavior. In *The collected works of L. S. Vygotsky. The history of the development of higher mental functions. Vol. 4*. (pp. 63–79). Robert W. Rieber (Ed.), trans. M. J. Hall. New York: Plenum.

Vygotsky, L. S. (1997c). *The collected works of L. S. Vygotsky. Volume 3: Problems of the theory and history of psychology*. R. W. Rieber and J. Wollock (Eds.), trans. R. van der Veer. New York: Plenum.

Vygotsky, L. S. (1998). *The collected works of L. S. Vygotsky. Volume 5: Child psychology*. R. W. Rieber (Ed.), trans. M. J. Hall. New York: Plenum.

Vygotsky, L. S. (1999). *The collected works of L. S. Vygotsky. Volume 6: Scientific legacy*. R. W. Rieber (Ed.), trans. M. J. Hall. New York: Plenum.

Vygotski, L. S. (Vygotsky) (2001). *A construção do pensamento e linguagem* [Thought and language]. São Paulo: Martins Fontes.

Vygotsky, L. S. (2004). Imagination and creativity in childhood. *Journal of Russian and East European Psychology, 42*(1), 7–97.

Vygotski, L. S. (Vygotsky) (2014). *Obras escogidas II – Pensamiento y Lenguaje: conferencias sobre psicología* [Selected works II: Thought and language. Conferences on psychology]. Madrid: Machado Libros.

4

THE GERM CELL OF VYGOTSKY'S SCIENCE

Andy Blunden

"Psychology is in need of its own *Das Kapital*," wrote Vygotsky in 1928 (1928a/1997, p. 330), observing that "the whole of *Das Kapital* is written according to this method," (p. 320), the method in which Marx identifies the 'cell' of bourgeois society - an exchange of commodities - and then unfolds from an analysis of the contradictions within this single cell, the entire process of bourgeois society. Vygotsky was the first to grasp *Das Kapital* in this way, and his recovery and application of the method of 'analysis by units' is his most important legacy.

What Vygotsky did was to produce *one* study which would function as an exemplar for research in psychology; that one study addressed the age-old problem of the relation between thinking and speech, and by solving this *one problem* in an exemplary fashion, he created a paradigm for research in all domains of psychology and, as a matter of fact, in *all* the sciences. Indeed, Vygotsky left us as many as *five* different exemplars of analysis by units.

But first let us reflect on the historical origins of this idea.

Origins of the concept of 'cell' as a method of analysis

The idea of the 'cell' originates with the philosopher of history, Johann Gottfried Herder (1744–1803). In his effort to understand the differences between peoples, Herder introduced the idea of a *Schwerpunkt* ('strong point'). This idea is probably better known nowadays in its formulation by Marx:

> There is in every social formation a particular branch of production which determines the position and importance of all the others ... as though light of a particular hue were cast upon everything, tingeing all other colors and modifying their specific features.
>
> *(1857/1993, pp. 106–7)*

Herder's friend Johann Wolfgang von Goethe (1749–1832) sought to utilize this idea in his study of botany during his Italian journey in 1786 in order to understand the continuity and differences between the plants found in different parts of the country.

Goethe came to the idea of an *Urphänomen* – not a law or principle, but a simple, archetypal phenomenon in which all the essential features of a whole complex process are manifest. In Goethe's own words:

> The *Urphänomen* is not to be regarded as a basic theorem leading to a variety of consequences, but rather as a basic manifestation enveloping the specifications of form for the beholder.
>
> *(1795/1988, p. 106)*

> Empirical observation must first teach us what parts are common to all animals, and how these parts differ. The idea must govern the whole, it must abstract the general picture in a genetic way. Once such an Urphänomen is established, even if only provisionally, we may test it quite adequately by applying the customary methods of comparison.
>
> *(Cited in Naydler, 1827/1996, p. 118)*

This meant that in order to understand a complex process as an integral whole or *Gestalt*, we have to identify and understand just its smallest part – a radical departure from the 'Newtonian' approach to science based on discovering intangible forces and hidden laws.

It is widely agreed that the idea that Goethe was working towards was the cell of an organism, but it wasn't until microscopes became powerful enough to reveal the microstructure of organisms that Schleiden and Schwann were able to formulate the cell theory of biology in 1839. The cell is the unit of analysis of biology and, alongside Darwin's idea of evolution by natural selection, constitutes the foundation of biology.

The philosopher Hegel took up Goethe's idea and gave it a firm logical foundation in his *Science of Logic*, in which the place of the cell was now taken by the concept. The *Logic* describes the formation and development of concepts in three books. Book one, known as the "Logic of Being," describes the process in which the basic regularities are abstracted from the flow of immediate perception in the form of a mass of measures. Book two, the "Logic of Essence," describes the emergence of theories trying to make sense of this data, with each theory being contested by opposing theories and both then being overtaken by others, digging successively deeper, and building up a theoretical picture of the phenomenon, until … book three, the "Logic of the Concept," begins when, in a kind of Aha! moment, an abstract concept emerges which captures the phenomenon as a whole at its simplest and most abstract level. Beginning from this abstract concept – the cell – the phenomenon is then reconstructed as a *Gestalt* by unfolding the contradictions inherent in this cell as it interacts with other cells.

Note that each of these phases has the form of a movement from abstract to concrete (abstract in the sense of simple and isolated), *and* from concrete to abstract (concrete in the sense of immediate and real). "Being": from perceptions to measures; "Essence": from measures to a concept; "Concept": from a simple concept to a rich and concrete concept of the whole.

Marx renders this idea particularly transparent in the famous passage of the *Grundrisse*, "The method of political economy."

> Along the first path the full conception was evaporated to yield an abstract determination; along the second, the abstract determinations lead towards a reproduction of the concrete by way of thought.
>
> *(1857/1993, p. 100)*

Taking as given the collection of the data on which the science rests, Marx here refers to the two phases in the development of a science as represented by Hegel in the logics of essence and concept. The first of these phases corresponds to the decades Marx spent in the 'immanent critique' of the theories of political economy, leading to the discovery of the cell; the second phase is the 'dialectical reconstruction' of political economy in *Capital*, beginning from the analysis of exchange of commodities in Chapter 1. Anyone who has read Vygotsky cannot fail to have noted how he too approaches every single problem historically, working through the various theories which have hitherto been used to comprehend the phenomenon, and deriving from this immanent critique a unifying concept to which the various theorists seem to have been working. Like Marx, Vygotsky does not counterpose his own theory to that of others, but draws out of the history of the science what he deems to be the essential tendency.

In his "Notes on Adolph Wagner," Marx says: "I did not start out from the 'concept of value.' ... What I start out from is the simplest social form in the which the labor product is presented in contemporary society, and this is 'the commodity'" (1881/2010, p. 544). The commodity is a *form* of value, but 'value' is an intangible, not "a geometrical, a chemical, or any other natural property" (Marx, 1867/2010, p. 47) – but a suprasensible quality of commodities, and as such is unsuited for the role of *Urphänomen*. Value is a 'social relation' which can only be grasped conceptually. Nonetheless, the commodity is a form of value which, thanks to everyday experience, *can be grasped viscerally*. This means that the critique of the concept of commodity works upon relations which can be grasped viscerally by reader and writer alike. By beginning with the (concept of) commodity, Marx mobilizes the readers' visceral understanding of commodities, and as he leads us to each successive relation, so long as that relation exists in social practice, then not only is the writer's intuition validated by the *existence* of that relation, but it also allows the reader to securely grasp the logical exposition. Marx's decision to begin not with 'value' but with the 'commodity' illustrates Marx's debt to Goethe as well as Hegel.

It should be noted that only the first three chapters of *Capital* deal with simple commodity production. In Chapter 4, Marx derives the first, abstract concept of 'capital' which is to be the real subject matter of the book. Capital is an aggregate of commodities, but is a distinct unit, which subsumes under itself simple commodity production and thereafter capital accumulation gives a new direction to the development of economic life. The remainder of *Capital* is, in Hegel's sense, 'book two' of *Capital*.

Marx had been able to appropriate Hegel's method, but neither the naturalist-poet Goethe, nor the philosopher Hegel, nor the communist Marx could have a significant impact on the course of natural scientific activity during the nineteenth century. How could this achievement of classical German philosophy be transformed into methods for the resolution of the problems in the various branches of science?

Science proceeded piecemeal, and not according to the grand plan of Hegel's *Encyclopedia of the Philosophical Sciences*. The natural sciences were in general able to make progress by problem-solving in the separate disciplines, with occasional unexpected breakthroughs but no overall conception guiding their work. Cultural and political life proved resistant to this piecemeal approach, however. It took almost a century from Hegel's death in 1831, through the efforts of German natural science, French social theory and the American pragmatism, before a practical, laboratory method for understanding how individual human beings appropriated the cultural practices of their time was finally accomplished by Lev Vygotsky, thanks to the methodological conquests of Hegel and Marx and the cultural conditions created in the wake of the Russian Revolution.

The method of double stimulation

The key insight which opened up the possibility for a psychology adequate to the rich and complex cultural life of human beings was the formation of a basic unit of analysis or germ cell of cultural learning. This is the problem which had so far proved intractable.

Until Vygotsky's breakthrough, psychology had been split between those like Helmholtz who approached it with 'brass instruments,' as if it were a branch of the natural sciences, and those like Dilthey who saw psychology as a branch of the 'human sciences.' Recognizing that the mind was formed by the joint actions of physiology and culture, Wundt had even proposed that there be two separate psychologies: one carried out in the laboratory with the aid of introspection, the other by the study of literature and art. In the twentieth century, psychology was split between behaviorists who denied the existence of consciousness and saw psychology in terms of reflexes and 'empirical psychologists' who studied the mind by means of introspection. The 'brass instrument' methods hitherto employed in psychology laboratories were capable of investigating only the most elementary and primitive reflexes which humans have in common with the animals, while introspection was incapable of providing the objective data needed for the development of a science. Contra behaviorism, consciousness not only exists but is the subject matter of psychology, without which human behavior is incomprehensible; consciousness – like history, for example – cannot be observed *directly*, but only as mediated through its connection with physiology and behavior, both of which are objective.

Vygotsky solved these problems with the experimental method of double stimulation.

This was first formulated by Vygotsky in conjunction with Alexander Luria in 1928 (see Luria, 1928/1994, and Vygotsky, 1928b/1994). An experimental subject, typically a child, would be presented with a problem, such as memorizing a series of words, and as they were trying to solve it, the researcher would present them with an artifact, perhaps a picture-card, to use as a means in solving the problem. In this simple scenario, we have the germ cell of cultural development and activity.

In Figure 4.1, *A* represents a person who confronts an object or problem, *B*, and *X* is a sign, an artifact introduced into the scenario by a collaborator, as a means of solving the problem. This simple germ cell captures the essential relation of people to their culture: a problem set by another person is solved by using an artifact (in this case, a sign) drawn from the cultural environment. In the process of appropriating the use of the given artifact, the subject's psychology is enhanced by the creation of a new reflex, associating *B* with *X*. Vygotsky has set up here an extremely simple scenario that can be sensuously experienced and therefore grasped viscerally, without the need of a preexisting overarching theory. But in this simple setup we have both the immediate situation of an individual confronting a problem and the entire cultural history of the subject's environment represented in the artifact-solution. It is a unit of analysis which is a unity of the individual psyche and an entire cultural history.

The meaning of the term 'double stimulation' is illustrated in the diagram. *A* is subject to two stimuli at the same time, both the object itself, $A \rightarrow B$, and the auxiliary stimulus, $A \rightarrow X$, which is associated with the object, $X \rightarrow B$. Thus the subject responds to the object *B* in two ways at once, the immediate perception of the object, $A \rightarrow B$, and the sign, $A \rightarrow X$. Each of these reactions is a perfectly natural reflex. It is the mediated reaction $A \rightarrow X \rightarrow B$, which is *socially constructed* and which gives *meaning* to the object, *B*, a meaning acquired from the culture, thanks to the collaboration with the other person, in this case, the researcher. *X* may be an image on a card which reminds the subject of the word to be remembered, for example, or it may be a written word giving the name of the object. This idea, in which all our relations to the environment are taken to be *mediated*, is directly linked to Hegel's *Logic*. "There is nothing," says Hegel, "nothing in heaven, or in nature or mind or anywhere else which does not equally contain both immediacy

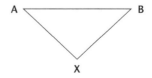

FIGURE 4.1 The method of double stimulation

and mediation" (1816/1969, p. 68). It is by using cultural signs and tools to solve problems thrown up in life in collaboration with others that people learn and become cultured citizens of their community, introducing mediating signs and other artifacts into their relation with their immediate environment.

Using this experimental setup, Vygotsky was able to observe whether and how children of different ages were able to use which kind of memory-cards to improve their performance in memorizing tasks and, by this means demonstrated, for example, the qualitative difference between how small children remember and how adults remember. By appropriating elements of their culture in the course of their development, people completely restructure their consciousness.

This first unit of analysis, the 'artifact-mediated action,' is the first germ cell developed for psychological research by Vygotsky.

Word meaning

In 1931, Vygotsky came to the conclusion that the archetypal cultural artifact through which people appropriated the culture of their community was not just any artifact, but *the spoken word*. After all, every physiologically able child spontaneously learns to speak, while many never master literacy, and speech had emerged contemporaneously with labor (the use of tool-artifacts) in the very evolution of the human species. Signs, such as the written word, were a later invention, corresponding to transition to class society and civilization. So it was that, in 1934, Vygotsky composed his last and definitive work, *Thinking and Speech* (1934a/1987).

In the first chapter of *Thinking and Speech*, Vygotsky presents the one and only exposition of analysis by units, and in this instance his chosen unit is 'word meaning' – a unity of speech and thinking, of sound and meaning. A word is a unity of sound and meaning because a sound without a meaning is not a word and a meaning without sound is not a word – word has to be both. Word meaning is equally a unity of generalization and social interaction, of thinking and communication. A word is a unit because it is the smallest discrete instance of such a unity.

This unit has to be understood as a 'sign-mediated action,' though as Vygotsky insists, word meaning is not a *subset* of the larger category of artifact-mediated actions. Rather, the relation between tool-use and sign-use is genetic. The archetype of a 'sign', according to Vygotsky, is a mnemonic symbol, such as a knot in a handkerchief or a notch in a message stick, and these signs developed historically into the written word several thousand years ago. Sign-mediated actions, such as the use of written words, arose historically as an extension of tool-mediated actions. Speech, however, arose in close connection with the development of labor in the very process of human evolution. The use of symbolic artifacts, such as writing, therefore has to be understood as something phylogenetically and ontogenetically distinct from speech that co-evolved as part of the labor process, which according to Engels (1876/1987), marked the evolution of the human species.

In his discussion of tool-use, Vygotsky distinguishes between 'technical tools' and 'psychological tools.' Tools in the normal sense, technical tools, are used to operate upon matter, whereas psychological tools are used to work on the mind, and these include "language, different forms of numeration and counting, mnemotechnic techniques, algebraic symbolism, works of art, writing, schemes, diagrams, maps, blueprints, all sorts of conventional signs, etc." (Vygotsky, 1930/1997, p. 85). Using a (technical) tool has profound psychological effects because tool-use widens the scope of a person's activity and expands their horizon of experience but it does not 'work on the mind' in the same sense as does a psychological tool. Psychological tools developed alongside and as an extension of the development of technical tools.

It is important to emphasize that speech, that is to say acting with a word, is an *action*; to *mean* something, that is, word meaning, is an action. 'Word meaning' does not refer to an entry in the dictionary; it is the action in which an intention is carried out using a meaningful word as a means. It is for this reason that in the definitive translation, the book is titled *Thinking and Speech* and not *Thought and Language* as was the first English translation.

Just as Marx analyzed the commodity as early as 1843, but took until 1859 to realize that the commodity had to be taken as a unit of analysis, Vygotsky pointed to the importance of analyzing speech in his first published work (1924/1997) but took a further decade to settle on the spoken word, the simplest act of 'psychological exchange', as the unit of analysis for his major work.

Using this unit of analysis, Vygotsky analyzed the development of the *intellect*; that is, of verbal thought. The unit of 'practical intellect' is a tool-use and has a distinct path of development, side by side with (verbal) intellect, whose unit is a word meaning.

Although word meaning is the basic unit of the intellect, a larger, 'molar' unit is required to understand the structure and development of the intellect. This molar unit is the concept, which is an aggregate of many word meanings. The center of Vygotsky's analysis in *Thinking and Speech* is the formation of concepts, which only reach a fully developed form in late adolescence. Vygotsky's task then was to trace the development of the intellect from infancy to adulthood by observing the development of speech.

Vygotsky summarizes his study of the emergence of speech in young children as follows:

1. As we found in our analysis of the phylogenetic development of thinking and speech, we find that these two processes have different roots in ontogenesis.
2. Just as we can identify a "pre-speech" stage in the development of the child's thinking, we can identify a "pre-intellectual stage" in the development of his speech.
3. Up to a certain point, speech and thinking develop along different lines and independently of one another.
4. At a certain point, the two lines cross: thinking becomes verbal and speech intellectual.

(1934a/1987, p. 112)

FIGURE 4.2   Double helix of speech and thinking

Vygotsky traces the changes in word meaning from the first emergence of speech in the form of 'unconscious', 'expressive' speech to 'communicative' speech, calling upon adults for assistance, to 'egocentric' speech in which the child gives itself audible instructions or commentary, with the child taking the place of the adult in commanding their own behavior, to egocentric speech which becomes more and more curtailed and predicative, passing over into 'inner speech' and later – as he notes in the final chapter of *Thinking and Speech* – thinking that goes *beyond* speech with the most developed forms of thinking no longer tied to putting one word after another. The changing form of word meaning allowed Vygotsky to trace the emergence and construction of the verbal intellect and thereby understand its essential nature.

The development of thinking and speech takes the form of a double helix (see Figure 4.2).

I use his model of co-development to represent Vygotsky's understanding of the complex development of all the higher forms of activity acquired by human beings.

By use of a germ cell that is open to observation and tracing its internalization as it is gradually transformed into something private and inaccessible to observation, Vygotsky created an objective scientific basis for cultural psychology. This was an astounding achievement.

Formation of concepts

In his study of the formation of concepts in the fifth and sixth chapters of *Thinking and Speech*, Vygotsky describes experiments using the method of double stimulation by setting children sorting tasks. Children were invited to sort a variety of blocks of different sizes, shapes and colors into groups that were 'the same.' The problem could be solved by looking at nonsense words written on the base of the blocks. The children were only gradually introduced to these clues so that the researchers could observe the children's actions in forming better and better groups, aided by reference to the signs. Vygotsky was able to describe a number of discrete types of concepts, according to the different ways children sorted the blocks. Each of these concepts were identified as a *form of action*, rather than as a logical structure as Hegel might have categorized them; and Vygotsky did not reify them as mental functions or capacities – they were just forms of action. Thus, by using sign-mediated actions as his unit, Vygotsky was able to study the emergence of concepts, the units of the verbal intellect. These concepts, constructed in the laboratory on the basis of features of the objects being sorted, were not yet true concepts, but exhibited the type of concepts which arise among children, who have not yet left the family home and entered the world of adult concerns.

True concepts, acquired through instruction in some real-world institution, and actual concepts, developed through participation in both everyday and professional life, are yet different forms of activity. These Vygotsky investigated through experiments involving speech. Typically, young people would be asked to complete a narrative sentence with "because …" or "although …," researchers observing their efforts to verbalize causal relations with which they were well accustomed, with conscious awareness. The insight from these experiments is that a child, or even a domesticated animal, can learn to respond rationally to a situation, demonstrating an implicit understanding of the relevant causal connections between events. However, the ability to isolate this relation in a form of thought and, with conscious awareness, to use the thought form (concept) as a unit in reasoning is something characteristically human – conceptual thought. True concepts, transmitted through the generations by cultural institutions, professions, and so on, are invariably carried by words which are part of a real language. So a concept is the conscious awareness of a form of activity organized around a word.

By characterizing concepts in this way, as formations of artifact-mediated activity, Vygotsky laid the basis for an interdisciplinary science. Social formations are made up of a variety of forms of activity, each of which is apprehended as a concept, and these concepts together constitute the culture of the given community. And yet Vygotsky has given us a down-to-earth laboratory method for studying how people acquire these concepts.

Note that just as Marx did not take 'value' as some intangible quality but, rather, began with a specific type of social action, exchange, Vygotsky did not take 'concept' to be some intangible mental entity but, rather, a specific type of social action. And this is true of all Vygotsky's units of analysis – they are specific, observable forms of activity.

Note that in the above, we have seen *two* units: word meaning and concept. The 'larger' or molar unit, concept, arises on the basis of the 'smaller' or molecular unit, word meaning. Words only exhibit their full meaning as part of a system of meanings constituted by the concept they evoke, and conversely, concepts exist only in and through the large number of word meanings and other artifact-mediated actions associated with them. Nonetheless, Vygotsky showed that children learn to use words long before they master conceptual thinking, at which point their speech activity is transformed.

This process, whereby a molar unit of activity arises on the basis of the action of a molecular unit, is a common feature of the analysis of processes by units. It is found in Marx's critique of political economy with commodity and then capital, and in activity theory where the molecular unit is an artifact-mediated action and the molar unit is an activity. The method of analysis by units allows the researcher to trace step by step how the more developed unit emerges out of the action of the fundamental units.

Germ cell and unit of analysis

The term Marx used for the concept of 'cell-form' is referred to in cultural-historical activity theory (CHAT) by two different terms: 'unit of analysis,' and 'germ cell.' These are two different expressions for the same concept, but they indicate two different aspects of the same concept.

Germ cell indicates the germ from which more complex forms develop, just as the embryo grows into the mature organism. For example, actual exchange of commodities is rarely seen in modern capitalist society, where everything is bought and sold, not literally traded. But Marx showed how, historically, once a community starts producing for exchange, perhaps on its borders or with passing merchants, it is more or less inevitably drawn into the world market, and with that the need for a universal measure of value. Thus, a universal commodity (C), emerges - gold, paper money, credit and so forth all 'unfold' themselves from the original simple exchange. This first unit, CC, through the mediation of money (M), opens up into CMC in which a person sells in order to buy, but from this mediating element there arises a whole class of people who buy in order to sell at a profit: MCM, and thus arises *capital*, a new unit of value, a new social relation which arises on the basis of the 'logic' of that simple relation, *exchange*. With the emergence of capital – people buying in order to sell at a profit – economic life is reorganized, with production of commodities now subsumed under capital and reoriented towards the accumulation of capital rather than simply the cooperative provision of human needs. The 'germ cell' of capital, MCM, exhibits this course of development in embryo.

Likewise, in psychology, the simple word meaning, when developed in the course of discourse, gives rise to more developed forms of thinking and speech, namely concepts. "Germ cell" emphasizes this aspect of *development*, the relation between the simple undeveloped relation, on the one hand, and on the other hand, the mature, concrete relation.

Vygotsky appropriated the term 'unit of analysis' from social science, in which it meant the 'resolution of the analytical microscope', so to speak, the smallest entity which is taken account of in a given theory. In mainstream social science the unit of analysis is usually taken to be individuals, sometimes groups, classes or even nations. The difference between how Vygotsky uses the term is that for him, the unit of analysis already represents a *concept of the whole*. That is, he merged this analytical concept with Goethe's idea of the *Urphänomen* as a representation of a *Gestalt*.

I will illustrate how the idea of a unit of analysis figured in Marx's work. The young Marx was outraged by the treatment of the poor, by censorship and other social issues, but realized that he knew nothing of the root causes of these phenomena. Thus he turned to a study of political economy. Twenty-five years later, when he wrote *Das Kapital*, 'bourgeois society' was now conceived of as an integral whole, a market place – just millions and millions of commodity exchanges, and nothing else; other phenomena, such as censorship, political corruption, cruelty, now came to be seen as *inessential* and contingent. By taking commodity exchange as the unit, the whole, the *Gestalt* was now redefined and was not coextensive with his original conception of the whole. This is the other aspect to the concept of cell – it means taking the whole process to be nothing other than millions and millions of this one simple relation, a relation which can be grasped viscerally, without the need for abstract theories and forces and so on. The unit of analysis expresses the results of analysis in terms of a relation between the whole and the part; the whole is *nothing but* millions and millions of the same unit of analysis. It is possible to see the water cycle – rain, rivers, ocean, evaporation, clouds and back down again as rain – is one whole process, a *Gestalt*, because all these are nothing but billions and billions of the same unit: H_2O molecules.

So when we gain a certain insight into a complex process, with an *Aha!* moment, that the process is nothing but such and such a simple action or relation, then this is the *starting point* for a truly scientific understanding of the process, an understanding which allows us to understand not just as a process with this or that features, but as a whole, as a *Gestalt*.

Thus the germ cell and the unit of analysis are one and the same thing – be it a commodity exchange or a meaningful word – but in one case the developmental aspect is emphasized and in the other case the analytical aspect is emphasized.

Five applications of the method of analysis by units

'Unit of analysis' is a relative term: analysis of what? A unit of analysis is always used for the analysis of some specific problem or phenomenon. Frequently, writers only ever analyze one phenomenon and devote their lives to that issue. For example, according to Robert Brandom, Kant takes judgment as the unit of experience, Frege takes the smallest expression to which pragmatic force can be attached, and Wittgenstein, the smallest expression whose utterance makes a move in a language game. In line with this analytical tradition, Brandom takes the proposition as his unit of analysis. Hegel uses a different concept for the unit of analysis for each of the books in his *Encyclopedia of the Philosophical Sciences*.

Vygotsky's work covered five different domains of psychological research. He used the unit of sign-mediated actions to analyze a range of distinct psychological functions, such as will, attention, memory, and so on. And he used word meaning to study verbal intelligence and concept formation. In addition to these, Vygotsky found a unit of analysis for three other areas of research.

Perezhivanie is an untranslatable Russian word meaning 'an experience' together with the 'catharsis' entailed in surviving and processing that experience. One and the same event does not have the same significance for every person, so *perezhivaniya* are 'lived experiences' which depend not only on characteristics of the event itself, but also on characteristics of the individual. Vygotsky writes that alongside heredity, it is *perezhivaniya* that forms the personality, and understanding the personality as a process rather than a product, he claims that *perezhivaniya* are units of the personality. *Perezhivaniya* stand out from the general background of experience, have a beginning and an end and, throughout the course of the experience, have a unity and a certain intense emotional color. *Perezhivaniya* have a very definite psychological form. Reflect on your own life, remember those seminal experiences, the daring moves you got away with, the public humiliations you suffered, the reprimands, injustices, or accolades you received – your personality is the aggregate of all these *perezhivaniya*, and analysis of them would give a therapist or psychiatrist insight into your personality. It is these *perezhivaniya* that make up the story you tell yourself of your own life, your identity.

Vygotsky deals only briefly with *perezhivanie* in a lecture called "The problem of the environment"; in this, he defines a *perezhivanie* as a "unity of environmental and personal features" (1934b/1994, p. 343). This expression has been the source of some confusion. A personal feature might be a child's age, and an environmental feature might be the age of school entry; neither of these features in themselves shape the personality of a child, but *taken together*, they self-evidently factor in the forming of the child's personality. Further, *perezhivanie* is often translated as "lived experience," which in contemporary social science is taken to be entirely subjective, whereas *perezhivaniya* have objective as well as subjective sides. *Perezhivanie* does not mean 'experience' – the Russian word for this is *opit* – because *perezhivaniya* are episodes which stand out from the background of experience and include the active contribution of the subject and its aesthetic character.

Vygotsky devoted much of his efforts to working with children affected with a variety of disabilities. In those days, the Soviet government grouped all kinds of disability together under the heading of 'defectology.' But Vygotsky did not see the defect as being on the side of the subject; rather, the defect was in the relation between the subject and the cultural environment, including the failure of the community to provide for the full participation of the subject in social life. For every defect, there is a compensation. That compensation is a combination of measures on the part of the community to facilitate the participation of the subject, and the psychological adjustment made on the part of the subject to overcome the barrier to their participation. Vygotsky took the unit of analysis for defectology as the unity of the defect and the compensation – the 'defect-compensation.' Vygotsky's writings on defectology are in volume 2 of his *Collected Works*. To a great extent, Vygotsky appropriated Alfred Adler's work on the 'inferiority complex.'

In his work on child development, Vygotsky developed the concept of 'social situation of development.' Vygotsky insisted that the social situation is not just a series of factors – age of mother, salary and occupation of father, number of siblings, etc. – it is a *specific situation*. Each of these situations have a definite name in a given culture, such as 'infant' or 'elementary school child', etc. Each of these situations places certain expectations on the child, and their specific needs are met in a corresponding and appropriate way. The child is more or less obliged to fit into this role. In the process of normal development, however, at a certain point the child develops needs and desires which cannot be met within the current social situation and a crisis breaks out in the family group, both the child and its carers. The child may become difficult and rebellious, and if the family and carers respond, the child and the whole situation will undergo a transformation and a new social situation will be established with the child occupying a new social position. Child development is constituted by this specific series of situations, both family and child going through a series of culturally specific transformations in which the child eventually develops into an independent adult. The social situation of development is a unity of the child and its carers in a specific caring relationship.

In each of the areas of psychological research into which Vygotsky delved, his aim was to establish a unit of analysis. He was not always successful; for example, his study of the emotions failed to arrive at a unit of analysis before his death in 1934. But he did discover five units: artifact-mediated actions, meaningful words, *perezhivaniya*, defect-compensations, and social situations of development.

The importance of Vygotsky for social theory

Hegel, Marx, and Vygotsky each made an important development in the methodology invented by Goethe. Hegel replaced the *Urphänomen* with the abstract concept which could be an object of reasoning, rather than merely intuition. Marx insisted that the real subject was social practice rather than thought, and critique could only reconstruct what was given in social practice. Consequently, rather than an abstract concept such as 'value', the germ cell would be a practical action such as commodity exchange. In his critique of psychology, Vygotsky showed that this germ cell had to be a discrete, finite, observable interaction. Whereas Marx left us only one instantiation of this method, because Vygotsky applied the method to the solution of five different problems and provided five different instances of a 'germ cell', he made the idea explicit and the method reproducible.

Vygotsky was a psychologist – in particular, a cultural psychologist – not a social theorist. He approached the cultural formation of the psyche (as mentioned above) by means of a study of the collaborative use of artifacts that originate in the wider culture, in some social situation, also the product of the wider culture. But he did not investigate the processes of formation of the social environment itself. These were problems that were taken up by the Activity Theorists whose work followed on from Vygotsky's. Although the Activity Theorists made important developments, none of them were able to consistently maintain Vygotsky's method of analysis by units.

Nonetheless, through the method of analysis by units and, in particular, through the unit artifact-mediated action, Vygotsky has given social theorists an approach that can fully integrate the sciences of the individual and the social and historical sciences. Rather than psychology on one side and social theory on the other, Vygotsky has given us the opportunity for a genuinely interdisciplinary science. Concepts are equally the unit of a culture and the unit of the intellect, and Vygotsky's research on concepts in *Thinking and Speech* shows us how we can understand concepts not as invisible thought forms, but as forms of activity. Vygotsky's approach is a powerful alternative to the 'ideology critique' which is the usual fare in Marxist social theory. It suggests an approach which can generate new insights into the complex social problems of today.

References

Engels, F. (1876/1987). The part played by labor in the transition from ape to man. In *Marx and Engels collected works: Volume 25* (pp. 452–464). London: Lawrence & Wishart.

Goethe, J. W. v (1795/1988). Outline for a general introduction to comparative anatomy. In *Goethe: The collected works. Volume 12: Scientific Studies*, D. Miller (Trans.). Princeton: Princeton University Press.

Hegel, G. W. F. (1816/1969). *Science of logic*, A. V. Miller (Trans.). London: George Allen & Unwin.

Luria, A. (1928/1994). The problem of the cultural behavior of the child. In R. van der Veer and J. Valsiner (Eds.), *The Vygotsky reader* (pp. 46–56). Oxford: Blackwell.

Marx, K. (1857/1993). *Grundrisse*, M. Nicolaus (Trans.). London: Penguin

Marx, K. (1867/2010). Capital: Volume 1. In *Marx and Engels collected works: Volume 35*. London: Lawrence & Wishart.

Marx, K. (1881/2010). Marginal notes on Adolph Wagner. In *Marx and Engels collected works: Volume 25* (pp. 531–559). London: Lawrence & Wishart.

Naydler, J. (Ed.) (1827/1996). *Goethe on science: An anthology of Goethe's scientific writings*. Edinburgh: Floris Books.

Vygotsky, L. S. (1924/1997). The methods of reflexological and psychological investigation. In *The collected works of L. S. Vygotsky: Volume 3*, R. W. Rieber and J. Wollock (Eds.), R. van der Veer (Trans.), (pp. 35–50). New York: Plenum Press.

Vygotsky, L. S. (1928a/1997). The historical meaning of the crisis in psychology: A methodological investigation. In *The collected works of L. S. Vygotsky: Volume 3*, R. W. Rieber and J. Wollock (Eds.), R. van der Veer (Trans.), (pp. 233–344). New York: Plenum Press.

Vygotsky, L. (1928b/1994). The problem of the cultural development of the child. In R. van der Veer and J. Valsiner (Eds.), *The Vygotsky reader* (pp. 57–72). Oxford: Blackwell.

Vygotsky, L. (1930/1997). The instrumental method in psychology. In *The collected works of L. S. Vygotsky: Volume 3*, R. W. Rieber and J. Wollock (Eds.), R. van der Veer (Trans.), (pp. 85–90). New York: Plenum Press.

Vygotsky, L. (1934a/1987). Thinking and speech. In *The collected works of L. S. Vygotsky: Volume 1*, R. W. Rieber and A. S. Carton (Eds.), N. Minick (Trans.), (pp. 39–288). New York: Plenum Press.

Vygotsky, L. (1934b/1994). The problem of the environment. In R. van der Veer and J. Valsiner (Eds.), *The Vygotsky reader* (pp. 338–354). Oxford: Blackwell.

5

WHAT MAKES VYGOTSKY'S THEORY OF PSYCHOLOGY A *MARXIST* THEORY?

Peter Feigenbaum

In the unpublished essay Vygotsky wrote in the late 1920s entitled "The historical meaning of the crisis in psychology: A methodological investigation" (1997a), he conducted an extensive and intensive analysis of the methods used by the leading schools of psychology. His conclusion was that as a science, psychology is fatally flawed because it is internally divided over the issue of methodology and, hence, basic philosophy. There are essentially *two* psychologies, he asserted: one that uses 'natural scientific' methods based on the philosophy of materialism and one that employs 'spiritualistic' introspective methods based on the philosophy of idealism. He argued compellingly that only the materialist approach is capable of providing a proper foundation for the science of psychology because its methods are objective (although indirect), whereas the subjective methods of the idealist approach are most usefully applied to artistic and aesthetic activities. Essentially, psychology must jettison idealism as a fundamental philosophy, he claimed, if it ever hopes to become a true science (ibid., p. 324).

In that same essay, Vygotsky committed himself to the task of building a *Marxist* science of psychology that not only embraces materialism but also the philosophy of dialectics, which has the potential to describe and explain developmental processes and emergent qualities that psychological theories based on mechanistic principles (such as behaviorism and reflexology) simply cannot. The first step in building a Marxist psychology, he proposed, is to establish a *general theory* of psychology based on the principles of dialectical materialism. Just as Marx and Engels (1848/1976) created a theory of 'historical materialism' by applying the principles and methods of dialectical materialism to the history of society, Marxist psychologists must create a theory of 'psychological materialism' by applying the principles and methods of dialectical materialism to the history of psychology. In addition, building a general theory of psychology crucially depends on establishing appropriate *methods*, he insisted, for it is through methods that theories are brought into direct contact with empirical facts. When Vygotsky wrote that essay, both the general theory of psychology and the corresponding methods to which he referred existed only as historical goals.

By what measures, then, are we to evaluate the Marxist character of the general theory of psychology and the unit of analysis (i.e., the general method) that Vygotsky (1934/1987) put forward several years later, just before his untimely death in 1934? It won't suffice to simply put Marx's theory of the development of political economy (Marx and Engels, 1848/1976) side by side with Vygotsky's theory of the development of verbal thinking and compare their contents; the essence of Marxism lies not in the particular content area studied but in the application of the philosophy of dialectical materialism to that content area. On the other hand, despite the considerable concrete differences between political economy and verbal thinking, both phenomena share the distinction of being a culturally universal human social activity characterized by interpersonal transactions that involve human-made objects of exchange. So there may be a benefit to comparing the two theories on *formal* grounds. Ultimately, to assess Vygotsky's theory from the perspective of how well dialectical materialism was used in its construction, I believe the best evidence to look for would be: the choice of subject matter (i.e., the focus and unit of analysis); the consistency with which the dialectical method of analysis and synthesis is applied to the established facts; and the consistency between the theory and the methods.

My aim in this chapter is to assess the Marxist character of Vygotsky's (1934/1987) theory of the development of verbal thinking in childhood. Care must be exercised so as to avoid falling into the same trap as some of Vygotsky's critics, whom he chastised for overgeneralizing Marxist concepts (Vygotsky, 1997a). He warned that a theory of psychological materialism can only be created by Marxist psychologists working down in the trenches; nothing useful is accomplished by outsiders to the science who cleverly string together quotations from Marx focused at a high level of generalization and then apply those generalities to psychology. Therefore, because Vygotsky's theory must first be described and explained before it can be assessed, I play the role of tour guide. My qualifications consist mainly in being a Marxist who later also became a developmental psychologist – and a follower of Vygotsky. Of course, even though I point to objective evidence, my choice of facts necessarily reflects my own individual understanding of Marxism and Vygotskian psychology.

One last digression: regardless of whether Vygotsky succeeded in his mission, rest assured that it was his *intention* to build a science of psychology consistent with Marx's theory and modeled on Marx's method. Vygotsky self-identified as a Marxist and expressed in numerous passages his commitment to its principles and to its veracity. For example, he was dedicated to the truth: "Our science will become Marxist to the degree that it becomes truthful and scientific" (ibid., p. 341). He also believed in the validity of the theory of historical materialism:

> We are dialecticians. We do not at all think that the developmental path of science follows a straight line, and if it has had zigzags, returns, and loops we

> understand their historical significance and consider them to be necessary links in our chain, inevitable stages of our path, just as capitalism is an inevitable stage on the road toward socialism.
>
> *(Ibid., p. 336)*

Moreover, he discerned what was essential to Marx's method. Regarding the creation of a general theory, Vygotsky noted:

> In order to create such intermediate theories – methodologies, general sciences – we must reveal the *essence* of the given area of phenomena, the laws of their change, their qualitative and quantitative characteristics, their causality, we must create categories and concepts appropriate to it, in short, we must create our *own Das Kapital.*
>
> *(Ibid., p. 330)*

In terms of establishing a central focus for his new science, Vygotsky closely followed Marx's approach:

> The whole of *Das Kapital* is written according to this method. Marx analyses the "cell" of bourgeois society – the form of the commodity value – and shows that a mature body can be more easily studied than a cell. He discerns the structure of the whole social order and all economical formations in this cell.
>
> *(Ibid., p. 320)*

Seizing on this crucial concept, Vygotsky then set an analogous goal for the new science of psychology: "He who can decipher the meaning of the cell of psychology, *the mechanism of one reaction*, has found the key to all psychology" (ibid., p. 320, emphasis added).

Overview

Vygotsky's (1934/1987) theory of child development, which is encapsulated in his final book *Thinking and Speech* but supplemented by many other writings and lectures, is as broad and sweeping as it is deep and penetrating. It is based on a complex analysis of history; it embraces the biological and sociocultural sources of individual psychological development; it ties conceptual development to the development of spoken language (interpersonal speech); it maps out biological stages and interleaved periods of sociocultural engagement and development; it places the *subjective meaning* of words at the center of investigation; it recognizes the phenomenon of talking to oneself (personal speech) as the key to the development of the 'higher mental functions'; and it even delves into developmental details, positing very specific claims about particular linguistic changes that occur in 'private' speech (the vocalized form of personal speech) during its structural transformation into 'inner' speech (the silent, subvocalized form of personal speech).

I have organized our tour of Vygotsky's theory into five topic areas. The first is Vygotsky's analysis of history, which distinguishes between the anthropological, social, and personal lines of history. The biological and sociocultural sources of individual psychological development are presented next. From the vantage point of this second topic – the unity and conflict of 'thinking' and 'speaking' – the full sweep of the theory is first revealed. I describe how the tension between thinking and speaking plays out across a sequence of distinct biological stages and distinct developmental periods. 'Word meaning,' Vygotsky's methodological unit of analysis for researching the development of speaking and thinking, is the third topical focus. I describe how this unit of analysis applies to verbal thinking at different periods in development and at different scales of analysis. Personal speech, the fourth area, is the process whereby verbal thinking becomes personalized. The phenomenon of 'private' speech (talking aloud to oneself as opposed to another person) represents the first step in a child's 'internalization' or personalization of speech communication. Private speech is a transitional stage in which verbal thinking is *functionally* internalized. The fifth and final stop on our tour is a review of the specific claims that Vygotsky put forward in reference to the *structural* internalization of personal speech – that is, its physical transformation into subvocalized or silent 'inner' speech. Inner speech conversation typically takes the form of a narration inside our heads, and it is the psychological activity that underlies the development of self-control and the higher mental functions. I conclude by noting the formal resemblances between the developmental process and the sequence of periods that Marx outlined for political economy (see Marx and Engels, 1848/1976) and that Vygotsky described for verbal thinking.

Vygotsky's analysis of history

According to Sylvia Scribner (1997), Vygotsky used history as a means to envision human psychological development from multiple perspectives. For one thing, he distinguished between phylogeny (biological evolution based on natural selection) and general history (human history). General history includes the anthropological origins of humans (starting several million years ago with the dawn of hominids) as well as recent human history (starting approximately 10,000 years ago with the dawn of civilization). Vygotsky based his sociohistorical analysis of psychological development partly on Engels' (1927/1940) account of the anthropological origins of humans and partly on Marx and Engels' (1848/1976) theory of the development of political economy and class-divided society. Vygotsky considered modern human psychological processes, such as voluntary attention and logical reasoning, to be discontinuous with the elementary, biologically evolved psychological processes possessed by most animals. The higher mental functions in humans cannot be explained by natural laws alone, he insisted. Instead, their roots are to be found in the specifically human *labor* activities that follow the laws and regularities of the development of human culture.

Engels (1927/1940) asserted that as our hominid ancestors became increasingly dependent for their survival on the manufacture and use of stone tools, they inadvertently began a process of selective breeding that favored offspring with hands better adapted to working with stone tools. Thus, stone tool technology – a cultural development – is seen as a major cause of the physical transformation of apes into humans. According to Scribner (1997), Vygotsky embraced the Marxist view of human origins in which natural selection gradually gave way to man-made selection; he concurred that human beings began to create the conditions for their own development. Marx's theory (Marx and Engels, 1848/1976) describes the continued development of these man-made conditions during the past 10,000 years of social history. This period is marked by the division of society into antagonistic social classes. Vygotsky's (1934/1987) understanding of the role of culture in the development of human psychology led him to propose that, under the conditions of class struggle, the same psychological processes would develop *differently* depending on one's social class.

A second level of historical analysis employed by Vygotsky pertains to the life history of the individual in society (Scribner, 1997). In contrast to General history, in which biological development is eventually displaced by cultural development, in the history of an individual, both systems of development co-occur and are fused. Children grow and develop biologically at the same time as they acquire uniquely cultural tools – most importantly, speech communication. The rules for exchanging speech utterances are learned through conversational interaction with verbally competent adults or older children. Transforming a child's biologically inherited system of psychological functioning into a cultural system of psychological functioning requires that adults take a leading role – a fact amply documented by Vygotsky's disciples (Karpov, 2005). That the end product of the child development process – i.e., a competent adult speaker and thinker – is a necessary ingredient in the learning situation of every young child makes the ontogenetic level of analysis stand in sharp contrast to the phylogenetic level. More important still is the fact that the cultural line of development appears *twice* in the history of every individual: first in the form of *social* experience and then in the form of *personal* experience. Vygotsky (1934/1987) placed great emphasis on the transformation of interpsychological functioning into intrapsychological functioning, elevating it to the status of a psychological law.

A third use of history that Vygotsky applied in his theory-building concerns the ways in which the development of particular psychological systems differs when compared across timelines (Scribner, 1997). For example, he hypothesized about differences in the process of memory development in different historical contexts: within the history of an individual in society, within the history of human societies, and within the evolution of the human species. Vygotsky believed it is fruitful to compare particular psychological functions in people who differ by age (such as child and adult), society (peasant and industrialized), and historical epoch (primitive and modern). Although politically controversial, he also believed it is informative to study the psychological differences between educated and uneducated populations (Luria, 1976).

To recap, Vygotsky provided an approach to theory-building that is capable of integrating and coordinating all levels of history into one overarching explanatory account of the biological-sociological formation of the human mind. One may be tempted – and rightly so – to consider this grand design as deserving of the name 'Vygotsky's theory.' Nonetheless, the scope of this chapter is limited to his ontogenetic theory in particular, to the theory of the development of verbal thinking in individual children. At the very least, this brief exposure to Vygotsky's comprehensive view of history establishes some context for understanding and appreciating his ontogenetic theory.

Before leaving this topic, I want to note the Marxist character of Vygotsky's analysis of history. By placing such emphasis and importance on the role of history in building a general theory of psychological development, Vygotsky maximally exploited the potential of the philosophy of materialism to furnish concrete evidence. Material objects (including people) interact and develop over time and bear concrete traces of their history within them – traces that constitute empirical evidence. Consequently, by using all of history (inorganic, organic, evolutionary, human, sociocultural, and individual) as a material foundation for building a general theory of psychology, Vygotsky vastly enlarged the scope of empirical evidence available for testing such a theory.

Thinking and speaking

A major postulate of Vygotsky's (1934/1987) theory is that the biologically inherited system of thinking and the culturally inherited system of speaking, which are initially separate systems in the life of a newborn, unite during infancy to form a new psychological activity: 'verbal thinking.' How does this unity come about? It occurs when an infant weds the two functions together by *intentionally uttering his or her first words to an adult as part of a mutually meaningful conversational exchange*. Over time, a child's naïve verbal thinking undergoes a developmental transformation because the systems of thinking and speaking are on different developmental trajectories: thinking is initially holistic and tends toward articulation, whereas speaking is initially fragmented and tends toward elaboration. Vygotsky wrote, "Though they form a unity, the inner, meaningful, semantic aspect of speech is associated with different laws of movement than its external, auditory aspect" (ibid., p. 250). More specifically:

> the development of the semantic and external aspects of speech move in opposite directions. The semantic aspect of speech develops from the whole to the part or from the sentence to the word. The external aspect of speech moves from the part to the whole or from the word to the sentence.
>
> *(Ibid., p. 250)*

This antagonism, which makes their unity tricky to manage, is the motor that propels the development of verbal thinking. In dialectical terminology, this phenomenon is a typical example of the 'unity and conflict of opposites.'

Given the practical and societal importance of verbal thinking – specifically, how it enables adults to communicate and organize thoughts and activities via speech – developing children face a formidable challenge. They must learn to navigate the antagonistic movements of the underlying systems in order to become fluent in their native tongue and participate competently in this crucial communal activity. To master adult speech communication, a child has to not only acquire the word-sequencing rules for producing and comprehending complex linguistic structures, but also grasp the meaning-making rules for appropriately deploying and recognizing these same linguistic structures in conversation. Developmentally, each linguistic structure that a child acquires sets in motion a cognitive reorganization aimed at understanding how that new structure is meaningfully used in communication. The recursive cycles of acquisition and understanding play out over time, leading to a series of increasingly more developed forms of verbal thinking between infancy and adolescence – at which point most children achieve verbal fluency.

Based on several crucial discussions in chapters 5, 6, and 7 of *Thinking and Speech* (Vygotsky, 1934/1987), the development of verbal thinking can be understood as consisting mainly of four distinct developmental periods. With regard to the speech system, four separate but related *linguistic* structures are acquired in the following chronological order: words, phrases, sentences, and (for lack of a better term) narratives. Each new structure builds on the previous ones, which are nested within it. Together they form a hierarchy or upside-down tree structure, with the narrative being the most developed of the four linguistic structures and occupying the highest node of the hierarchy. With regard to the thinking system, four separate but related *semantic* structures ('structures of generalization') develop in the following chronological order: 'syncretic heaps,' 'complexes,' 'pre-concepts,' and 'concepts.' Each of these structures also builds on and incorporates the previously developed ones. Now comes the most interesting part: when thinking and speaking converge in infancy to form the system of verbal thinking, a correspondence *in time* is thus established between the two subsystems such that: acquisition of the first words becomes bound up with syncretic thinking; months later, infants acquire phrase structures which become the means for engaging in complexive thinking; still later, children acquire sentence grammar, supplying a propositional basis for preconceptual thinking; and finally, at about age 7, most children acquire narrative structures, providing a discursive foundation for the mastery of generalization and conceptual thinking.

The timing of these developmental periods has been pinned down rather precisely by Toomela (2003). In terms of biological development, he reported that Vygotsky identified six distinct critical stages in the maturation of the central nervous system of an individual: the first is at birth, and the others occur in the first, third, seventh, thirteenth, and seventeenth years. Citing recent studies on genetic variability, brain growth, and electrophysiological maturation, together with behavioral-developmental data, Toomela confirmed the timing of these biological stages and added two more to the list, one at 6 months and the other at 18 months. Between each of these stages, relatively stable periods occur between growth spurts, in which the appropriate conditions exist for adult–child social interactions of increasing complexity and for a developing child to internalize these social interactions and transform them into personal experience and understanding. To sum up, the four developmental periods that give rise to four qualitatively distinct formations in the development of verbal thinking occur at: 12–18 months (first words/syncretic thinking); 18 months to 3 years (phrases/complexive thinking); 3 to 7 years (sentences/preconceptual thinking); and 7 to 12 years (narratives/conceptual thinking).

Resemblances can be seen between Marx's theory (Marx and Engels, 1848/1976) of the development of political economy and Vygotsky's (1934/1987) theory of the development of verbal thinking. For one thing, both theories are predicated on the notion that the phenomena under investigation consist of two initially separate and antagonistic systems that merge into one, forging an uneasy unity in which each subsystem causes the other to develop. For Marx, the two systems that are united in conflict are politics and economics; for Vygotsky, they are thinking and speaking. A second resemblance between the two theories is the notion that the respective phenomena develop through a series of distinct periods, each characterized by a distinct developmental form possessing increasingly more complex qualities than the previous forms. This comparison is pursued more fully once the phenomenon of personal speech and its special role in development have been properly introduced.

Word meaning

'Word meaning' is Vygotsky's (1934/1987) unit of analysis – and general method – for studying the development of verbal thinking in childhood. 'Word' refers to the outward, objective, cultural, linguistic side of the activity of verbal thinking, while 'meaning' refers to the inward, subjective, personal, semantic side. The essence of the phenomenon of verbal thinking is not in its subsystems, however, but in their unity – in the special qualities that emerge when thinking and speaking behave in a complementary, symbiotic fashion and function as one activity. Their unity is what makes word meaning an irreducible unit.

In creating his Marxist theory of psychology, Vygotsky's (1997a) aim was to follow Marx's method of seeking out the 'cell' of psychology that would reveal the structure of the whole system of verbal thinking. He chose word meaning as that cell but left no explicit instructions as to where and how to apply this unit of analysis to data. Furthermore, word meaning can be applied to the process of verbal thinking from numerous perspectives, such as the phylogenetic, ontogenetic, and microgenetic scales of analysis. For example, one can study the development of the meaning of a particular word in terms of the history of a language, or from the point of view of the personal history of an individual, or in the context of a short-term learning situation. In a very real sense, word meaning is like a fractal because it exists at multiple levels of organization and can even be nested within itself. It applies equally well to all manifestations of the process of verbal thinking, from its most particular to its most general expression. Therefore, if word meaning is to be usefully applied to the scientific study of verbal thinking at each stage in a child's development, it must be both a conceptually coherent and yet practically flexible unit.

To envision what Vygotsky was attempting to accomplish by the use of word meaning, it is helpful to take a step back and consider his theory more broadly. In addition to conceiving of every individual person as a 'microcosm' of the society (or more precisely, the social class) in which he or she was born and raised, Vygotsky also conceived of *speech communication* as a social microcosm – as the crucial social process wherein adults induct children into the cultural world of verbal thinking. The emphasis here is less on speech as an *object* and more on communication as a *process*. Vygotsky (1934/1987) theorized that in order for individuals to successfully relate to one another in the objective social process of speech communication, they must necessarily subordinate their individual, subjective viewpoints to an intermediary sign or word, whose socially determined meaning is a *generalization* that can be shared. Thus, social communication (speaking) and conceptual generalization (thinking) are simply two sides of the same coin. 'Social interaction,' 'communication,' and 'verbalization' are the three qualities of verbal thinking that Vygotsky (ibid., p. 49) regarded as essential to any analysis of word meaning.

Consider the process of conversation between two individuals (designated A and B) as analogous to throwing and catching a ball: A initiates a conversational exchange by uttering speech (the throw), which B listens to and comprehends (the catch); then B responds to the comprehended utterance by producing a second utterance (the return throw), which A listens to and comprehends (the return catch). This simple reciprocal exchange, which is the essence of discourse (Stubbs, 1983), can be symbolically represented as $A > B > B > A$. One can look at this process from two radically different perspectives, however. One perspective focuses on the *interpersonal* activity (throwing and catching), or the movement from $A > B$ or from $B > A$, in which an individual utterance serves as a mediator or vehicle for conveying a thought from one person to another. From a contrasting perspective, however – namely, the linguistic and conceptual connection between two utterances in a conversation – it is the *intrapersonal* activity of $B > B$ (catching and throwing) that serves as the mediator or glue. Simply put, it is a *person* that links one utterance to another utterance in a conversation (or text). For Vygotsky, it is *the developing child* that occupies the central focus of analysis, thereby locating the development of word meaning squarely in the center of the $A > B > B > A$ communicative interchange. The child's developmental task is to internalize and personalize this logical formula by learning how every single utterance *responds* to a previous utterance and, simultaneously, *initiates* the next one in the chain. The fact that the interpersonal process of verbal thinking could also be an incubator for a child's personal development of verbal thinking suggests that Vygotsky came close indeed to pinning down the elusive 'cell' of psychology that he was seeking – 'the mechanism of one reaction.'

Bakhtin (1986) proposed the persuasive idea of parsing dialog or conversation into 'utterance' units, or speaking turns. The boundaries between one utterance and another are easy to distinguish because each utterance is produced by a different speaker. Because an utterance is defined not by its contents but by its boundaries with surrounding utterances in the conversation, its length and linguistic structure are free to vary widely. By Bakhtin's definition, an utterance can be as small as a single word or as long and involved as a formal lecture. Thus, while an utterance is a rigidly fixed linguistic unit from the perspective of dialog, its internal linguistic structure is extremely elastic. Consequently, Bakhtin's 'utterance' has the potential to provide the constancy and flexibility that Vygotsky sought from word meaning as his unit of analysis.

Finally, intimately and inseparably related to word meaning is the phenomenon of 'sense,' which is essentially the *communicative context of use* that speakers and listeners must jointly reference in order to interpret particular word meanings. Every speech communication consists of two tiers, with the *literal* meaning of a speech utterance constituting the first tier and the *context of use* constituting the second, which serves to qualify the meaning of the first tier (such as when a statement is delivered sarcastically to invoke the opposite of its literal meaning). Vygotsky (1934/1987) provided only a few examples of sense, and at present there is no agreed metric for identifying sense that researchers can use to evaluate the development of word meaning. But because word meaning is always contextualized and situated, it is as important to track sense as it is to track word meaning.

In summary, word meaning is as much a unit of thinking as it is a unit of speaking. Because Vygotsky died before elaborating and articulating his theory in sufficient detail to establish clearer linkages to concrete data (a task he bequeathed to the rest of us), there is currently no consensus about how to apply word meaning or sense to children's speech in such a way as to support programmatic empirical research.

Personal speech

In order to have a complete picture of Vygotsky's (1934/1987) theory, there is one more aspect that you need to understand: the differentiation of personal speech from interpersonal speech. Whereas other psychologists envisioned the development of children's thinking as proceeding from egocentric to socialized (e.g., Piaget, 1923/1955), Vygotsky postulated that thinking develops from socialized to personalized. Of all the cultural competencies that children master interpersonally and then internalize or personalize, none is more essential than communicative competence with speech. Internalizing interpersonal speech, however, also entails internalizing an ensemble of communicative *perspectives*. A struggle necessarily ensues to differentiate one's personal point of view – one's 'I' – from that of one's (internalized) community (Vygotsky, 1997b). You might say that it takes a collective to form a mind, but it takes an individual to personalize it. The main venue for conducting this psychological struggle, of course, is in conversations with oneself. And so, in addition to the four developmental periods (outlined earlier) two more can be overlaid upon them: a transitional period of 'private' speech (18 months to 7 years) and a mature period of 'inner' speech (7 to 12 years).

Personal speech is an appropriation: children commandeer the conversational routines that they learn from their experiences talking to others and redeploy them for personal thinking. In a nutshell, children start talking out loud to themselves in situations that require them to think. Private speech is the first stage in the personalization of speech communication; it is a transitional stage sandwiched developmentally between interpersonal speech and silent inner speech. Structurally, private speech is identical to interpersonal speech insofar as both are vocalized and audible to a listener, but functionally, it is identical to inner speech insofar as both serve as an instrument of personal mental activity. This contradiction between form and function is the feature of private speech that makes it unstable and transitory. Because its purpose is for thinking and not speaking, private speech is not conversationally adapted for use by others as is interpersonal speech. Instead, private speech is a personal response to a private thought and therefore contains no shared topic of conversation – it is pure commentary, or predication. Consequently, as speech, it is incomprehensible to others (Piaget, 1923/1955).

In the preschool period, private speech tends to lag behind a child's actions, serving as an echo or *reflection* of activity. During the school years, however, as a child develops some mastery in the use of speech, private speech begins to serve a higher function – as a force for *directing* activity. In addition to serving the functions of word play, fantasy play, and describing one's own activity, private speech gradually assumes a *planning* function in which solutions to problems are worked out verbally in advance of physical action. The shifting of private speech from *after* one's activity to *before* it marks the start of a new psychological system: the development of the 'higher mental functions.' Because verbal thinking is the driving force in human psychological development, the personalization of verbal thinking brings all the other mental functions with it. The gradual internalization of memory, cognition, volitional control, affect, and other psychological functions begins with private speech. An entirely new psychological system based on verbal discourse, logical reasoning, and volitional attention is brought into existence when a child develops private speech and begins to use it as an instrument to take perspectives and to objectively comprehend his or her subjective experience of objects, events, and social relations.

The structural transformation of private speech into inner speech

The final stop on our tour concerns the *structural* internalization of personal speech – that is, the physical transformation of private speech into silent inner speech. Inner speech is *sub*vocalized, which means it is audible only to the speaker. In inner speech, one *thinks* words rather than speaks them. Unlike interpersonal speech, which is fully expanded in form, inner speech is highly abbreviated, containing only those key words essential to a particular communication. Vygotsky (1934/1987) recognized that the abbreviated linguistic structure of inner speech is the result of a developmental process that begins with private speech – hence, private speech development is a window into the structure of inner speech. He was the first and only psychologist to propose a direct developmental connection between private speech and inner speech; he alone recognized that humans are not born with inner speech but, instead, develop it during childhood. That is why he referred to the disappearance of private speech (at about age 7) as a sign of its movement 'underground.'

This is one of the few areas in which Vygotsky put forward some rather specific empirical claims. For example, he hypothesized that the abbreviation of private speech follows a special logic such that words associated with the semantic topic (or subject) of conversation cease to be vocalized, leaving only those words related to the semantic comment (or predicate) (ibid., p. 267). He also claimed that the number of words uttered in the private speech mode reduces with age. Recent research in the West supports these and other Vygotskian hypotheses about private speech development (see Winsler *et al.*, 2009, for a review). Unfortunately, not all of Vygotsky's claims about private speech have been put to the test yet because empirical work using word meaning as a metric is lacking.

What value does the development of personal speech add to verbal thinking? The answer is that it provides a crucial learning opportunity not available in the interpersonal mode of speech. With regard to any single utterance of interpersonal speech, a child is always restricted to playing *either* a listening role *or* a speaking role – such as asking a question *or* answering one – but never both roles. To develop a complete understanding of discourse, however, a child needs to experience asking *and* answering the same question because that activity encompasses the reciprocal movement between conversational initiation and conversational response. A child must actively engage in the entire $A > B > B > A$ interaction in order to experience the complete logic of dialog.

To conclude this topic, after personal speech splits off from interpersonal speech, and after it transforms from private speech into inner speech, personal speech is reunited with interpersonal speech. This reunion occurs because inner speech has a crucial role to play in the conduct of everyday conversation: utterances must be adapted to specific circumstances and people, and the interpretation of others' utterances requires thinking and reflection – cognitive functions for which inner speech is well designed. Subjectively, inner speech conversation is typically experienced as an ongoing voice, a narration that insinuates itself into our personal thinking, imbuing it with analysis, reflection, commentary, affect, valuation, and even self-awareness. Inner speech is the culmination – the ultimate form – of the internalization of verbal thinking. With inner speech, new psychological potential is unleashed.

Summary and conclusion

This whirlwind tour of Vygotsky's (1934/1987) theory covered most of the highlights, but regrettably I was forced to pass over some rather important topics that delve even deeper. For those whose appetite for Vygotsky's theory has now been whet, I refer you to the work of Holbrook Mahn (2012), who has assembled a rather comprehensive conceptual model.

All that remains now is to complete the assessment of the dialectical-materialist character of Vygotsky's (1934/1987) theory. To that end, I believe that a comparison of the *formal* features of his theory with those of Marx's theory (Marx and Engels, 1848/1976) is informative.

First, both theories posit a series of developmental periods in which the phenomena under investigation take ever more complex forms as a result of the underlying conflict of opposites. Common to both theories is an initial and brief 'primitive' phase in which the respective systems of political economy and verbal thinking are first established. For Marx, this is the period of 'primitive' communism; for Vygotsky, it is the period of 'naïve' interpersonal speech (words/syncretic thinking). Then, a major division begins between the social and private paths of development. For Marx, a society splits into antagonistic social classes characterized by the 'rulers' and the 'ruled' in which wealth is privatized and accumulates in the hands of the rulers; for Vygotsky, a child's verbal thinking splits into antagonistic speech modes characterized by personal and interpersonal speech in which understanding is personalized and accumulates in the child's developing mind. In Marx's theory, this division takes the increasingly more developed forms of slavery, feudalism, and capitalism, with capitalism representing the highest stage in the development of the value form of the commodity (i.e., money). In Vygotsky's theory, the division takes the successive forms of complexive thinking in phrases, preconceptual thinking in sentences, and conceptual thinking in narratives, with conceptual thinking representing the highest stage in the development of verbal thinking (i.e., inner speech). Finally, both theories exhibit a phase in which the private and social strands of development are reunited, resulting in qualities not present in earlier periods. For Marx, this is the period of socialism and advanced communism, in which class division has been eliminated and the benefits of political and economic development are enjoyed by all. For Vygotsky, this is the period in which the personal and interpersonal modes of speech interact symbiotically, enabling the young adult to communicate competently with other adults in the community.

Marx's (1847/1976, 1867/1967) special analysis of the capitalist stage – particularly, the analysis of 'use value' and 'exchange value' – also has striking parallels in Vygotsky's (1934/1987) theory. For Marx, analysis of the use value and exchange value of commodities in commercial transactions reveals the nature of economic value; for Vygotsky, analysis of the sign properties (use value) and symbolic properties (exchange value) of speech utterances in communicative transactions exposes the nature of semiotic value, or subjective meaning. For Marx, a buyer confronts every commodity as a use value that satisfies some practical consumer need, while a seller confronts every commodity as an exchange value that can be traded; for Vygotsky, a listener confronts every utterance as a use value that conveys a conversational topic (initiation), while a speaker confronts every utterance as an exchange value that conveys a conversational comment (response). For Marx, the form of commodity value develops historically, from human beings (in slavery) to land (in feudalism) and finally to money (in capitalism); for Vygotsky, the form of semiotic value – word meaning – also develops, from complexive thinking (in phrases) to preconceptual thinking (in sentences) and finally to conceptual thinking (in inner speech narratives).

Finally, note the parallels between the two theories with regard to the most highly developed form of value, which for Marx (1867/1967) was money and for Vygotsky (1934/1987) was inner speech. Both theorists proposed a gradual conversion of use value into exchange value: Marx represented the conversion of commodities into money with the formula $CMC > MCM$, in which money shifts from playing a minor role as a means of exchange to playing the dominant role as the goal of exchange; Vygotsky discussed a similar conversion in verbal thinking in which meaning gradually shifts from playing a minor role as a means of exchange to playing the dominant role as the goal of exchange. This conversion could be represented as $WMW > MWM$. In both theories, development proceeds from the particular to the general: money and word meaning both mature into generalized expressions of value in their respective spheres of circulation.

In conclusion, there are sufficient formal parallels between the theories of Marx and Vygotsky to suggest that very similar philosophical approaches were used in their construction. In terms of the choice of subject matter, both theories regard cooperative social activity, particularly turn-taking and exchange, as the basis for human development. Both theories posit human-made objects as the materials being exchanged: commodities for Marx and word meanings for Vygotsky. With regard to methods, both theories employ dialectical analysis and synthesis to explain their respective phenomena, leading to close formal similarities in their respective descriptions of internal dynamics and developmental periods. The consistency with which Vygotsky (1934/1987) applied the dialectical method to child development is visible in his analysis of history and in his deft treatment of the many antagonistic processes comprising the process of child development, such as thinking and speaking, word and meaning, social and personal, and inner and outer. As for the consistency displayed between Vygotsky's theory and his methods, no glaring contradictions surfaced on our tour, although a more thorough examination is warranted.

I hope this chapter provides at least a preliminary answer to the question posed by the title. Beyond the issue of Marxist pedigree, however, I believe the more important questions we should be asking about Vygotsky's theory are: How well does it fit the established facts of child development?; Does it accurately predict facts yet to be discovered?

References

Bakhtin, M. M. (1986). *Speech genres and other late essays.* V. W. McGee (Trans.). Austin, TX: University of Texas Press.

Engels, F. (1940). The part played by labour in the transition from ape to man. In C. Dutt (Ed. and Trans.), *Dialectics of nature* (pp. 279–296). New York: International Publishers. (Original work published 1927).

Karpov, Y. V. (2005). *The neo-Vygotskian approach to child development.* Cambridge: Cambridge University Press.

Luria, A. R. (1976). *Cognitive development: Its cultural and social foundations.* M. Cole (Ed.), M. Lopez-Morillas, and L. Soltaroff (Trans.). Cambridge, MA: Harvard University Press.

Mahn, H. (2012). Vygotsky's analysis of children's meaning making processes. *International Journal of Educational Psychology, 1*(2), 100–126.

Marx, K. (1967). *Capital: A critique of political economy. Volume 1: The process of capitalist production.* F. Engels (Ed.), S. Moore and E. Aveling (Trans.). New York: International Publishers. (Original work published 1867).

Marx, K. (1976). The poverty of philosophy: Answer to the *Philosophy of Poverty* by M. Proudhon. In *Karl Marx Frederick Engels collected works: Volume 6.* F. Knight (Trans.), (pp. 105–212). New York: International Publishers. (Original work published 1847).

Marx, K., and Engels, F. (1976). Manifesto of the communist party. In *Karl Marx Frederick Engels collected works: Volume 6* (pp. 477–519). New York: International Publishers. (Original work published 1848).

Piaget, J. (1955). *The language and thought of the child*, M. Gabain (Trans.). New York: Meridian. (Original work published 1923).

Scribner, S. (1997). Vygotsky's uses of history. In E. Tobach, R. J. Falmagne, M. B. Parlee, L. M. W. Martin, and A. S. Kapelman (Eds.), *Mind and social practice* (pp. 241–265). Cambridge: Cambridge University Press.

Stubbs, M. (1983). *Discourse analysis: The sociolinguistic analysis of natural language.* Chicago: The University of Chicago Press.

Toomela, A. (2003). Development of symbol meaning and the emergence of the semiotically mediated mind. In A. Toomela (Ed.), *Cultural guidance in the development of the human mind* (pp. 163–210). Westport, CT: Ablex Publishing.

Vygotsky, L. S. (1987). Thinking and speech. In *The collected works of L. S. Vygotsky: Volume 1. Problems of general psychology.* R. W. Rieber and A. S. Carton (Eds.), N. Minick (Trans.), (pp. 375–383). New York: Plenum Press. (Original work published 1934).

Vygotsky, L. S. (1997a). The historical meaning of the crisis in psychology: A methodological investigation. In *The collected works of L. S. Vygotsky. Volume 3: Problems of the theory and history of psychology*, R. W. Rieber and J. Wollock (Eds.), R. van der Veer (Trans.), (pp. 233–344). New York: Plenum Press. (Original work unpublished).

Vygotsky, L. S. (1997b). Conclusion; Further research; Development of personality and world view in the child. In *The collected works of L. S. Vygotsky. Volume 4: The history of the development of higher mental functions*, R. W. Rieber (Ed.), M. J. Hall (Trans.), (pp. 241–252). New York: Plenum Press. (Original work unpublished).

Winsler, A., Fernyhough, C., and Montero, I. (Eds.) (2009). *Private speech, executive functioning, and the development of verbal self-regulation.* New York: Cambridge University Press.

6

IMAGINATION AND CREATIVE ACTIVITY

Ontological and epistemological principles of Vygotsky's contributions

Kátia Maheirie and Andréa Vieira Zanella

Lev. S. Vygotsky's writings have been read and discussed over the past years by researchers in different areas and in relation to several theoretical references (Kozulin, 1990; Ratner, 1991; Veresov, 1999; Pino, 2000; Rogoff, 2003; van der Veer, 2007; Valsiner, 2007; and others). His contributions to psychology, education, and art are sustained in ontological, anthropologic, and epistemological discussions, broadening the spectrum of researchers that find in his writings the foundations for problematization of contemporary issues.

The various ways his writings are appropriate and the profusion of perspectives that are founded in his contributions, which sometimes can be contradictory, from our understanding, are testimony to the relevance of his ideas. He is an author who, on the one hand, shows the marks of his time – evidenced, for instance, in his own lexicon of the advances in pre-revolutionary Russian physiology that characterizes some of his texts – and on the other hand, transcends the thresholds of that historical moment and the advances in science until then. How he created his ideas can be the key for the comprehension of this actuality: while Vygotsky conversed with interlocutors of various epistemological orientations, a creative reading enabled him to host or refute, partially or integrally, different contributions. It is necessary to comprehend that this dialogue, attentive to the fruitful aspects in the thinking of each author with whom he debated, was possible because it sustained a specific ontological and epistemological matrix assumed by Vygotsky: the historical materialism and the dialectical, open, and nonessential conception of the world.

Vygotsky takes on Marx's thinking and shows evidence of this in his writings, though not via the use of direct quotations. In "The historical meaning of the crisis in psychology" (Vygotsky, 1991), concluded by the author in 1926, Vygotsky's analysis, according to van der Veer and Valsiner (1991), of what had been accomplished in terms of construction of a new psychology founded in historical materialism and dialectical principles is critical of his antecessors for their mechanistic appropriation of Marx's writing, as evidenced in their persistent use of quotations. His work is characterized, as a consequence, by the inventive way he appropriates and presents the understanding of subject and world as reciprocally constitutive, posing a challenge to those who approach Marx's writing obliquely rather than directly.

An example of the inventive connection Vygotsky establishes with Marx's writings is found in his paraphrasing, "The psychological nature of the person is the sum of social relations" (Vygotsky, 2000, p. 27). In reading his many writings, we can comprehend that this is about a set of configurations in each person that are always diverse, with different intonations, creatively formed, which grants the condition of being at the same time a singular and collective person, subject to the period and conditions the person lives in and, concomitantly, its artifice. The social context, in turn, is a human production; it is history that brings the marks of other times and always updates itself in a constant reinvention process, even though this might be tense and complex.

Our interest in this creative dimension of human existence led us to develop studies of the dialogue of social psychology with art (Zanella and Maheirie, 2010; Zanella, 2013a, 2013b; Zanella and Wedekin, 2015; Maheirie, 2003, 2015; Maheirie et al., 2015; among others) since Vygotsky's crucial texts are about art (Vygotsky, 1971, 1995), aesthetical education (Vygotsky, 2001), and childhood imagination and creativity (Vygotsky, 2009). We consider the ontological, anthropological, and epistemological matrix chosen by the author himself as an indispensable source for the appropriation of his writings due to the fact that this is fundamental for the comprehension of mutual constitution between subject and society and because it cross-references and sustains his theoretical framework.

We are aware of the criticism shown by some authors to the strict entailment of Marx's writing in Vygotsky's contributions and of the disregard of other parties with whom he had conversed (Veresov, 2005). Certainly, Marx's writings were not his only references; however, in our view, the ontological, anthropological, and epistemological principles that sustain his ideas are founded in that spectrum. Aiming to contribute with studies that follow this direction – like those developed by Toulmin (1978), Shuare (1990), Newman and Holzman (1993), Pino (2000), and the authors that are participating in this collection – our purpose is to make visible the way that anthological, anthropological, and epistemological principles of Marx's work apply in Vygotsky's discussions of imagination and creative activity.

Procedures

In order to give visibility to the presence of a Marxist frame in Vygotsky's writings and the inventive way in which it is processed, we chose as the focus of our analysis the work *Imagination and Creativity in Childhood*. In this book, written in 1930, the author discloses his ideas about those processes to educators and the general public. According to Prestes and Tunes (2012), in this book, Vygotsky presents in a concise form the main discussions developed in *The Psychology of Art*, a book written five years earlier. As it is a work marked by a certain informality in the narrative, it provides an important source for our work in that the ontological, anthropological, and epistemological fundaments are embodied in the words and discussions. Consistent with Vygotsky's criticism of the authors who, up until then, had tried to build a Marxist psychology resting on quotations from Marx's writing, Vygotsky does not directly reference Marx's historical materialism and dialectics; however, these fundaments are engrained in Vygotsky's concepts and in the development of his arguments.

In this book, Vygotsky approaches the concepts of fantasy and imagination; the relations between imagination and reality; how creative activity is processed or its cycle, as it is referred to; the difficulties that are expected; the characteristics of imagination and creative activity in infancy, in adolescence, and in adult life; literary and theatrical creativity and drawing in childhood. These are interconnected subjects but are presented in chapters that open up each of them to endless possibilities for connections, if the search is for the traces of interlocutors on whose work the arguments are constructed.

Aware of the complexity of this assignment, we chose to analyze the initial chapters of the book, which highlight that each individual's potential for creative activity is fundamental for the transformation of the world and oneself. Vygotsky came to this understanding through interweaving of psychological, physiological, sociological, philosophical, and anthropological discussions, communicating complex issues in an accessible way. Though apparently simple, this work demonstrates Vygotsky's value in general and for this chapter specifically.

The link between Vygotsky's ideas and those of Marx is evident, according to Veresov (2005), from different perspectives and Marxist authors. We understand that this diversity suggests a plurality of possible readings of a work which shows itself as a challenge to any attempt at prescription or closing. This is why it is necessary to go back to Marx's writings, which is what we chose to do.

Some questions mark the analysis and relations that we establish between Vygotsky and Marx, and it is appropriate to present them here. When an author affirms the conditions that enable the emergence of a being, in this case, the human being, he is characterizing the ontological aspects of this being. In other words, he is characterizing the conditions for this being to be specifically human. Thus, the guiding aspects of the ontological conception of a human revolve around questions such as: What characterizes this being? What makes this being different from other beings around the world? What is its specificity? What is common and not common between the human being, the being of things, and the being of nature? We argue that the ontological position in Vygotsky's writing is the same as that presented in Marx's work, the key aspect being the contraposition to essentialist conceptions of being.

The ontological aspects of a theory are, in general, the philosopher's focus of attention, and they certainly develop a more precise insight than we in the area of psychology could. However, tracking the ontological principles of an idea or work is consistent to the epistemological perspective of historical materialism and dialectics as well as the methodological discussions presented by Vygotsky. This is indicated in the following:

> The zoologist, with the insignificant residue of a fossil animal bone, reconstructs its skeleton and, in addition, its way of life. An old coin, which at first lacks real value, allows the archeologist to know a complex historical problem. The historian who deciphers a hieroglyph drawn on a rock penetrates into the depths of missing centuries. The doctor establishes a diagnosis of a disease based on a few symptoms. Since the last few years, psychology has been overcoming the fear in front of daily appreciation of phenomena and learning by insignificant minutiae – residues of phenomena as Freud once said that required major attention for the psychology of daily life – to frequently discover important psychological documents.
>
> *(Vygotsky, 1995, p. 64)*

Following tracks, therefore, is an important path in the search for connections that can help understand facts which are often dispersed; comprehension of them is made clearer when the way they are interrelated, how they dialogue, and how they open possibilities for other paths are evident.

From the anthropological point of view, for Marx, just as for Vygotsky, the conception of how a being is transformed into a human being is consistent with an open and unfinished view of subjectivity and objectification processes, based on concrete life experience. The conception of history, which defines him and is defined by him, contemplates progressive and regressive movements (Sartre, 1984), intertwining past and future on the basis of concrete conditions of present and leaping beyond that.

This makes both authors defend the epistemological position that knowledge must go beyond the product to consider, mainly, the process. In turn, the product itself is the condensation of a process, which can be explored.

Traces of the ontological aspects of imagination and creative activity

Right at the beginning of *Imagination and Creativity in Childhood*, Vygotsky (2009, p. 13) introduces the idea that the human brain is characterized by an enormous plasticity because it is able to transform its structure through excitation, as well as conserving past experience, thus facilitating its reproduction:

> if the brain's activity were limited merely to retaining previous experience, a human being would be a creature who could adapt primarily to familiar, stable conditions of the environment. All new or unexpected changes in the environment not encountered in his previous experience would fail to induce the appropriate adaptive reactions in humans.[1]

By analyzing this excerpt from the first pages of the text, we see that Vygotsky announces the capacity of the human being to go beyond the determinations imposed by nature and previous conditions to the current experience, just as they are able to exercise mimesis, affirming its possibility of entering another function.

The relation between previous and coming experiences, between what has already happened and been accomplished and the possibility of something new, is highlighted in this discussion. The statement of the plasticity of the brain, a theme used by Vygotsky in some of his writings and developed by Alexander R. Lúria (1966), brings to the field of neurophysiology and psychology the perspective of history as a process, as a continuous movement, whether in relation to the history of society in general or any particular person. Since it is a movement, history is supported in previous achievements and in the conditions of possibilities of its own reinvention, conditions that are also historically built.

This perspective of history is clear in Marx's writings and provides evidence for the link between the thinking of this author and Vygotsky. On one hand, the past appears as history, socially developed, with landscapes, objects, ideas consisting in concrete conditions that anticipate and determine events. These conditions, it is worth mentioning, do not refer merely to the economic aspect, but to the whole material and immaterial patrimony of humanity. Marx (1852) writes:

> Men make their own history, but they do not make it as they please; they do not make it under self-selected circumstances, but under circumstances existing already, given and transmitted from the past. The tradition of all dead generations weighs like a nightmare on the brains of the living.[2]

Therefore, the past is always present and makes its mark in everything that surrounds us, everything that guides our existence in our own body, our ways of thinking, feeling, communicating, and acting. However, the ontological condition of the human being can not be reduced to an appropriation of the past, and this is the second point that we highlight: the past consists of and is updated in current objective conditions, which are necessarily directed towards some future through a fundamental and complex process that is the capacity of projecting and projection itself. The following details a fundamental characteristic of the human being, outlined by Marx and assumed by Vygotsky. Marx (2013) writes:

> A spider conducts operations that resemble those of a weaver, and a bee puts to shame many an architect in the construction of her cells. But what distinguishes the worst architect from the best of bees is this, that the architect raises his structure in imagination before he erects it in reality. At the end of every labour-process, we get a result that already existed in the imagination of the labourer at its commencement. He not only effects a change of form in the material on which he works, but he also realises a purpose of his own that gives the law to his modus operandi, and to which he must subordinate his will.[3]

This ontological characteristic of the human being present in Marx's work points out the projecting condition of the work of any subject through imagination – thus differing from the activity of any animal.

Basing itself on this dynamic conception of the being and the history, the brain assumes, in Vygotsky's discussions, an inventive character. It is not a repository of synapses, but an active organ that, from the challenges that are presented by society, rearranges what was already established, establishes new connections, opens paths for other possibilities: "The brain is not only the organ that stores and retrieves our previous experience, it is also the organ that combines and creatively reworks elements of this past experience and uses them to generate new propositions and new behavior" (Vygotsky, 2009, p. 14).[4]

Just as in the work of Marx, we find in Vygotsky affirmation of the condition of the human being as a creative being that, thanks to the creative capacity of the brain, is able, in current days, to project themself in a future anchored in their own and the collective's experiences and achievements of the past. For him, "it is precisely human creative activity that makes the human being a creature oriented toward the future, creating the future and thus altering his own present" (Vygotsky, 2009, p. 14).[5]

The human is a social being, producing themself in the collective: anthropological aspects of imagination and creativity

Creation is not an individual activity even though it is part of the human condition. According to Vygotsky (2009), in order to create, we root ourselves in previous experiences and in the available material of the present, these being, at the same time, the synthesis of events that enabled the current conditions. Those materials and experiences are recombined by imagination and aimed at new materials that synthesize them in a singular way. So there is a social element in each and every creation because the past experiences on which it is based belong not just to the person doing the creating. Creations are collective productions, the work of all human beings, embodied in all concrete and symbolic material that is used in the act of creation.

Another important aspect pointed out by Vygotsky regarding the process of creation is that it presents itself in each and every human situation, being produced by any and every person, thus dispelling the essentialist connotation generally attributed to it:

> creativity is present, in actuality, not only when great historical works are born but also whenever a person imagines, combines, alters, and creates something new, no matter how small a drop in the bucket this new thing appears compared to the works of geniuses. When we consider the phenomenon of collective creativity, which combines all these drops of individual creativity that frequently are insignificant in themselves, we readily understand what an enormous percentage of what has been created by

humanity is a product of the anonymous collective creative work of unknown inventors.

(Vygotsky, 2009, pp. 15–16)[6]

This conception is present in Marx's work when, in collaboration with Engels, he states the importance of "consciously [treating] all natural premises as the creatures of hitherto existing men, [stripping] them of their natural character and [subjugating] them to the power of the united individuals" (Marx and Engels, 1998, p. 87).[7]

These current claims are revolutionary and hard to assume in a contemporary universe in which meritocratic discussions, the logic of the market, the essentialist conceptions of the human being, and the opposition between individual and social, collective and singular, prevail. What Vygotsky (1995, p. 368) highlights in his discussion about imagination and creative activity is this condition of otherness of the human existence, the fact that "each person is to some degree a measure of the society, or rather class, to which he belongs, for the whole totality of social relationships is reflected in him."[8] Each person is, at the same time, both expression and fundament of the relations of which they are part and in which they participate, as well as social relations in general, collectively produced and historically written in the present.

Regarding processes and products in imagination and creation: epistemological aspects

Imagination, according to Vygotsky (2009), is a condition for creative activity. Using the concepts of fantasy and imagination indistinctly, Vygotsky states that creativity is the process in which every person traces fragments of their experience and other people's experiences, of various times and places, and combines these creatively. In this sense, creative activity is the objectification of imagination, resulting in an objective product that emerges through a process. This way of thinking of creation as a procedural activity requires a perspective that is also procedural in order to know it, and this characterizes the epistemological aspect of Vygotsky's work.

In order to describe the creation process, Vygotsky (2009) points out four fundamental linkages between reality and imagination. The first linkage regards the fact that imagination cuts out from reality the elements necessary to compose it. These elements were already there as a result of previous experiences, yet recombined through imaginative exercise. It is possible to find the traces of this idea in historical materialism and dialectical logic, and the following excerpt gives evidence of this relation:

> Men are the producers of their conceptions, ideas, etc. – real, active men, as they are conditioned by a definite development of their productive forces and of the intercourse corresponding to these, up to its furthest forms.
>
> [...] We set out from real, active men, and on the basis of their real life-process we demonstrate the development of the ideological reflexes and

echoes of this life-process. The phantoms formed in the human brain are also, necessarily, sublimates of their material life-process, which is empirically verifiable and bound to material premises.

(Marx and Engels, 1998, p. 19)[9]

By emphasizing where experience plays a role in imaginary production, Vygotsky introduces complexity through historical materialism, showing the transforming, acting, and mutual character of the constraints of reality. The existing element is the condition for the creative activity necessary for its transformation. It is not possible to create out of nothing, just as it is not possible to create without acknowledging the concrete, historical, and socially produced conditions that are to be created. Therefore, every act of imagination, even though it denies reality and projects possibilities, sustains it.

Highlighting this form of link between imagination and reality, Vygotsky (2009, p. 22) concludes by stating how important it is to analyze the process in order to understand the product "because this experience provides the material from which the products of fantasy are constructed."[10] From this, he argues that is necessary to increase the child's experience in order to provide solid foundations for creative activity, reaffirming the misconception that reality and imagination are opposed to one another and intertwining this to other psychological processes such as memory and cognition.

It is from this first link between imagination and reality that the second is derived. In this, the product of fantasy brings an amplified experience of the entire social context relevant to the subject. We produce our fantasies not only from our own experiences, but also using the experiences of others, known to us by their narration or description. With this type of link, Vygotsky (2009, p. 11) reaffirms that "in the everyday life that surrounds us, creativity is an essential condition for existence and all that goes beyond the rut of routine and involves innovation, albeit only a tiny amount, owes its existence to the human creative process."[11] Through this linkage, experience and imagination are fed in a mutual way.

In order to know the process of creation, it is worth drawing attention to the emotional link present in imagination, which characterizes the third form of relation between imagination and reality. Vygotsky (2009, p. 26) affirms that every emotion produces an image that corresponds to itself and that the configuration of these images generates an associated emotional sign: "The images of imagination also provide an internal language for our emotion."[12] Thus, if on one side, the emotion generates images, on the other, the images produce emotions. Such is the bond between emotion and fantasy that through it we not only produce but also recreate objects in different fields of the arts while also, in the position of spectator, generating sensations.

The fourth form of bond between imagination and reality refers to the objectification of the process, its transformation into product, characterized as crystalized fantasy or creativity itself. Such objectification, the materialized imagination, puts itself in the real as a new object, as condensed human experience that can become appropriate in various ways. It is, thus, a new element available to imagination and creative processes. That is, the product derives from the process, which generates new products that propel the creation of new processes, showing that collective life feeds singular life mutually and incessantly.

Certainly, in his theory about imagination and creation processes, just as in his other writings about the development and processes of learning, Vygotsky produces a materialistic and dialectical intelligibility. For this intelligibility, a nonessential method, not mechanistic but procedural, open, unfinished, and seized in its incompleteness and complexity is proposed by him (for questions about method in Vygotsky, see Ratner, 1997, 2002, and Zanella *et al.*, 2007).

Marx, with an even more intense focus on the anthropological and ontological aspects of the human (Lukács, 1979), used to make important methodological pronouncements in his writing, especially when considering the analysis of different forms of development and the connection between these forms (Marx, 2013) or in examining the idea of the world as a sum of processes in which objectivity results from the synthesis of many factors.

So creativity is a human condition that happens in the web of relations among subjects in specific social contexts. It is a complex activity that occurs throughout the process, similar to gestation: its products result from a long period and necessarily involve the anonymous collective in the co-authorship of production.

Final considerations

In their sixth thesis on Feuerbach, Marx and Engels (1998, p. 101) point out that: "the essence of man is no abstraction inherent in each single individual. In reality, it is the ensemble of the social relations."[13] This understanding is present in Vygotsky's writing. He opposes all essentialism when it comes to the nature of human existence and, therefore, each and every explanation that deposes from history the complex and diverse realities in which man lives and which are inexorably based on the achievements of other times; these are the basis of his understanding of each person and the collectivity in which he participates.

If the dimension of expression refers to previous experiences, then culture affirms, in general terms, the foundational aspect, the inventive condition of each person, their potential to create other conditions, to reinvent ways of living and being in association with others. After all, "Only in community [with others has each] individual the means of cultivating his gifts in all directions" (Marx and Engels, 1998, p. 101).[14]

As we have demonstrated in this chapter, these topics form part of Vygotsky's discussion of imagination and creativity. They also appear in many of Vygotsky's other writings – whether about art, the development of the human psyche, or the psychology of his time – which represent the core of historical-cultural psychology. Nevertheless, the presence of Marx's ontological, anthropological, and epistemological perspectives in Vygotsky's work is not immediately clear; it is necessary to trace their origin. This task requires a dialectical logic that is developed in an open, unfinished, and inventive way (Sartre, 1984). We have presented in this chapter what we have been able to find during our search for the traces of Marx in Vygotsky's *Imagination and Creativity in Childhood*. We hope that this will build on the legacy of this author and indicate promising paths for understanding the processes of imagination and creativity.

Notes

1 Quotation from: Vygotsky, L. S. (1990). Imagination and creativity in childhood, *Soviet Psychology*, 28(1), 84–96.
2 Quotation from: https://www.marxists.org/archive/marx/works/1852/18th-brumaire/index.htm
3 Quotation from: https://www.marxists.org/archive/marx/works/download/pdf/Capital-Volume-I.pdf
4 Quotation from: Vygotsky, L. S. (1990). Imagination and creativity in childhood, *Soviet Psychology*, 28(1), 84–96.
5 Ibid.
6 Ibid.
7 Quotation from: https://www.marxists.org/archive/marx/works/download/Marx_The_German_Ideology.
8 Quotation from: Vygotsky, L. S. (1997). *The collected works of L. S. Vygotsky: Volume 3* (ed. R.W. Rieber and J. Wollock; trans. R. van der Veer). New York: Plenum, p. 317.
9 Quotation from: https://www.marxists.org/archive/marx/works/download/Marx_The_German_Ideology.
10 Quotation from: Vygotsky, L. S. (1990). Imagination and creativity in childhood, *Soviet Psychology*, 28(1), 84–96.
11 Ibid.
12 Ibid.
13 Quotation from: https://www.marxists.org/archive/marx/works/1845/theses/index.htm
14 Quotation from: https://www.marxists.org/archive/marx/works/download/Marx_The_German_Ideology

References

Kozulin, A. (1990). *Vygotsky's psychology: A biography of ideas*. Cambridge: Harvard University Press.
Lukács, G. (1979). Ontologia do ser social [Ontology of the social being] Os princípios ontológicos fundamentais de Marx. São Paulo: Ciências Humanas.
Lúria, A. R. (1966). *Human brain and psychological processes*. New York: Harper & Row.
Maheirie, K. (2003). O processo de criação no fazer musical: uma objetivação da subjetividade, a partir dos trabalhos de Sartre e Vygotsky [The process of creating the musical: An objectification of subjectivity, based on Sartre and Vygotsky], *Psicologia em Estudo, Maringá*, 8(2), 147–153.
Maheirie, K. (2015). O fotografar e as experiências coletivas em Centros de Referência em Assistência Social [The shooting and collective experiences in Reference Centers for

Social Assistance]. In: Aluísio Ferreira de Lima, Deborah Christina Antunes, and Marcelo Gustavo Aguiar Calwegare (Org.). *A psicologia social e os atuais desafios ético-políticos no Brasil* [Social psychology and current ethical and political challenges in Brazil]. Porto Alegre: ABRAPSO, pp. 364–374.

Maheirie, K., Smolka, A. L. B., Strapazzon, A., Carvalho, C. S., and Massaro, F. K. (2015). Imaginação e processos de criação na perspectiva histórico-cultural: análise (de uma experiência [Imagination and creative processes in the cultural-historical perspective: Analysis of an experience], *Estudos de Psicologia (PUCCAMP. Impresso)*, 32(1), 49–61.

Marx, K. (1852). *The eighteenth Brumaire of Louis Bonaparte*, Chapter 1. Available at: https://www.marxists.org/portugues/marx/1852/brumario/cap01.htm (accessed December 1, 2016).

Marx, K. (2013). *O Capital: crítica da economia política. Livro I* [Capital: A critique of political economy. Book I]. São Paulo: Boitempo.

Marx, K., and Engels, F. (1998). A ideologia alemã [The German ideology]. São Paulo: Martins Fontes.

Newman, F., and Holzman, L. (1993). *Lev Vygotsky: Revolutionary scientist*. London: Routledge.

Pino, A. (2000). O social e o cultural na obra de Vigotski. (The social and cultural work in Vygotsky), *Rev. Educação e Sociedade*, 21(71), 45–78.

Prestes, Z., and Tunes, E. (2012). A trajetória de obras de Vigotski: um longo percurso até os originais [The trajectory of works by Vygotsky: A long journey to the originals], *Estudos de psicologia (Campinas)*, 29(3), 327–340.

Ratner, C. (1991). *Vygotsky's sociohistorical psychology and its contemporary applications*. New York: Plenum.

Ratner, C. (1997). *Cultural psychology and qualitative methodology: Theoretical and empirical considerations*. New York: Plenum.

Ratner, C. (2002). *Cultural psychology: Theory and method*. New York: Kluwer Academic/Plenum.

Rogoff, B. (2003). *The cultural nature of human development*. New York: Oxford University Press.

Sartre, J. P. (1984). *Questão de Método* [Method of issue]. São Paulo: Abril Cultural.

Shuare, M. (1990). *La psicología soviética tal cómo yo la veo* [The soviet psychology as I see it]. Moscow: Editorial Progresso.

Toulmin, S. (1978). The Mozart of psychology, *The New York Review of Books*, 25(14).

Valsiner, J. (2007). *Culture in minds and societies*. New Delhi: Sage.

van der Veer, R. (2007). *Lev Vygotsky: Continuum library of educational thought*. London: Continuum.

van der Veer, R., and Valsiner, J. (1991). *Understanding Vygotsky: A quest for synthesis*. Oxford: Blackwell.

Veresov, N. (1999). *Undiscovered Vygotsky: Etudes on the pre-history of cultural-historical psychology*. Frankfurt am Main: Peter Lang.

Veresov, N. (2005). Marxist and non-Marxist aspects of the cultural-historical psychology of L. S. Vygotsky, *Outlines*, 7(1), 31–49.

Vygotsky, L. S. (1971). *The psychology of art*. Cambridge, MA: MIT Press.

Vygotsky, L. S. (1991). *Obras escogidas I* [Selected works I]. Madrid: M. E. C./Visor.

Vygotsky, L. S. (1995). *Obras Escogidas: Vol. 3. Problemas del desarollo de la psique* [Selected works: Volume 3: Problems of the theory and history of psychology]. Madrid: Visor.

Vygotsky, L. S. (2000). Manuscrito de 1929, *Educação & Sociedade*, 21(71), 21–44.

Vygotsky, L. S. (2001). A educação estética [The aesthetic education]. In *Psicologia edagógica* [Educational psychology] (pp. 225–248). Porto Alegre: Artmed.

Vygotsky, L. S. (2009). *Imaginação e criação na infância: ensaio psicológico* [Imagination and creativity in childhood: Psychology essay]. São Paulo: Ática.

Zanella, A. V. (2013a). *Perguntar, registrar, escrever: inquietações metodológicas* [Ask, register, write: Methodological concerns], 1st ed. Porto Alere: Editora da UFRGS.

Zanella, A. V. (2013b). Youth, art and city: Research and political intervention in social psychology, *Revista de Estudios Urbanos y Ciencias Sociales*, 3(1), 105–116.

Zanella, A. V., and Maheirie, K. (Org.) (2010). *Diálogos em psicologia social e arte* [Dialogues in social psychology and art], 1st ed. Curitiba: CRV.

Zanella, A. V., and Wedekin, L. (Org.) (2015). *Visita à Bienal: diálogos Bakhti(Vigotski)anos* [Visit to the Biennial: Bakhti (Vigotski) dialogues]. Curitiba: CRV.

Zanella, A. V., Reis, A. C, Titon, A., Urnau, L. C., and Dassoler, T. (2007). Questões de método em textos de Vygotski: contribuições à pesquisa em psicologia [Method issues in Vygotsky's texts: Contributions to psychology research]. *Psicologia & Sociedade*, 19(2) 25–33.

7

MATERIALIST DIALECTICS IN VYGOTSKY'S METHODOLOGICAL FRAMEWORK

Implications for applied linguistics research

James P. Lantolf

Packer (2008, p. 8) pointed out that when Vygotsky's works first appeared in English, cultural-historical psychologists observed a connection with Marx's analysis of capitalist society; however, before long, with a few exceptions (e.g., Toulmin, 1978), extensive mention of Marx's influence disappeared from their scholarship. Packer noted that "even when the references to Marx have been acknowledged, there has been little consensus about their significance" (2008, p. 9). For instance, Chaiklin's (2011, p. 139) comparative analysis of the respective methodological perspectives of Lewin and Vygotsky briefly mentioned Vygotsky's goal of building a Marxist psychology. Clearly, however, the influence of Marx on Vygotsky's thinking is amply documented in the pages of his *Collected Works*, especially in what is arguably his most overt commitment to Marx's analytical methodology, 'The historical meaning of the crisis in psychology: A methodological investigation' (Vygotsky, 1997a).

In what follows, I address specific features of Vygotsky's general methodological framework grounded in Marx's analytical approach and the implications of this framework for how Vygotsky conceived of concrete research procedures and what counted as scientific explanation. I then discuss applied linguistics (henceforth AL) research in which Vygotsky's theory and methodological framework has been influential. I also consider the consequences and implications of AL research which continues to follow the hard science model, a perspective that Vygotsky forcefully resisted.

Vygotsky and standardized scientific research methodology

Vygotsky recognized that the crisis in psychology constituted two interrelated problems – one ontological and the other epistemological. While the ontological crisis was certainly a thorny issue, the epistemological crisis, in some respects, was and continues to be a more complex problem because it goes to the heart of what it means for psychologists to engage in scientific research.

Vygotsky pointed out that in the final analysis, there existed two incommensurable psychologies: one materialist, focusing on human behavior "as a unique form of movement," and the other idealist, concentrating on "the mind as non-movement" (1997a, p. 315). He concluded that it would be impossible to create a single science about two completely divergent forms of being and incorporating divergent epistemological stances (1997a, p. 314). Vygotsky, relying on Engels' discussion of dialectics in nature (see Novack, 1978), argued that dialectics is not something one applies to an object of study; rather, one discovers dialectal relations in the object of study through an appropriate analytical procedure, which of course necessitates a discussion of epistemology and research method.

Vygotsky understood that it would have been unproductive for Marx to mount an analysis of capitalist society by merely searching for instances of dialectical laws (e.g., interpenetration of opposites, leap from quantitative to qualitative change, development through contradictions, negation of negation). He recognized that for Marx to penetrate the structure of capitalism, it had been necessary to formulate the intermediate theory of historical materialism through which dialectical laws operate along with an appropriate analytical methodology (Vygotsky, 1997a, p. 331). Influenced by his reading of Marx, Vygotsky argued for the need to create a general theory of psychology as an intermediate theory that required the formulation of its own principles, concepts, laws, and methodology firmly anchored in general principles of dialectical materialism. While principles of dialectics are assumed to function in all domains of reality (an ontological assumption), dialectics is at the same time a way of thinking about and analyzing any domain of reality (an epistemological assumption). As Vygotsky succinctly put it, "Psychology is in need of its own *Das Kapital*—its own concepts of class, basis, value, etc.—in which it might express, describe and study its object" (1997a, p. 330); "we must develop a theory of psychological materialism" (1997a, p. 331). In Marx's methodology, Vygotsky found inspiration and guidance for building the methodological framework for a theory of general psychology. In the next section, I discuss aspects of Marx's methodological framework, and in the section that follows, I consider how these were adapted by Vygotsky and what the implications were for Vygotsky's proposals for a concrete research method.

Before moving on, however, it is helpful to clarify the distinction between methodology and method. Toomela described this very effectively. According to him, methodology is "a philosophy of scientific cognition" (2015, p. 106). It is a mode of inquiry that determines why a particular study is to be carried out in the first place. Given that the object of scientific inquiry is comprised of "processes and structures" that are not open to direct observation, it guides the researcher's semiotic construction and interpretation of those processes and structures that are the focus of the inquiry (2015, p. 106). Finally, it determines the nature of explanation and whether a study achieves its goal or not. Method, on the other hand, comprises the "procedure of study, the technical actions to be performed," and as such it justifies selection of participants, equipment, and materials and how these are to be implemented as well as determining "the procedures of data interpretation" (2015, p. 106).

Dialectics and the philosophy of internal relations

To introduce his comparison of the philosophies of external and internal relations, Ollman asked the age-old question: "'Which came first, the chicken or the egg?'" (2015, p. 8). If we perceive the chicken and the egg from an externalist stance, they are two separate and distinct entities and, according to Ollman, the question is unanswerable. However, the internalist perspective contends that the chicken and egg are "two moments in the development of the same one"; therefore, Ollman stated the answer to the question is "the other" (2015, p. 8). Marx's analysis of the production/consumption relation included in the *Grundrisse* elegantly reflects the internalist position whereby "production is also immediately consumption" and "consumption is also immediately production" (1939/1973, p. 90). The act of eating is simultaneously the consumption of food and the production of the body. Also, in *Capital* (1867/1992), Marx argued that the production of commodities is at the same time the consumption of raw materials and the machinery involved in the production process.

Ollman (2015) described the philosophy of external relations as both the common-sense and social science perspective that dominates much of the thinking in modern (capitalist) society. This contends that there are 'things,' or 'factors' (if one is a social scientist), and relations, both of which "are logically independent of each other" (2015, p. 10). Any change that may occur is assumed to be external to the thing itself, and therefore "its new form is treated as independent of what it was earlier" (2015, p. 10). Reality is conceived of as being essentially static, and change is only attended to when things bump into each other or into us with sufficient force to have an impact.

In the philosophy of internal relations, "change and relations are the basic building materials" of reality (2015, p. 10). What externalists take to be 'things' are, from the internalist viewpoint, processes and relations. For externalists, while the whole may be comprised of parts, it is nothing more than the sum total of its parts. Following this, in much social science research, including in mainstream psychology, society is conceived of as a mere collection of individuals. Internalists, on the other hand, contend that not only are wholes more than the sum of their parts but also the whole is found in the parts. Said another way, the whole (society) and the parts (individuals) are two modes of the same existential phenomenon (Avineri, 1968, p. 89). In Marx's theory, the whole-in-part relation takes 'commodity' as the cell or unit of analysis for understanding capitalism. In the same way, Vygotsky proposed 'word meaning' as the unit of analysis for the study of consciousness. In his later writings, Vygotsky (1935/1994) explored the possibility of *perezhivanie*, or 'experienced reality,' as the analytical unit to appropriately capture the dialectical unity of emotion and reason that reflected the full personality of an individual.

Marx's internalist orientation allowed him to uncover the details of the multiple interactions among capital, labor, value, credit, interest, rent, money, and wages as part of the web of dialectical relations comprising the structure of industrial capitalism in his time. As Harvey (2010, 2013) pointed out, what one discovers in Marx's masterwork is not so much the working out of the analysis *per se* but the results of the analysis, intended for public consumption as a 'textbook' explicating the complexities of capitalist society. According to Ollman, "without an adequate grasp of the conceptual 'tools' with which Marx achieved his results, we have little chance to make the most effective use out of what he has to teach" (2015, pp. 11–12). Marx's analytical tools are presented with considerable detail in the *Grundrisse* (Marx, 1939/1973), a collection of his notes that was not published until after Vygotsky's death. It seems then that Vygotsky was able to understand Marx's analytical tools through his reading of *Capital* and Marx's other writings. Indeed, Luria (1979) lauded Vygotsky as having greater knowledge of Marx's theory than any other member of their research group.

Marx's methodology

In this section, I present an overview of the methodology that Marx deployed in his analysis of capitalist society. I highlight particular components of the methodology that I believe to be most relevant for Vygotsky's methodology. To carry out the task, I rely primarily on the superb exegesis of Marx's methodology laid out in chapters 8 and 9 of Ollman's (2003) monograph on dialectics in Marx.

According to Ollman (2003, p. 140), Marx's methodology encompasses six components, the first of which is commitment to a materialist ontology whereby the world is conceived of as real and separate from humans and comprised of interrelated parts that make up the whole such that the whole is expressed through, gives meaning to, shapes, and imparts specific functions to the individual parts. The second component is epistemology, comprised of several subcomponents: perception (including not just sensory input but also mental and emotional activity), abstraction, conceptualization of what is abstracted into new or redefined concepts (e.g., surplus value, labor power, commodity, credit), and orientation to the proposition that social context must be part of all explanations. The third component is inquiry into the laws of dialectics operating in capitalist society via the concepts uncovered as a result of abstraction and analyzed through the study of history 'backwards' (and forwards). The fourth component is the intellectual reconstruction of what is uncovered through inquiry, where the results of the analysis are unified for the understanding of the researcher in notebooks, such as the *Grundrisse*, and other writings with the self as primary audience. The fifth component is exposition of the results of the analysis for others to comprehend (e.g., *Capital*). The sixth and final component is praxis, which unites theory and activity to test, change, and thereby more deeply understand reality.

I focus my discussion on components two, three, and six as, in my view, analysis through abstraction, the study of history backwards and forwards, and praxis profoundly shaped Vygotsky's understanding of how to construct the methodology and method of general psychology. It is worth pointing out, nevertheless, that many of Vygotsky's writings included in the *Collected Works* as well as recently uncovered manuscripts (see Zavershneva, 2016) reveal that much of what he wrote reflects the fourth component of Marx's methodology – working out the researcher's own understanding of the analysis. One could also make the reasonable argument that *Thinking and Speech* represents Vygotsky's attempt to realize the fifth component of Marx's methodology, as is evidenced in its preface where Vygotsky oriented the reader to the fact that the work synthesizes the results of previous research.

Abstraction

Marx argued that "reality may be in one piece when lived, but to be thought about and communicated it must be parceled out" (Ollman, 2003, p. 60). The process through which Marx segmented reality into manageable analytical units is "abstraction" (Ollman, 2015, p. 15). There is nothing remarkable about abstraction *per se* since it is the normal process through which humans break down "reality into manageable parts" in order to make sense of it (Ollman, 2003, p. 60). As Ollman noted, however, most of us are unaware not only that we abstract but that we do so in terms of the "mental units" that are part of our "cultural inheritance" (2003, p. 61). Marx, however, used abstraction intentionally and rationally, and in four different, interrelated, ways. Most importantly, he considered abstraction as a process for mentally segmenting reality into those constructs considered to be most relevant for thinking about his object of study. He also used it according to its nominal meaning in order to describe the results of the process of abstracting parts of relations that formed his object of study. He used it in a third sense to reference mental units that are 'ill-fitting,' overly narrow, or too superficial to permit an appropriate analysis. In this sense, abstractions function as units of ideology. Finally, he used abstraction to refer to a specific "organization of elements in the real world," as opposed to mental units (Ollman, 2003, p. 61). These could be highly visible or they could be invisible – for instance, when social relations are fetishized as separate entities (e.g., surplus value as a social relation between labor and capital hidden in the price of a commodity).

History

According to Packer (2008, p. 9), Marx's approach to history is the most important of his influences on Vygotsky. Normally, history is construed as a narrative that explains what happens by beginning in the past and moving to the present. Marx, however, proposed a different approach to history as an analytical methodology. He argued that it is possible to develop a more accurate account of how the present came to be by beginning an analysis from the "vantage point of the present" (Ollman, 2003, p. 115). This would allow the analyst to abstract those processes that are relevant in constructing the current state of affairs and to ignore those that are irrelevant. In essence, Marx proposed studying history 'backwards.' Rather than starting from the conditions that lead to change and concluding with the change that occurred, Marx began with the results of change (i.e., modern capitalist society) and worked backwards to uncover the preconditions that give rise to the results (Ollman, 2003, p. 116). According to Ollman, studying history backwards

> is a matter of asking where the situation under hand comes from and what had to happen for it to acquire just these qualities. ... Knowing how the "story" came out, placing such knowledge at the start of our investigation, sets up criteria for relevance as well as research priorities.
>
> *(2003, p. 118)*

This analytical approach allowed Marx to delve far more deeply into the myriad of relations that comprised modern industrial capitalism and ultimately explain, for instance, the contemporary relation between capital and wage labor as "two movements in the process of becoming" and, simultaneously, "aspects of a single movement" (Ollman, 2003, p. 117).

Marx also proposed the study of history forwards; in this, he attempted to find evidence of socialism (the future) inside capitalism. Here he operated with different levels of extension – near future (neo-formations of capitalism), middle future (socialism), and far future (communism). He carried out his analysis through a four-step process: first, he identified the primary relations of contemporary capitalism; next he undertook to locate the preconditions for these relations in the past; then he projected the relations "reformulated as contradictions, from the past, through the present, and into the [near, middle, and distant] future"; finally, he adopted the vantage point of the projected socialist and communist future to re-examine the present as preconditions for the future (Ollman, 2003, p. 161). The preconditions for the future already existing in capitalism include unions, public education, municipal hospitals, cooperatives, social security, single-payer health care, etc. According to Ollman (2003, p. 159), even preconditions that do not appear to be connected with socialist society should be included, such as extreme wealth and extreme poverty, inequality, and unemployment. We could also include progressive income tax and state control of credit through a central bank (see Harvey, 2014).

Praxis

The final component of Marx's methodology considered here is 'praxis,' where one's theoretical stance is brought into the world with the purpose of more deeply understanding it, testing the theory, and eventually changing reality itself (Ollman, 2003, p. 157). In praxis, philosophy ceases to be contemplative and becomes practical. Or foreshadowing Vygotsky with regard to psychology, philosophy becomes applied philosophy (Avineri, 1968, p. 129). I return to this topic when discussing Vygotsky's integration of praxis into general psychology.

Vygotsky's methodology and method

Vygotsky argued forcefully that while the extension of experimental research into psychology, imported from the natural sciences, might be appropriate for the study of elementary (i.e., biological) mental functions, stimulus–response experiments, whether employing introspection or reaction time measures, are inappropriate for the study of higher (i.e., culturally structured) mental functions. Human psychological behavior is qualitatively different from that of animals; therefore, blindly transporting methods from the natural into the human sciences "created the appearance of science" but in fact "concealed a total impotence in the face of the studied facts" (Vygotsky, 1997a, p. 280).

Contemporary social science research, including experimental research, essentially follows the same experimental procedures, although with perhaps somewhat more sophistication, as formulated by Wundt, to address a wide array of problems, including those that for Vygotsky are in the domain of higher mental functions. It is interesting that although social science research, and psychology in particular, rejected behaviorism, it managed to salvage the experimental method by relabeling stimulus–response as 'independent–dependent' variables (see Blumer, 1956). Indeed, the experimental method has become so pervasive in the social sciences that in his 1975 presidential address to the American Sociological Association, Lewis Coser (1975, p. 693), lamenting the lack of emphasis on theoretical substance in favor of methodological rigor in preparing the then next generation of sociologists, referenced an earlier publication (McGrath and Altman, 1966) in which the authors remarked that "one way to publish rapidly is to apply the [same] procedure, task, or piece of equipment over and over, introducing new variables or slight modification of old variables, and thereby generate a host of studies rather quickly." In Coser's opinion, this research approach eschews inquiry into "problems about which data are hard to come by" in favor of problems that are less intractable for experimentation to handle, resulting in either "the piling up of useless information" or "tunnel vision in which some problems are explored exhaustively while others are not even perceived" (1975, p. 693).

For Vygotsky, to construct a theory of general psychology, it would not be enough to establish a methodological framework for how psychologists should cognize their object of study. It would be equally necessary to specify how research should be conducted on the concrete level. This is precisely what he proposed to do with regard to the different domains of history that he believed psychology had to include within the scope of its research into higher-order thinking (see Scribner, 1985). While Vygotsky considered it essential to follow Marx's approach to analysis and commitment to historical explanation, he understood the relevance of experimentation for scientific research. Bringing the three components (analysis, history, and experimentation) together, Vygotsky proposed what he called the "experimental-developmental" method (see Vygotsky, 1978).

The key to the new method is history, but history in the way Marx used it in his analysis of capitalism – history backwards or, citing Marx, "the 'reverse' method"

(Vygotsky, 1997a, p. 235). Vygotsky argued that "A certain state of development and the process itself can only be fully understood when we know the endpoint of the process, the result, the direction it took, and the form into which the given process developed" (1997a, p. 235). The endpoint of the process at the level of individuals is fully formed adult thinking, which he described as "fossilized" (Vygotsky, 1978). The problem with fossilized, or automatized, thinking is that it is difficult, if not impossible, to distinguish lower (biological) from higher (cultural) contributions to the overall process – a fundamental failure of stimulus–response experimentation that Vygotsky laid squarely at Titchener's doorstep. Therefore, he reasoned, psychological experimentation needed to uncover the origins of adult thinking as well as the nature of the process through which biology (the animal pole of the dialectic) and culture (its non-animal pole) formed the organic unity fossilized in adult consciousness. The 'experimental-developmental' method was, then, Vygotsky's proposal for introducing history into experimental research. He asserted that "developmental psychology, not experimental [i.e., stimulus–response research] psychology, provides the new approach to analysis that we need" (Vygotsky, 1978, p. 61).

This meant that the focus of psychological research had to shift from fully formed adult thinking to earlier stages in its history when the thinking process was being formed. Thus, childhood took center stage. Here Vygotsky proposed the "*functional method of double-stimulation*" (Vygotsky, 1978, p. 74, italics in original) – a two-stage procedure in which children of different ages (in some cases, adults were included) are given tasks assumed to be difficult and likely beyond their biologically endowed ability, and then they are provided with auxiliary artifacts (e.g., pieces of colored paper) that could potentially be integrated into the task solution. The researcher then observes if and how the children use the artifacts to support, or mediate, their solution to the problem. By studying children of different ages, Vygotsky reasoned it would be possible to trace the formation of higher order (i.e., cultural) thinking in adults as it develops over time; that is, through history.

All of this means that for Vygotsky, scientific explanation is fundamentally developmental (i.e., historical) in nature. It is therefore a mistake to characterize Vygotsky as a developmental psychologist on a par with his contemporary Jean Piaget. In the introductory chapter to *Mind and Society*, Cole and Scribner forewarned readers that by developmental method, Vygotsky is not referring to "a theory of child development" but to "the central method of psychological science" (1978, p. 7). John-Steiner and Souberman, in the afterword to the same volume, reiterated this crucial point when they stated that "to view this great Russian psychologist as primarily a student of child development would be an error" (1978, p. 128).

Given her apparent agreement with Cole that Vygotsky was not a developmental psychologist, Scribner oddly, in my opinion, argued that Vygotsky included "child history" among the historical strands he introduced into general psychology (1985, p. 138). Based on how Vygotsky conceptualized the experimental-developmental method, however, I propose that it would be more appropriate to change from 'child history' to 'adult history.' After all, Vygotsky was interested in the historical development of adult thinking, not with children *per se*.

It might be reading too much into Vygotsky to argue that he also followed Marx in studying history forward. Nevertheless, I would like to raise the possibility that in the zone of proximal development (ZPD), Vygotsky attempted to capture elements of the future in the present. Recall that for Marx, studying history forward was about uncovering elements of a socialist or communist future operating in contemporary capitalism. Development itself is always future oriented (i.e., something that is yet to happen) rather than about what has already fossilized as a consequence of previous development. Consequently, the future and the current state of a person's development comprise a dialectical relation in which the future is exposed and made visible through the person's response to mediation provided by others. Thus, according to Vygotsky, the relation is established between teaching-learning (*obuchenie*; see Cole, 2009) and development in which the former activity "sets in motion a variety of developmental processes that would be impossible" in its absence (Vygotsky, 1978, p. 90). Thus, the ZPD is concerned with uncovering evidence for and, simultaneously, provoking an individual's future mental processing.

Quantification?

Modern psychology, along with AL, highly values quantification as the *sine qua non* of scientific research. While qualitative research has attained a modicum of cachet, it is still seen as narrow, anecdotal, and lacking in generalizability. Following the lead of the natural sciences, psychology continues to conduct controlled experiments using increasingly sophisticated inferential statistics as its primary way to achieve generalizability. Toomela argued that Vygotsky was on solid ground in rejecting quantification in favor of qualitative interpretation because he understood that mathematical analysis may very well lack any "correspondence with the reality that underlies observed behaviors encoded in variables" (2015, p. 109). Mathematical methods, Toomela continued, are indifferent to the objects that are studied and, indeed, the objects can be replaced by other objects as long as the relations remain stable (2015, p. 109). Toomela insightfully pointed out that despite the fact mathematical methods are incapable of uncovering hidden structures and processes, the commitment to quantification is so powerful and pervasive in modern psychology that new fields characterized by method alone, such as mathematical and mixed-method psychologies, "turn science upside down; methods start to determine the questions that are asked" (2015, p. 111).

Despite his rejection of the natural science research model, Vygotsky nevertheless saw great value in observing phenomena under the artificial conditions of the laboratory. Thus, he proposed what for some is no doubt an oxymoron: qualitative experimentation whereby participant performance under lab conditions is subjected to rigorous qualitative analysis guided by a principled theoretical and methodological framework.

Praxis

Following Marx, Vygotsky argued that theory could no longer function independently and prior to practice, where practice was merely "the application" of theory that occurred "outside of science and came after science" (1997a, p. 305). On the contrary, practice was to be deeply integrated into the scientific enterprise as an equal partner with theory as it "sets the tasks and serves as the supreme judge of theory, as its truth criterion" (Vygotsky, 1997a, pp. 305–306). Accordingly, for Vygotsky (1997a), applied psychology is the key component in the solution to the crisis in psychology. Even though scientific experimentation is a kind of praxis because it entails the systematic manipulation of reality (see Sanchez Vasquez, 1977), Vygotsky clearly had a dedication to improving the life of society outside of the laboratory setting. In fact, it could be argued that from the perspective of practice, the world outside of the laboratory is itself an experimental setting where the same theory/practice dialectic operates.

Vygotsky and A. R. Luria, arguably his most influential colleague, saw education and clinical intervention as two activities where their research had the potential to improve the life of individuals and communities. Both scholars engaged in clinical research – Vygotsky with children suffering from various forms of biological and cultural deprivation as well as adults experiencing psychological disorders (see Vygotsky, 1993), and Luria with individuals suffering brain insult related to stroke or injuries incurred as a result of World War II (see Luria, 1973). Vygotsky considered education to be an activity that provokes "the artificial development" of the person to the extent that it systematically and intentionally "restructures all functions of behavior in a most essential manner" (1997b, p. 88). Education achieves its developmental goal because it exposes students to concepts that reflect the results of rigorous objective thinking and analysis while, at the same time, exposing the hidden ideologies at work in society (see Vygotsky, 1987). In assigning a central role to education in the development of the individual and the reformation of society, Vygotsky was no doubt influenced by Engels' (1877/1987) proposal that freedom entails in-depth knowledge of a particular subject – the type of knowledge that Vygotsky argued was primarily available through appropriately organized formal education.

Methodology and method in applied linguistics

In this section, I address two aspects of AL research that draw on Vygotsky's Marxist approach to methodology and method. The first deals with existing research informed by sociocultural theory, and the second has to do with the potential consequences of not taking account of Vygotsky's caution against wholesale importing of the methods of the natural sciences into social science research.

Sociocultural theory and second language learning research

Frawley and Lantolf (1985) were, to my knowledge, the first AL researchers to publish a paper on sociocultural theory (SCT) and second language (L2) performance. Their study analyzed the use of private speech to maintain and regain self-regulation among L2 adult and first language (L1) child speakers of English. Since that time, well over a thousand published works have appeared in the AL literature, informed by various concepts and principles of SCT. According to Lantolf and Beckett (2009), SCT-L2 research can be divided into two broad chronological eras, one representing work from 1985 to approximately 2003 and the other from the latter date to the present. The distinction between the eras resides in the fact that the early research primarily used SCT as a lens to examine L2 learning and use in everyday and educational settings. Some of the studies were mini ethnographic projects conducted in language classrooms, while others presented L2 learners with simple tasks such as constructing oral and written narratives based on picture stories, as used by Frawley and Lantolf (1985). Yet other studies used questionnaires, a method that was en vogue in the 1990s in AL.

Perhaps because of the response of reviewers but also because those applied linguists who were attracted to sociocultural theory had received training as quantitative, experimental researchers, a substantial number of these researchers pursued quasi-experimental studies that overlooked Vygotsky's methodological stance and his research method. Lantolf and Thorne (2006) included a discussion of this research in their overview of SCT-AL research.

Beginning with Negueruela's (2003) dissertation and publications emanating from it (e.g., Negueruela and Lantolf, 2006), a substantial number of SCT-L2 researchers adopted a praxis-based approach to second language developmental research. The majority of their studies were conducted in real-world classrooms rather than laboratory settings. The research was conducted as part of normal teaching activities typical of tertiary education in North America. Most of the research was situated within Gal'perin's approach to educational development, Systemic Theoretical Instruction (STI), which systematically organizes and concretizes Vygotsky's educational principles into an effective pedagogical approach (see Talyzina, 1981, and Haenen, 1996). The majority of this research adhered to Vygotsky's commitment to the study of history backwards in promoting the development of understanding and use of L2 conceptual knowledge to achieve communicative goals.

Karen Johnson and her colleague Paula Golombek (see Johnson, 2009, and Johnson and Golombek, 2016) described a praxis-based approach to language teacher education grounded in sociocultural and activity theory. Their approach was not focused on a particular language but, rather, sought to raise the awareness of language teachers to the consequences of their classroom behavior on student development. Instead of calling attention to knowledge of specific features of language, they viewed language on a broader level as social practice and undertake to make teachers aware of this way of thinking about what they are teaching while, at the same time, raising their awareness of the consequences of their classroom behavior on student language development. A group of scholars at Pompeu Fabra University in Barcelona, Spain established a program for primary and secondary teachers that integrated STI with elements of teacher education along the lines proposed by Johnson and Golombek (see Esteve *et al.*, in press).

Another strand of research that emerged from praxis-based methodology focused on dynamic assessment (DA). Inspired by Vygotsky's writing on the ZPD, DA unifies instruction and assessment into a seamless dialectical activity (see Haywood and Lidz, 2007). SCT-L2 research on DA was pioneered in Poehner's dissertation written in 2005 and appearing eventually as a monograph (Poehner, 2008). DA research has, by and large, adopted Vygotsky's perspective against quantification and measurement. Haywood and Lidz (2007) have argued that reliability measures and the bell curve are antithetical to DA, whose goal is to violate the very idea of a normal distribution in promoting development for all individuals. However, applied linguists accustomed to working within the psychometric tradition have found their attraction to statistical analysis difficult, if not impossible, to overcome; they have criticized language-focused DA research for violating principles of good assessment as an activity that may influence teaching but that must be conceptualized as separate from it – a clear commitment to externalist philosophy (see discussion in Lantolf, 2009, and Lantolf and Poehner, 2014). Within the past two years, SCT-AL researchers have moved into educational domains beyond the field of second languages. For instance, a dissertation by Kurtz (in progress) implemented an STI project in a course intended to develop the ability of international law students from civil and Sharia law legal cultures to reason analogically between the facts of a case, precedent cases, and statutes, typical in the practice of American common law.

Early as well as more recent praxis-based SCT-L2 research has always taken account of the importance of development (i.e., history). However, it has not been easy to convince colleagues working from an externalist perspective, including especially mainstream journal editors and reviewers, to accept the legitimacy of SCT research methods. While the situation has improved over the past three decades, we continue to confront doubts of reviewers regarding single case studies and, perhaps more importantly, how history is incorporated into the research. Many of the praxis-based classroom studies have covered sufficiently long temporal trajectories (typically 8 to 16 weeks) to be deemed acceptable as 'longitudinal' studies. However, when the time frame drops below 8 weeks, things become more problematic. For instance, the following critique was recently received by a former student who submitted a manuscript to a major AL journal: "the sample (one individual only) is too small and comparison groups/individuals are missing; a longitudinal investigation comprises more than two weeks; single snapshots of learner performance do not constitute appropriate evidence of learning and development." This reaction and critique leads me to consideration of the second aspect of Vygotsky's stance on experimentation and quantification – the consequences of an obsession with controlled experimentation in AL research.

Whither experimentation?

To conclude the chapter, I would like to consider a typical AL experimental study from the perspective of Vygotsky's warning against uncritically importing research methods from one science into another. As I noted earlier, the gold standard of AL research is controlled quantitative experimental research that seeks generalizability. My purpose is to illustrate the consequences of ignoring Vygotsky's criticism of what Stephen J. Gould (1996) calls "physics envy."

The study, reported in Hernández (2011), focused on Spanish discourse markers equivalent to the English 'then,' 'when,' 'therefore,' 'however,' 'on the other hand,' etc., which enhance textual coherence and cohesiveness. Although the study, carried out with 91 students enrolled in a university Spanish-language program, asked two research questions, only one of these is relevant for present purposes: "Does explicit instruction and input flood [extensive exposure to the discourse markers in natural texts] have a greater effect on learners' use of discourse markers than input flood alone?" (Hernández, 2011, p. 163).

The participants were distributed across three groups: Input Flood (IF), Input Flood plus Explicit Instruction (IF+EI), and Control Group. Instruction covered two 50-minute class sessions in the same week (Hernández, 2011, p. 165). Both experimental groups were given a review of how past tense verbal aspect is used in narration in Spanish. As part of their instruction, both groups reviewed use of past tense in narratives, and this was followed by exposure to three texts containing an artificially inflated number of discourse markers (i.e., the input flood). While reading the texts, the IF+EI group was asked to notice use of and to underline past tense verbs and discourse markers; the IF group followed the same procedure but for past tense verbs only. The two groups were then asked comprehension questions about the text by their teachers. They then engaged in the same communicative activities, which provided opportunities to use past tense and discourse markers.

Crucially, the IF+EI group received a handout with an 86-word paragraph ostensibly explaining use of discourse markers and including a list of 29 such markers and their English equivalents. A pretest was given to the three groups one week prior to instruction. A post-test was administered immediately after instruction and a delayed post-test given four weeks later. For comparison purposes, several native speakers of Spanish completed the same pretest task as the learners.

Hernández counted the frequency of discourse markers used by each group on all tests and subjected this to statistical analyses; this revealed no significant difference among the three groups on the pretest, significant differences between both experimental groups and the control group on the two post-tests, and most importantly, no significant differences between the experimental groups on either post-test. On this basis, Hernández concluded that supplementing input flood with explicit instruction "does not enhance the effect of IF alone" (2011, p. 175). It is worth mentioning that neither of the experimental groups showed anything close to the frequency of discourse markers used by the native speakers. Indeed, following instruction, the mean frequency of marker use on both post-tests was only slightly more than half of native production for both experimental groups.

The major point I want to raise goes to Hernández's assumption that providing students with a handout containing, at best, a very general overview of what discourse markers are and how they are used counts legitimately as explicit instruction. Clearly, from Vygotsky's perspective on educational praxis and on how explicit instruction is interpreted in Gal'perin's STI, Hernández's assumption has to be called into question. Equally worrying is how the results of the study have found their way into the general AL literature. In a recent monograph on instructed second language acquisition, Loewen summarized the findings of Hernández's study as follows:

> Hernández found that both groups improved significantly in their use of discourse markers during picture description tasks used as pretest and post-test, and again, there was *no additional improvement for the group that received explicit information about the target structure.*
>
> *(2015, p. 71, emphasis added)*

While Loewen referred here to "explicit information," which seems to be a wise decision on his part even though the quality of this information was questionable, at the outset of the same paragraph, he used Hernández's terminology "explicit instruction group" and referred to the study as one that "compared the effects of input flood and explicit *instruction* on the use of Spanish discourse markers" (2015, p. 71, emphasis added).

The message that Hernández's study and its uptake by Loewen sends to practitioners is: "Don't bother explaining things to learners; it is sufficient to provide them with a lot of evidence and allow them to figure things out on their own." The problem is that good experimentation does not necessarily make for good education. What would have happened if explicit instruction had comprised a deeper and more expansive explanation of the meaning and use of discourse markers and how they are used to structure texts? This would most likely have taken more than the few minutes the participants needed to read the one-page handout. But it would have contaminated the experiment because, for one thing, not only would the IF+EI group have had more time to learn, they would also have received better-quality instruction on a complex feature of the language. The appropriate conclusion to draw from the study is not that explicit instruction fails to enhance the quality of learning; rather, it is that when explicit instruction is restricted to a virtually useless handout for the sake of experimental orthodoxy, it fails to promote learning. The lesson of Vygotsky's skepticism regarding controlled quantitative experimentation in the social sciences is clear.

References

Avineri, S. (1968). *The social and political thought of Karl Marx*. Cambridge: Cambridge University Press.

Blumer, H. (1956). Sociological analysis and the "variable." *American Sociological Review*, 21(6), 683–690.

Chaiklin, S. (2011). Social scientific research and societal practice: Action research and cultural-historical research in methodological light from Kurt Lewin and Lev S. Vygotsky. *Mind, Culture, and Activity: An International Journal*, 18(2), 129–147.

Cole, M. (2009). The perils of translation: A first step in reconsidering Vygotsky's theory of development in relation to formal education. *Mind, Culture, and Activity: An International Journal*, 16(4), 291–295.

Cole, M., and Scribner, S. (1978). Introduction. In M. Cole, V. John-Steiner, S. Scribner, and E. Souberman (Eds.), *L. S. Vygotsky. Mind in society: The development of higher psychological processes* (pp. 1–14). Cambridge, MA: Harvard University Press.

Coser, L. A. (1975). Presidential address: Two methods in search of substance. *American Sociological Review*, 40(6), 691–700.

Engels, F. (1877/1987). Anti-Dühring. Herr Eugen Dühring's revolution in science. Part I: Philosophy. In *The collected works of L. S. Vygotsky, Volume 25* (pp. 33–134). New York: International Publishers.

Esteve, O., Fernandez, F., Martin-Peris, E., and Atienza, E. (In press). The integrated plurilingual approach: A didactic model providing guidance to Spanish schools for reconceptualizing the teaching of additional languages. *Language and Sociocultural Theory*.

Frawley, W., and Lantolf, J. P. (1985). Second language discourse: A Vygotskian perspective. *Applied Linguistics*, 6(1), 19–44.

Gould, S. J. (1996). *The mismeasure of man*. New York: Norton.

Haenen, J. (1996). *Piotr Gal'perin: Psychologist in Vygotsky's footsteps*. New York: Nova Science Publishers.

Harvey, D. (2010). *A companion to Marx's Capital*. London: Verso.

Harvey, D. (2013). *A companion to Marx's Capital: Volume 2*. London: Verso.

Harvey, D. (2014). *Seventeen contradictions and the end of capitalism*. London: Profile Books.

Haywood, C. H., and Lidz, C. S. (2007). *Dynamic assessment in practice: Clinical and educational applications*. Cambridge: Cambridge University Press.

Hernández, T. A. (2011). Re-examining the role of explicit instruction and input flood on the acquisition of Spanish discourse markers. *Language Teaching Research*, 15(2), 159–182.

Johnson, K. E. (2009). *Second language teacher education: A sociocultural perspective*. New York: Routledge.

Johnson, K. E., and Golombek, P. (2016). *Mindful L2 teacher education: A sociocultural perspective on cultivating teachers' professional development*. New York: Routledge.

John-Steiner, V., and Souberman, E. (1978). Afterword. In M. Cole, V. John-Steiner, S. Scribner, and E. Souberman (Eds.), *L. S. Vygotsky. Mind in society: The development of higher psychological processes* (pp. 121–133). Cambridge, MA: Harvard University Press.

Kurtz, L. (In progress). *Vygotsky goes to law school: A concept-based pedagogical intervention to promote legal reading and reasoning development in international LL.M. students*. Unpublished doctoral dissertation, Pennsylvania State University.

Lantolf, J. P. (2009). Dynamic assessment: The dialectical integration of instruction and assessment. *Language Teaching*, 42(3), 355–368.

Lantolf, J. P., and Thorne, S. L. (2006). *Sociocultural theory and the genesis of second language development.* Oxford: Oxford University Press.

Lantolf, J. P., and Beckett, T. (2009). Research timeline: Sociocultural theory and second language acquisition. *Language Teaching,* 42(4), 459–475.

Lantolf, J. P., and Poehner, M. E. (2014). *Sociocultural theory and the pedagogical imperative: Vygotskian praxis and the research/praxis divide.* New York: Routledge.

Loewen, S. (2015). *Instructed second language acquisition.* New York: Routledge.

Luria, A. R. (1973). *The working brain.* New York: Basic Books.

Luria, A. R. (1979). *The making of mind: A personal account of Soviet psychology,* ed. M. Cole and S. Cole. Cambridge, MA: Harvard University Press.

McGrath, J. E., and Altman, I. (1966). *Small group research: A synthesis and critique of the field.* New York: Holt, Rinehart and Winston.

Marx, K. (1867/1992). *Capital: A critique of political economy. Volume 1.* London: Penguin Books.

Marx, K. (1939/1973). *Grundrisse: Foundations of the critique of political economy.* London: Penguin Books.

Negueruela, E. (2003). *A sociocultural approach to the teaching-learning of second languages: Systemic-theoretical instruction and L2 development.* Unpublished doctoral dissertation, Pennsylvania State University.

Negueruela, E., and Lantolf, J. P. (2006). A concept-based approach to teaching Spanish grammar. In R. Salaberry and B. Lafford (Eds.), *Spanish second language acquisition: State of the art* (pp. 79–102). Washington, DC: Georgetown University Press.

Novack. G. (1978). *Polemics in Marxist philosophy.* New York: Pathfinder.

Ollman, B. (2003). *Dance of the dialectic: Steps in Marx's method.* Urbana, IL: University of Illinois Press.

Ollman, B. (2015). Marxism and the philosophy of internal relations; or, how to replace the mysterious "paradox" with "contradictions" that can be studied and resolved. *Capital and Class,* 39(1), 7–23.

Packer, M. J. (2008). Is Vygotsky relevant? Vygotsky's Marxist psychology. *Mind, Culture, and Activity: An International Journal,* 15(1), 8–31.

Poehner, M. E. (2008). *Dynamic assessment: A Vygotskian approach to understanding and promoting L2 development.* Berlin: Springer Verlag.

Sanchez Vasquez, A. (1977). *The philosophy of praxis.* London: Merlin Press.

Scribner, S. (1985). Vygotsky's use of history. In J. V. Wertsch (Ed.), *Culture, communication, and cognition: Vygotskian perspectives* (pp. 119–145). Cambridge: Cambridge University Press.

Talyzina, N. (1981). *The psychology of learning: Theories of learning and programed instruction.* Moscow: Progress Press.

Toomela, A. (2015). Methodology of cultural-historical psychology. In A. Yasnitsky, R. van der Veer, and M. Ferrari (Eds.), *The Cambridge handbook of cultural-historical psychology* (pp. 101–125). Cambridge: Cambridge University Press.

Toulmin, S. (1978). The Mozart of psychology: Review of *Mind in society: The development of higher psychological processes* (by L. S. Vygotsky, ed. M. Cole, V. John-Steiner, S. Scribner, and E. Souberman), *New York Review of Books,* 25(14), 51–57.

Vygotsky, L. S. (1935/1994). The problem of the environment. In R. van der Veer and J. Valsiner (Eds.), *The Vygotsky reader* (pp. 338–354). Oxford: Blackwell.

Vygotsky, L. S. (1978). *Mind in society: The development of higher psychological processes* (ed. M. Cole, V. John-Steiner, S. Scribner and E. Souberman). Cambridge, MA: Harvard University Press.

Vygotsky, L. S. (1987). *The collected works of L. S. Vygotsky. Volume 1: Problems of general psychology, including the volume Thinking and Speech*. New York: Plenum.

Vygotsky, L. S. (1993). *The collected works of L. S. Vygotsky. Volume 2: The fundamentals of defectology (Abnormal psychology and learning disabilities)*. New York: Plenum.

Vygotsky, L. S. (1997a). The historical meaning of the crisis in psychology: A methodological investigation. In R. W. Rieber and J. Wollock (Eds.), *The collected works of L. S. Vygotsky: Volume 3* (pp. 233–344). New York: Plenum.

Vygotsky, L. S. (1997b). The instrumental method in psychology. In R. W. Rieber and J. Wollock (Eds.), *The collected works of L. S. Vygotsky. Volume 3* (pp. 85–90). New York: Plenum.

Zavershneva, E. (2016). Vyotsky the unpublished: An overview of the personal archive (1912–1934). In A. Yasnitsky and R. van der Veer (Eds.), *Revisionist revolution in Vygotsky studies* (pp. 94–216). New York: Routledge.

8

CONSTRUCTIONIST INTERPRETATION OF VYGOTSKY

A theoretical–methodological study of the concept of language

Eduardo Moura da Costa and Silvana Calvo Tuleski

Studies on language have been part of the history of philosophy since its early days and transferred to psychology when it started to be developed as a science in the nineteenth century.

The linguistic turn occurred in the 1970s; this revived discussions about language in various scientific fields (Ibánez, 2004). The impact of this movement on psychology can be observed through the development of discursive psychology, the second revolution of cognitive psychology, and social constructionism, among other orientations.

Lev Vygotsky (1896–1934)[1] was a psychologist who highlighted the study of language. This theme was part of his intellectual trajectory since the beginning of his work, as can be verified by his interest in literature and by his first investigations in Gomel (van der Veer and Valsiner, 1991). In Vygotsky's historical-cultural psychology, language, as a genuinely human cultural instrument, has a central role in the development of consciousness and genuinely human psychological functions.

Having said that, a temporal coincidence can be noted between the 'discovery' of Vygotsky's work by the West and the intellectual movement that was formed in the 1970s, known as postmodernism. This movement involves the 'linguistic turn.'[2] Inside psychological science, for example, a strong critical movement was occurring in relation to the modern scientific view, especially against behaviorism and cognitivism. From the perspective of the critics, Vygotsky was seen as a great ally. His historical conception of development of superior psychological functions was seen as a strong weapon against biologizing, subjective, and reductionist visions of man.

However, according to authors such as Duarte (2001) and Tuleski (2008), in the process of appropriation of Vygotsky's theories, the Marxist basis of his work was misrepresented and there was even censorship in American publications. According to Duarte (2001), this aspect of Vygotsky's writing was put aside in favor of others, such as language, culture, interaction, internalization, and mediation. It is precisely in discussion of this problem – that is, the misrepresentation of Vygotsky's psychology and his Marxist fundaments – that we place this chapter.

In synthesis, it is possible to observe the emergence of different emphases and interpretations of language in the development of psychological studies. These different conceptions equally affected the psychologist's practice. As an example, the practice of the educational psychologist can change significantly according to different conceptions of the relation between thinking and language in human development. Furthermore, different orientations diverge regarding the role of language in clinical practice. We shed light on this issue through analysis of Vygotsky's constructionist appropriations.

Social constructionism and language

Vygotsky is considered one of the many predecessors of social constructionism (Castanõn, 2007; Guanes, 2006; López, 2003; López-Silva, 2013; Grandesso, 2000; Harré, 2000; Lock and Strong, 2010). Constructionist authors themselves, as well as Gergen (1995), Harré (2000), and Shotter (2001), mention the relation between their conceptions and the Soviet psychologist. Shotter (1993c) comes to the point to affirm that Vygotsky would be his and Harré's 'hero.'

López (2003), for example, affirms that the reinstatement of Vygotsky and other Soviet authors, such as Leontiev and Luria, by social constructionism was based on criticism of the predominant psychology and reflected Vygotsky's anti-cognitive and anti-mentalistic arguments. López-Silva (2013), on the other hand, highlights that Vygotsky, as well as other constructionist authors, would form part of the 'constructivist continuum.' For López-Silva, Vygotsky's ideas would be in a middle ground between radical constructivist ideas, which state it is the subject itself that constructs its reality, and constructionism, where reality is socially built.

By reason of the breadth and the many forms taken by social constructionism (Dazinger, 1997), for our discussion of Vygotsky's appropriation of the conception of language, we focus on the work of John Shotter (1989, 1993a, 1993b, 1993c, 1996, 2001). This English psychologist used much of Vygotsky's work in order to formulate his form of constructionism, which he called the "rhetorical-responsive" version (Shotter, 2001). Let us move on, then, to the discussion.

In general, according to Castanõn (2007), social constructionism is a result of a series of incorporations into psychology of different theoretical and philosophical bodies. Its most important intellectual forerunners are Peter Berger (1929–) and Thomas Luckmann (1927–2016), Thomas Kuhn (1922–1996) and Paul Feyerabend (1924–1994), Jacques Derrida (1930–2004), Lev Vygotsky, Ludwig Wittgenstein (1889–1951), and Richard Rorty (1931–2007). They constitute the central core of constructionism, but there are other diverse schools of thinking and authors that appeal to constructionists. González Rey (2003), for example, identifies Jacques Lacan (1901–1981) as an author who is almost always quoted by constructionists, and Harré (2000) mentions the personalism of William Stern (1871–1938) as another implied influence in some constructionist perspectives. A third example is Mikhail Bakhtin (1895–1975), whose importance was great for the rhetorical-responsive version of constructionism developed by Shotter (2001), which we enter into in detail further on.

In general, we can say that such a vision implies the idea that reality is the product of social, conversational, or discursive constructions and that our constructions of reality are always social and historical, not individual. In contrast to the representational model, knowledge is viewed as being constructed from relations. Social construction refers to the creation of senses by our collaborative activities (Gergen and Gergen, 2010). Shotter (2001), in turn, affirms that rather than focusing on the ways in which individuals get to know the objects or the world that surrounds them, constructionism is interested in explaining how these individuals first create and maintain determined forms of relating in practical life and then, from these forms of speaking, understand the circumstances of life. Such vision is coherent with the notion of Harré that "the primary human reality is conversation" (Harré, as quoted in Shotter, 2001, p. 11).[3] Therefore, for constructionism, the relation of man with his peers comes first and after this, his relation with the environment.

Gergen (1995) makes the constructionist emphasis clear in terms of language and discursive activity. According to him, "for the constructionist, terms for both world and mind are constituents of discursive practices; they are integers within language and thus themselves socially contested and negotiated" (Gergen, 1995, p. 61).[4]

From the perspective of social constructionism, knowledge would not be a direct reflection of the object by the subject; nor would it be a construction of the world by purely individual internal structures as proposed in, for example, radical constructionism. Shotter (2001) describes the constructionism produced by knowledge of a 'third type.' For him, third type knowledge is:

> a knowing from *within* a discursively constructed situation; that is, from within an event. As such, it is a form of knowledge whose nature cannot be described theoretically, in ways amenable to evidential support. Even to try to do so would be paradoxical: for we want an account of it from within the context of its use, and to assume that its nature could be described theoretically would still be to assume that it could be described in a context-free way.
>
> *(Shotter, 2001, p. 174, emphasis added)*[5]

For constructionists, it is in our interaction with others that we become autonomous beings. Using the notion of group action, Shotter explains social activity not in terms of the attributes of individuals but as a result of the situations in which people find themselves, which provide individuals with the ability to act. This concept was developed, going back to his first studies, through the elaboration of his rhetorical-responsive version of social constructionism (Shotter, 2001).

Shotter uses the term 'responsive' because, according to him, the capacity that we have, as individuals, of representing the world – that is, of describing the state of things (whether real or not) in the way that we do – comes from the fundamental and primary fact that we speak in response to those who surround us, regardless of the influence of the environment. With respect to 'rhetorical' character, he states:

> Indeed, a part of what we must learn in growing up, if we want to be perceived as speaking authoritatively about factual matters, is how to respond to the others around us should they challenge our claims. This is one of the reasons for calling it a *rhetorical* rather than a referential form of language: for more than merely claiming to depict a state of affairs, our ways of talking can "move" people to action, or change their perceptions.
>
> *(Shotter, 2001, p. 18)*[6]

Shotter argues that for Volosinov, Bakhtin, and Wittgenstein, the primarily rhetorical-responsive function of words follows Vygotsky's understanding; that is, the referential and representational function of speech is a secondary function. He notes that Volosinov, Bakhtin, and Wittgenstein fought the idea of comparing language to a system of mathematical signs. For Shotter, these authors "take utterances, or words in their speaking, rather than sentences, or patterns of already spoken words, as the basic unit of dialogic speech communication" (2001, p. 82).[7]

He also states that meaning, which is one of the components of language, is conditioned by its social use. In his version of constructionism, it is social relations that define knowledge about things, not empirical reality.

In order to approach this question, Shotter (2001) makes use of Wittgenstein's idea that the meaning of words appears in their use, using the metaphor of words as tools. Noting that Wittgenstein established the metaphor of 'language games,' Shotter explains that a metaphor does not represent any permanent order of language since it is, by its own nature, open to the determination by the context in which it is used. However, through metaphor, it is possible to create, in an artificial way, an order that did not exist before, describing an aspect of our use of language.

In addition to the ideas of Wittgenstein, Shotter also draws on Vygotsky's thinking. According to Lock and Strong (2010), Shotter's work in the 1970s elaborates on Vygotsky's ideas: first, symbols of external phenomena originate from interactions among individuals and, thereafter, shape their actions; second, this happens primarily because of our ability to spontaneously respond to one another and subsequently to voluntarily control our actions. The idea of 'group action' is directly related to this appropriation of Vygotsky's ideas. Shotter affirms that from group action, we develop skills spontaneously in a social context, which afterwards become voluntary. In other words, our ability to manipulate symbols is formed in our contact between each other.

He makes it clear that by focusing on "events within the contingent flow of continuous communicative interaction between human beings," he was following the vision of Green and other constructionists (Shotter, 2001, p. 19).[8] This would be a way to oppose the central vision of individual psyche (romantic and cognitive subjectivism) in favor of one centered in the characteristics already determined by the external world (objectivism, modernism, and behaviorism). According to Shotter, these two classical visions search to elucidate the mind or the world according to ahistorical principles.

His version of constructionism implies a move away from decontextualized interest in theoretical and explanatory 'psychology of mind' to an interest in practical and descriptive psychology of 'social-moral relations.' For this vision, the mind is no longer a thing but starts to be a rhetorical artifice, something that can be spoken in different moments and with different purposes. The main change coming out of psychology as a moral science would be the abandonment of:

> the attempt simply to discover our supposed "natural" natures, and a turning to the study of how we actually do treat each other as being in everyday life, communicative activities – a change which leads us to a concern with "making," with processes of "social construction."
>
> *(Shotter, 2001, p. 45)*[9]

This vision complies with that of Harré, for whom primary reality is made up of individuals in conversation. Shotter (2001) claims the relationship between oneself and others is the basis of the relationship between oneself and the world. Without interaction with others, individuals would not be responsible in their actions. In his vision, the 'me–world' relationship originates from the bidirectional rhetorical-responsive flow of activities between oneself and other. In other words, the way we talk with and understand other constitutes the manner in which we explain the world. Our me–world relationship is produced by our me–other relationship.

His view of what should transform psychology is completely based on rhetorical and discursive relations; hence, the importance of language conception for his rhetorical-responsive vision.

Shotter (2001) affirms, in his interpretation of Vygotsky's conception of language, that it does not represent reality but, through it, develops human relations in which we affect each other. By this 'instrument,' others would instruct us or convince us of how reality is and we could say that this corresponds to a naturalization of ideology. We intend to demonstrate, further on, that such an interpretation of Vygotsky's conception of language is misplaced.

According to Shotter (1996), Wittgenstein's position is similar to Vygotsky's; that is, the relationship between thinking and language is neither pre-formulated nor constant, but has an evolving course of development. Shotter (1996) refers to Vygotsky's famous passage in which he states that action rather than word begins this development, while the word is the end of the process. However, Shotter does not mention that for Vygotsky the evolution of the word is closely linked to the relation of production and social class division. That is, in the same way that activity is limited by the characteristics of reality, transformation of reality requires language and concepts that represent it satisfactorily.

In short, what Shotter (1989, 1993a, 1993b, 1996) is requesting, following Wittgenstein and Vygotsky, is a new focus in the study of human activity, a new place of operations, whatever it may be, that focuses on individuals' responding to one another in particular moments of interaction.

Having considered Shotter's perspective, we move on to discuss the Vygotsky's concepts.

Criticism of social constructionism's conception of language

One of the many criticisms of social constructionism focuses on its relativism. By limiting constructions to discursive exchanges between different 'communities' and by denying realism,[10] the perspective of constructionism approached irrationality. Even though Vygotsky would deny it, his idea of social construction is settled in an ontological and epistemological foundation that has consequences for the explanation of what man is, social relations, history, language, social changes, etc. With that being said, the intention here is to discuss merely one aspect of Vygotsky's theory, his language conception, in order to demonstrate the incoherence regarding other aspects of this theory.

In accordance with Shotter (2001), the different ways in which we talk about ourselves, in terms of recent events, lead us to experience the world in very different ways. Shotter took as his foundation the studies of Whorf[11] on the language of the Hopi in *confirming* his constructionist vision of language. He says that the way these North American people talk influences how they comprehend reality. According to Whorf, and Shotter (2001), words create things.

In Shotter's (2001) interpretation, Whorf verifies that conceptions of 'time' and 'space,' for example, are conditioned by the structure of private languages. Furthermore, cultural and behavioral norms also respect linguistic patterns. According to this author, European people have more metaphoric ways of speaking and the Hopi possess a more immediate language, which does not recognize the characteristics of time in the speech, for example. Nevertheless, he does not explain how the different forms of speaking would have originated.

As a result of Shotter's conclusion on the role of language for the Hopi, we asked ourselves: Is Shotter thus offering an idealistic view? In claiming that ways of comprehending the world arise from forms of language, wouldn't he be denying the fact that language appears and develops from the activity of transformation of material reality in each society? We believe that studies by Vygotsky (1996) and Vygotski and Luria (2007) can help us to answer these questions.

For these authors, the material is analogous to the psychological. Therefore, it can be expected that different stages of cultural development exist according to the material development of a society, in its different historical periods. In Vygotsky and Luria's words:

> It ... becomes obvious that the impact of this language and its various characteristics on the nature and structure of mental operations parallels that

of the properties of implements on the structure and makeup of the different types of work done by humans.

(1996, p. 126)[12]

Tuleski (2011) points out that intercultural studies by Vygotsky and Luria aimed to verify suppositions in Marx's theory, especially the concept of praxis. This asserts that the evolution of human superior psychological functioning resulted from human activity, which is instrumental and social and internalization of which results in consciousness. According to Tuleski:

> the fact that knowledge and consciousness emerge and structure themselves in the social environment means each individual has determined possibilities for development, conditioned by objective reality, which means also that different social-cultural environments offer distinct possibilities of development to the individuals within them.
>
> *(2011, p. 84)*

Tuleski (2011) highlights that Luria and Vygotsky's goal in their intercultural studies was to identify whether social and technological changes result in alterations in the thinking process. These authors understood that there were differences according to the stage of cultural development and not in terms of innate skills.[13]

According to Vygotsky and Luria (1996), the language of the primitive man was richer in detail than is ours. The justification is that primitive language was more narrowly attached to memory, becoming photographic, as if representing a drawing; a great number of concrete details disappear with language development.

In the language of Australian people, for example, the absence of words designates general concepts; however, these (languages) are flooded with many specific terms that precisely distinguish the individual traces and distinct character of objects (Vygotsky and Luria, 1996, p. 121).

These authors illustrate the advantages and disadvantages of this type of language. The advantage is that it creates a sign for all concrete objects, in such a way that men have no need of a 'replica' of the designated object. The disadvantage is that such a form of language overloads thinking with endless details and does not allow for the data from experience to be processed and synthesized.

The words of primitive men are no different from objects, but continue to be closely related to immediate sensorial perceptions (Vygotsky and Luria, 1996). In order to explain this relation, these authors give the example of a primitive man that was learning a European language. In the learning process, he refused to write something that was in fact occurring. This is because "The operations of language and counting prove possible only to the extent that they are connected to those concrete situations that gave to them" (Vygotsky and Luria, 1996, p. 124).[14]

Vygotsky and Luria see the thinking of primitive men in the same terms as their language: entirely "concrete, graphic and pictoral" (1996, p. 128),[15] a function of language based on images. With the cultural development of thinking and language, the eidetic character of language faded and it started to occupy a new level. Language had expressed the concrete details of the external world, but in moving away from the notion of the immediate concrete nature of reality, words came to be associated not with individual objects, but with sets of interrelated objects and ideas. Nevertheless, despite language referring to groups of objects, it cannot lose its individuality and singularity. The authors conclude that the thinking of primitive men would be at the stage of thinking by complexes.

The main point we want to highlight in the theorization of Vygotsky and Luria (1996) is the relation that they establish between language and the activities developed by primitive society. They affirm that the richness of vocabulary reflects the wealth of experience; that is, it is related to active adaptation of men in nature. "The real reason for these special features of primitive language therefore lies in technical requirements and vital necessity" (Vygotsky and Luria, 1996, p. 132).[16] The authors sum up the development of language in this manner:

> Fundamental progress in the development of thinking manifests itself in the transition from the first method of using words as proper names to a second method, whereby words serve as symbols for sets, and lastly to a third, involving the use of words as tools or means for the elaboration of concepts. Just as the cultural development of memory is closely linked to the history of the development of writing, so also the cultural development of thinking is quite as closely tied to the history of development of human language.
>
> *(Vygotsky and Luria, 1996, p. 133)*[17]

Therefore, the origin of language for Vygotsky and Luria is completely different than it is for Whorf, who was an influence on Shotter. Vygotsky and Luria, consistent with the Marxist method, start from the notion that it is work and language, socially created, that organize consciousness and not the other way round. In other words, it is not the way of speaking that determines the way of experiencing the world, but the inverse; that is, the starting point is the world itself, the organization of human material life. The various names given to things by primitive men, as indicated by Vygotsky and Luria (1996), prove this.

In essence, our intention was to stress that constructionism, in explaining the role of language in man's development, dislocating it from its origin, lost sight, intentionally or not, of the existing relation between men's activity and language and thinking development. As we saw, constructionism comprehends language as separate from material relations of social existence of a people, which is a lot different from what we see in the cultural studies developed by Vygotsky and Luria (1996, 2007).

Disregard for the category of 'work' in Vygotsky's psychology is one of the main factors that led to the constructionists' idealistic interpretation of language. The denial of this category brought many authors, such as Shotter, to adopt Vygotsky's concept of language as being unattached to material reality, to vital human activity.

Vygotsky's writings offer us clues to understanding the creation of artificial stimuli (signs), to stimulate the other and then oneself, through practical activity that has as its goal the survival of the organism itself through work. Thus, according to Vygotsky, work, as a vital human activity, is the foundation of the social being. The following passage does not avoid questions regarding the relation between language and work: "The rational, intentional conveyance of experience and thought to others requires a mediating system, the prototype of which is human speech born of the need of communication during work" (Vygotsky, 1934/1986, p. 7).

At another time, by speaking of the relation between language and objective reality in childhood development, Vygotsky says:

> In order to become a sign of a thing (word), the stimulus must be supported by the qualities of the object itself that is denoted. Not all things are equally important for the child in such play. The real qualities of the object and their sign meaning enter into complex structural interrelations in the play. Thus, for the child, the word is connected with the object through its qualities and included in a common structure with it.
>
> *(1999, p. 52)*

Constructionists say that not *everything* goes because men conventionally decide what knowledge is; in accordance with Shotter (2001), for example, people who surround us would avoid the chaos of *everything goes*. Nevertheless, according to Vygotsky, it is not this exactly because for him the stimuli–sign must support itself in the object, as explained in the quotation above. Therefore, we have here a clear difference between two positions.

The psychological development of concepts is another clear difference. For Vygotsky (1934/1986), there is no separation between language and the object it represents; the concept is not simply a photograph or representation, but the establishment of complex connections with other concepts, ultimately unveiling the full complexity of reality. Thus, concepts are not naturally given but, rather, formed out of internal development; neither can they be comprehended in an isolated fashion. In order to develop, the child needs school-based education. The true concept completes its development close to a transitional age, marking the passage of a syncretic analysis and structuring of the conception of the world and the personality of man. By developing concepts, the young person becomes independent from adults and comprehends the world on their own.

When Vygotsky (1934/1986) theorizes on the development of concepts, he is focusing on, above all, scientific concepts. He refers to Marx's famous assertion: if the form of manifestation and the essence of things directly coincided, all science would be unnecessary. Concepts would be dispensable if reflected as a mirror image in the object's appearance; however, the latter is always partial and does not capture totality. Capturing the essence of things implies the analysis of their multiple characteristics, and this is the function of 'scientific' concepts. On the other hand, for Vygotsky, 'spontaneous' concepts are those developed outside the school context, in daily social relations.

In accordance with Vygotsky (1934/1986), the content modifies the development of thinking. Real phenomena, thus, can only be properly represented by concepts. Discussing the development of thinking in the age of transition, Vygotsky affirms his position as follows:

> For this reason, those who consider abstract thinking as a removal from reality are wrong. On the contrary, abstract thinking primarily reflects the deepest and truest, the most complete and thorough disclosure of the reality opening up before the adolescent. Regarding the changes in content of the thinking of the adolescent, we cannot bypass one sphere that appears at this outstanding time of reconstruction of thinking as a whole. We are speaking of the awareness of one's own internal activity.
>
> *(1998a, p. 47)*

Shotter (1989) says that in the process of internalization of social relations, there is no need for representation of reality based on contextual proof. The idea that has been verbalized relies less on linguistic context each day because it is supported also by the new context that has been built linguistically. As can be seen, Shotter (1989) makes the mistake pointed out by Vygotsky in the quotation above.

Vigotski (1998b), in contrast to Shotter, believes that imagination cannot be understood without its relation with reality. He highlights that even animals could no longer survive if psychic activity is emancipated from reality. The same would be true for children: For a child, pleasure is connected to satisfaction of real needs (Vigotski, 1998b, p. 119).

Vigotski (1998b) affirms that the content of reality, mediated by concepts, also goes through social conscience. The author states that the development of the child is associated with the development of class psychology and ideology (Vygotsky, 1998a, p. 43). He (1998a) considers that changes do not occur only in the internal point of view of the individual. In his vision, identification with a class is the result of a life in community, in the process of which activities and interests become common.

The entering of the teenager into the political-social world makes him reflect intensely on the problems of existence, which demands the development of superior forms of thinking. Different from what constructionists like Shotter would have us believe, Vygotsky (1998a) affirms that the teenager is son of his social class and also active in it. Thus, Vygotsky (1998a) is referring to the concrete teenager and not to the abstract, by which we mean, he is referring to a subject that is the result of multiple determinations within social class relations.

As new studies show, the claim that the abstract thinking of the adolescent breaks away from the concrete, and from the visual, is incorrect: the development of thinking during this period is characterized not by the intellect's breaking of the connections to the concrete base that it is outgrowing, but by the fact that a completely new form of relation arises between abstract and concrete factors in thinking, a new form of merging and synthesis so that, at this time, elementary functions long since established – functions such as visual thinking, perception, or practical intellect of the child – appear before us in a completely new form (Vygotsky, 1998a, p. 37).

In summary, Shotter (1993a, 2001) is not entirely wrong in saying that we know the world through people that surround us. Vygotsky also shares this position, but as we highlighted, he is referring to the child's development. The problem with respect to Shotter is that he generalizes Vygotsky's explication of childhood development and extends it to adults. Vygotsky (1999) states that there is a fusion between objects and people only in small children. In his words, "Reactions to things and to people comprise in children's behavior an elementary, undifferentiated unity from which both actions directed toward the external world and social forms of behavior later evolve" (Vygotsky, 1999, pp. 20–21). Therefore, as already mentioned, it is clear that for them, there is 'syncretism of action' in early stages of childhood development, but, after this, the child enters in contact separately with the objective world and with the people that surround him.

Final considerations

The constructionist interpretation of Vygotsky is in line with the tendency already demonstrated by authors like Duarte (2001) and Tuleski (2008) to avoid any Marxist justification of Vygotsky and other contributors to historical-cultural psychology. Vygotsky's work suffered a process of 'de-ideologicalization' at the hands of many Western intellectuals, starting with readings made by North Americans that attempted to extract from Vygotsky's work any conflict between socialist and liberal understandings (Duarte, 2001).

Shotter sacrifices the fundamental methodological basis of Vygotsky's thinking. Vygotsky states:

> It is this feeling of a system, the sense of a [common] style, the understanding that each particular statement is linked with and dependent upon the central idea of the whole system of which it forms a part, which is absent in the essentially eclectic attempts at combining the parts of two or more systems that are heterogeneous and diverse in scientific origin and composition.
>
> *(1997, p. 259)*

Constructionism is characterized by eclecticism. It juxtaposes authors completely conflicted with each other in order to justify *a priori* formulations without respecting the heterogeneous elements of different systems. The totality of the theories of thinkers such as Vygotsky, Bahktin, Wittgenstein, and Foucault, among others, is torn apart in order to fit into the constructionist panorama.

Constructionists such as Shotter, anchored in the work of Vygotsky and Bakhtin, transform language, describing it as having an existence *independent* of the material reality that produces it. According to McNally (1999), such an understanding of language expresses a new type of idealism, characterized by the poststructuralistics, postmodernists and post-Marxists. Believing that language exists only in social interaction, as the constructionists do, does not exempt them from seeing it independently. By comprehending that language results from material reproduction of man, it is possible to overcome this conception.

> Language, like consciousness, is not a separate and detached realm of human existence; rather, it is an expressive dimension of this existence. As such, it is permeated by the conflicts, tensions, and contradictions of real life. The new idealism sees none of this. By treating language "as a system of abstract grammatical categories," in Bakhtin's words, rather than understanding it as "ideologically saturated," as "contradiction-ridden, tension-filled," idealism impoverishes our understanding of the relations between language, life, history, and society. The new idealism may claim to understand ideology, conflict, contradiction, and resistance, but it has in a sense done one step futher than the old idealism, not just abstracting language but in effect transforming society itself into a linguistic system.
>
> *(McNally, 1999, p. 46)*[18]

Marx and Engels (1932/1974) reflect Hegel in their belief that with the criticism of ideas, human beings would be released. We can think of constructionism as a revival and exacerbation of this type of idealism, with the difference being that its adherents critique the discursive and relational forms of ideas that, for all intents and purposes, mean to disconnect ideas from materiality. In the words of Marx and Engels, "They [Young Hegelians] forgot, however, that they themselves are opposing nothing but phrases to phrases, and that they are in no way combating the real existing world since they are combating solely the phrases of this world" (1974, p. 36). The 'real existing world' that connects to the postmodern parts, as we sketched above, is a world manipulated by bourgeoisie ideology.

It is worth pointing out that the different conception of language in constructionism and in Vygotsky's work appears in an attempt at articulation between Vygotsky's conception and that of Wittgenstein. According to Coutinho (2010), Wittgenstein expresses an idealistic subjective vision by comprehending language as closed to the individual. This author would start from a clearly solipsistic view by proposing that our world is limited by language.

In essence, we detected that Shotter's conclusions were exactly what Vygotsky criticized. He mutilated heterogeneous elements of different theories in order to justify a vision that bears little similarity to the original theories. Therefore, after all we have presented here, it is clear that integration between these two views is impossible.

Notes

1 By translating the Russian alphabet to the Western, differences can be observed in the spelling of the author's name. We adopt "y" in place of "i" in our discussion, but we preserve the different spellings used in Brazilian or Spanish editions when citing works.

2 In general, the expression 'linguistic turn' designates a change that occurred in philosophy and in other human and social sciences, which, as the name itself suggests, corresponds to the lack of attention paid to the role of language in the phenomena that these disciplines studied. Ferdinand de Saussure (1857–1913) was responsible for breaking with the old philological tradition and instituting the modern linguistics. He developed concepts and methods that entailed rigorous study of language considered *through itself and in itself* (Ibáñez, 2004).

3 Quotation from Shotter, J. (2002) *Conversational realities: Constructing life through language*. London: Sage, p. 40.

4 Quotation from Gergen, K. J. (1994). *Realities and relationships: Soundings in social construction*. Cambridge, MA: Harvard University Press, p. 68.

5 Quotation from Shotter, J. (2002) *Conversational realities*.

6 Ibid., p. 6.

7 Ibid., p. 51.

8 Ibid., p. 7.

9 Ibid.

10 Critical realism affirms that there is a world (reality) outside the subject that knows it; social constructionism starts from the perspective that reality is a social construction invented by men.

11 Benjamin Lee Whorf (1897–1941) was an American linguist that, jointly with Edward Sapir (1884–1939), created the Sapir-Whorf hypothesis. This hypothesis points out that different ways of seeing the world depend on the forms that languages take in different cultures.

12 Quotation from Luria, A. R. and Vygotsky, L. S. (1992). *Ape, primitive man, and child: Essays in the history of behavior*, trans. E. Rossiter. Orlando, FL: Deutsch, pp. 66–67.

13 It is worth mentioning that such studies served to accuse Vygotsky and other authors of *racism*. With regard to this, Tuleski affirms: "Only a wrong understanding of the fundaments under which historical cultural theory was placed could give space to a racist interpretation based on the genetic or organic inferiority of such populations" (2011, p. 85).

14 Quotation from Luria, A. R. and Vygotsky, L. S. (1992). *Ape, primitive man, and child: Essays in the history of behavior*, p. 65.

15 Ibid., p. 68.

16 Ibid., p. 71.

17 Ibid.

18 Quotation from McNally, D. (1997). Language, history and class struggle. In *In Defense of History: Marxism and the Postmodern Agenda*, ed. E. M. Wood and J. B. Foster (pp. 26–42). New York: Monthly Review Press, p. 39.

References

Castañon, G. A. (2007). *Psicologia Pós-Moderna? Uma crítica epistemológica do construcionismo social* [Postmodern psychology? An epistemological critique of social constructionism]. Rio de Janeiro: Booklink.

Coutinho, C. N. (2010). *O estruturalismo e a miséria da razão* [The structuralism and misery of reason], 2nd ed. São Paulo: Expressão Popular.

Danziger, K. (1997). The varieties of social construction. *Theory and Psychology*, 7 (3), 399–411.

Duarte, N. (2001). *Vigotski e o "aprender a aprender": críticas às apropriações neoliberais e pós-modernas da teoria vigotskiana* [Vygotsky and "learning to learn": Criticism of neoliberal appropriations and postmodern theory of Vygotsky]. Campinas: Autores Associados.

Gergen, K. (1995). *Realidades y relaciones: Aproximaciones a la construcción social* [Realities and relationships: Soundings in social construction]. Barcelona: Paidós.

Gergen, K. J., and Gergen, M. (2010). *Construcionismo social: um convite ao diálogo* [Social construction: Entering the dialogue]. Rio de Janeiro: Instituto Noos.

González Rey, F. L. (2003). A subjetividade e as teorias de inspiração social na psicologia [Subjectivity and theories of social inspiration in psychology]. In F. L. González Rey, *Sujeito e subjetividade: uma aproximação histórico-cultural* [Subject and subjectivity: A historical-cultural approach] (pp. 121–199). São Paulo: Pioneira Thomson Learning.

Grandesso, M. (2000). *Sobre a reconstrução do significado: uma análise epistemológica e hermenêutica* [On the reconstruction of meaning: An epistemological analysis and hermeneutics]. São Paulo: Casa do Psicólogo.

Guanaes, C. (2006). *A construção da mudança em terapia de grupo: um enfoque construcionista social* [The construction of change in group therapy: A social constructionist approach]. São Paulo: Vetor.

Harré, R. (2000). Personalism in the context of a social constructionist psychology: Stern and Vygotsky. *Theory and Psychology*, 10 (6), 731–748.

Ibáñez, T. (2004). O "giro linguístico" [The "linguistic turn"]. In L. Iñiguez (Coord.), *Manual de análise do discurso em ciências sociais* [Discourse analysis manual in social sciences], 2nd ed. Rio de Janeiro: Editora Vozes.

Lock, A., and Strong, T. (2010). *Social constructionism: Sources and stirrings in theory and practice.* New York: Cambridge University Press.

López, E. E. J. (2003). Mirada caleidoscópica al construccionismo social [Kaleidoscopic look at social constructionism]. *Política y Sociedad*, 40 (1), 5–14.

López-Silva, P. (2013). Realidades, construcciones y dilemas: una revisión filosófica al construccionismo social [Realities, buildings and dilemmas: A philosophical review of social constructionism]. *Cinta moebio*, 46, 9–25.

McNally, D. (1999). Língua, história e luta de classes [Language, history and class struggle]. In: E. M. Wood and J. B. Foster (Eds.), *Em defesa da história: Marxismo e pós-modernismo* [In defense of history: Marxism and the postmodernist agenda]. Rio de Janeiro: Jorge Zahar.

Marx, K. and Engels, F. (1974). *The German ideology*, ed. C. J. Arthur. London: Lawrence & Wishart. (Original work published 1932).

Shotter, J. (1989). Vygotsky's psychology: Joint activity in a developmental zone. *New Ideas in Psychology*, 7 (2), 185–204.

Shotter, J. (1993a). Bakhtin and Vygotsky: Internalization as a boundary phenomenon. *New Ideas in Psychology*, 11 (3), 379–390.

Shotter, J. (1993b). Vygotsky: The social negotiation of semiotic mediation. *New Ideas in Psychology*, 11 (1), 61–75.

Shotter, J. (1993c). Harré, Vygotsky, Bakhtin, Vico, Wittgenstein: Academic discourses and conversational realities. *Journal for the Theory of Social Behavior*, 23 (4), 459–482.

Shotter, J. (1996). Talk of saying, showing, gesturing, and feeling in Wittgenstein and Vygotsky. *The Communication Review*, 1 (4), 471–495.

Shotter, J. (2001). *Realidades conversacionales: La construcción de la vida a través del lenguaje* [Conversational realities: Constructing life through language]. Madrid: Amorrortu Editores.

Tuleski, S. C. (2008). *Vygotski: a construção de uma psicologia marxista* [Vygotsky: The construction of a Marxist psychology], 2nd ed. Maringá: Eduem.

Tuleski, S. C. (2011). *A relação entre texto e contexto na obra de Luria: apontamentos para uma leitura marxista* [The relationship between text and context in the work of Luria: Notes for a Marxist reading]. Maringá: Eduem.

van der Veer, R., and Valsiner, J. (1991). *Understanding Vygotsky: A quest for synthesis*. Oxford: Blackwell.

Vygotsky, L. S. (1986). *Thought and Language*. Cambridge, MA: MIT Press. (Original work published 1934).

Vygotsky, L. S. (1997). The historical meaning of the crisis in psychology: A methodological investigation. In: *The collected works of L. S. Vygotsky: Volume 3* (pp. 233–345). New York: Plenum.

Vygotsky, L. S. (1998a). Development of thinking and formation of concepts in the adolescent. In: *The collected works of L. S. Vygotsky: Volume 5* (pp. 29–82). New York: Springer/Plenum Press.

Vigotski, L. S. (Vygotsky) (1998b). A imaginação e seu desenvolvimento na infância [Imagination and its development in childhood]. In: L. S. Vigotski, *O desenvolvimento psicológico na infância* [Psychological development in childhood]. São Paulo: Martins Fontes.

Vygotsky, L. S. (1999). Tool and sign in the development of the child. In: *The collected works of L. S. Vygotsky: Volume 6* (pp. 1–69). Springer/Plenum Press: New York.

Vygotsky, L. S., and Luria, A. R. (1996). *Estudos sobre a história do comportamento: símios, homem primitivo e criança* [Ape, primitive man, and child: Essays in the history of behavior]. Porto Alegre: Artes Médicas.

Vygotski, L. S. (Vygotsky), and Luria, A. R. (2007). *El instrumento y el signo en el desarrollo del niño* [Tool and sign in the development of the child]. Madrid: Fundación Infancia y Aprendizaje.

INDEX

Taylor & Francis eBooks

Helping you to choose the right eBooks for your Library

Add Routledge titles to your library's digital collection today. Taylor and Francis ebooks contains over 50,000 titles in the Humanities, Social Sciences, Behavioural Sciences, Built Environment and Law.

Choose from a range of subject packages or create your own!

Benefits for you

- » Free MARC records
- » COUNTER-compliant usage statistics
- » Flexible purchase and pricing options
- » All titles DRM-free.

Benefits for your user

- » Off-site, anytime access via Athens or referring URL
- » Print or copy pages or chapters
- » Full content search
- » Bookmark, highlight and annotate text
- » Access to thousands of pages of quality research at the click of a button.

REQUEST YOUR **FREE** INSTITUTIONAL TRIAL TODAY

Free Trials Available
We offer free trials to qualifying academic, corporate and government customers.

eCollections – Choose from over 30 subject eCollections, including:

Archaeology	Language Learning
Architecture	Law
Asian Studies	Literature
Business & Management	Media & Communication
Classical Studies	Middle East Studies
Construction	Music
Creative & Media Arts	Philosophy
Criminology & Criminal Justice	Planning
Economics	Politics
Education	Psychology & Mental Health
Energy	Religion
Engineering	Security
English Language & Linguistics	Social Work
Environment & Sustainability	Sociology
Geography	Sport
Health Studies	Theatre & Performance
History	Tourism, Hospitality & Events

For more information, pricing enquiries or to order a free trial, please contact your local sales team:
www.tandfebooks.com/page/sales

The home of
Routledge books

www.tandfebooks.com